Strange Bedfellows

Strange Bedfellows

Surprising Text Pairs and Lessons for Reading and Writing Across Genres

Carol Rawlings Miller

Foreword by Jim Burke

HEINEMANN • Portsmouth, NH

Heinemann

361 Hanover Street

Portsmouth, NH 03801–3912

www.heinemann.com

Offices and agents throughout the world

The author and publisher wish to thank those who have generously given permission to reprint borrowed material:

"I Have a Dream" by Martin Luther King Jr. Reprinted by arrangement with The Heirs to the Estate of Martin Luther King Jr., c/o Writers House as agent for the proprietor, New York. Copyright © 1963 Dr. Martin Luther King Jr.; copyright © 1991 Coretta Scott King.

"9.11.01" from *At the Same Time: Essays & Speeches* by Susan Sontag. Copyright © 2007 by The Estate of Susan Sontag. Reprinted by permission of Farrar, Straus and Giroux, LLC.

Melissa Byles, "An Open Letter to Susan Sontag" (www.albany.edu/offcourse/fall01/letters .html). Reprinted by permission of Offcourse.

Credits continue on page vi.

Library of Congress Cataloging-in-Publication Data
Miller, Carol Rawlings.
   Strange bedfellows : surprising text pairs and lessons for reading and writing across genres / Carol Rawlings Miller ; foreword by Jim Burke.
       p.   cm.
   Includes bibliographical references.
   ISBN-13: 978-0-325-01371-8
   ISBN-10: 0-325-01371-3
  1. College readers. 2. English language—Rhetoric—Problems, exercises, etc. 3. Report writing—Problems, exercises, etc. 4. Reading comprehension—Problems, exercises, etc. I. Title.
   PE1417.M48537 2008
   808'.0427—dc22
                                                                      2008031505

Editor: Wendy Murray
Production editor: Sonja S. Chapman
Cover and interior design: Lisa Fowler
Compositor: Eric Rosenbloom, Kirby Mountain Composition
Manufacturing: Steve Bernier

Printed in the United States of America on acid-free paper

12 11 10 09 08 VP 1 2 3 4 5

THIS IS FOR MY STUDENTS,

WHO TAUGHT ME TO TEACH,

AND FOR MY PARENTS,

CHARLES AND JOAN RAWLINGS,

WHO TAUGHT ME TO READ.

Contents

PART **1** PERSUASION POLITICS

PART **2** WARTIME

Acknowledgments

I would like to extend a grateful thank-you to the Heinemann team and Saint Ann's School for their support of all kinds with this project. And many, many thanks and much more to editor extraordinaire, mother hen, and guardian angel of this project, Wendy Murray. Thanks are also due to Jillan Scahill and Sonja Chapman for their indispensable assistance.

I would also like to acknowledge support from Gail Brousal, James Busby, Ruth Chapman, Elisa Chavez, Sarah Crichton, Michael Donohue, Elizabeth Fodaski, Nicole Hartnett, William Hogeland, Melissa Kantor, Thomas Kingsely, Pamela Clarke Keogh, Matthew Laufer, Victor Marchioro, Jeanne Miller, Milton Miller, David Murgio, Dana Okeson, Annie Rawlings, Charles Rawlings, Eddie Rawlings, Joan Rawlings, Denise Rinaldo, Robert Swacker, Laura Trevelyan, Mary Watson, Larry Weiss, Toni Yagoda, and Ken and Isabelle Zeidner. I would like to express special gratitude to Ragan O'Malley, Head Librarian at Saint Ann's School, for her kind support and assistance with research. And most especially I want to thank my husband, James Miller (for making the coffee), and my son, Jack (for making me laugh).

Foreword

We read for the conversations that texts invite us to have about the world, human nature, and ourselves. Every text is an invitation to converse, and we bring to these encounters a different urgency and perspective at various stages of our lives. We live in a world now where these encounters include those so different from ourselves—or so it seems at first. As Carol Rawlings Miller proves in this wonderful book *Strange Bedfellows*, there are often surprising harmonies between seemingly discordant voices. She challenges our ideas about literature and life by putting texts that talk back to each other literally side by side for us to examine. In so doing, Miller plays the role of matchmaker, bringing together voices and ideas, topics and texts, to create couples we could not have imagined. Her work here, in all ways, embodies what Arthur Applebee calls "curriculum as conversation."

It is, however, much more than a polite textual tea party where these different authors sit around tables talking easily about [persuasion] politics or wartime or cultural identity. Carol Rawlings Miller has arranged these works around heftier, edgier ideas, using these diverse texts to answer or at least respond to essential questions appropriate to our times and the world around us. *Read this, and then let's talk*, Miller seems to be saying. Enough with the hand wringing about pedagogy; put complex, fabulous texts in students' hands, ask good questions, and fire up their intellects. Miller leads us—and in turn our students—into longstanding and urgent conversations that have become all too scarce in many classrooms in recent years, places where the curriculum has become all too safe, too plain. When she pairs Martin Luther King and Shakespeare, there is a resounding cymbal crash in the head, as there is when Miller serves up speeches by Susan Sontag and George W. Bush. A stranger set of bedfellows has not been seen in some time.

Carol Rawlings Miller puts forth much more here than a rousing collection to share with students. In recent years, English education has undergone a host of challenges and changes, many in response to the demands of the workplace and postsecondary institutions. There is, appropriately, a demand for students to be able to synthesize multiple perspectives, to critically examine different sides of an argument, and to convey these understandings through coherent, rhetorically effective writing both on the page and the screen. In *Strange Bedfellows*, the texts, while the heart of the book, are merely the beginning of a lively mix that can be used to work on genre, rhetoric, and writing. Miller has also assembled an array of types of texts through which to examine the big ideas in this book. It is not, in other words, a typical anthology of essays, but is, instead, a varied bunch of speeches, poems, articles, editorials, lyrics, and, of course, essays. Through these different genres, Miller creates many opportunities to develop what I have referred to elsewhere as "textual intelligence," which means, in short, the knowledge of not only how to make sense of various texts but also an ability to construct a variety of types of texts for a range of purposes. Smart readers parlay their hard-won skills to become smart writers.

In fact, the reading-writing connection is a big push in this book. Because she is a classroom teacher, she is always trying to accomplish much more than merely inviting interesting people to talk to her students. Every text and pair here is accompanied by questions and prompts, suggested assignments and strategies that work to improve students' abilities as readers, writers, and thinkers. Throughout the country high schools are being asked to teach students more expository prose, to develop greater expository writing skills so when they arrive at college, they are prepared to not only read but to write about and discuss with intelligence what they read. Carol Rawlings Miller has written a book that will help both the experienced and the novice teacher do all these things. Perhaps most important, she has created a course of study that will bring back to the classroom something of the fire it once had but which recent movements have dampened. Anytime Barack Obama and Arnold Schwarzenegger come together you know it will be not just an interesting conversation but a great class.

—Jim Burke
Author of *The English Teacher's Companion*

Introduction

How do students become readers? My experience is that the proverbial best teacher is experience. Give a student a compelling, historic, unforgettable text and you might wind up with a reader. Why? Because the texts themselves create people who want to read. Through them readers come to know a sustenance and stimulation that is really like nothing else. Reading pulls us in deeply.

Eclectic texts comprise this collection. I have juxtaposed writings in a variety of configurations meant in various ways to push and pull students, to educate and delight, as Horace once so usefully said. And I give strategies for teaching reading and for the interpretation and analysis of intellectually engaging material. The responsive, skeptical, curious reader is my goal as a teacher—I selected texts and created reading and writing activities here with that prize in mind.

The specific premise of *Strange Bedfellows: Surprising Text Pairs and Lessons for Reading and Writing Across Genres* is that the juxtaposition of texts has a pedagogic efficacy that is remarkable. A few days spent on some of these texts might radicalize a student's awareness of language. What is rhetoric? What is persuasion? The study of the "I Have a Dream" speech and "St. Crispin's Day" speech, for example, teaches students easily, emblematic as they are of persuasive speech.

Juxtaposing texts can work with a variety of abilities and ages, though I first noticed its power when I was teaching a review for the English AP in Language and Composition. I saw how quickly students' reading sharpened when they had done even a few practice essays on paired texts. They could suddenly understand diction more clearly and notice strategies for structure and argumentation more quickly. They became more aware of rhetoric. They learned how to approach unfamiliar terrain more confidently, and their sophistication, in a related development, seemed to grow naturally and quickly.

Further, the relative shortness of these readings is an important part of the story. The study of reading often privileges long works. We spend long weeks on the road with this novel and that play and well we should. This is a part of literacy that builds stamina and an ability to shoulder long arcs of complexity. But an overemphasis on long works misses an opportunity. Short readings lend themselves to reading aloud in class. An entire short work, such as a personal essay or an editorial, provides examples of structure, of how pieces should have a beginning, middle, and end. Short works can make expository writing more accessible for some students; it simply narrows the field they are writing in, creating a certain kind of focus perforce.

Genuine literacy is, I think, created by a wide range of challenges, and here, as elsewhere in life, variety has a virtue all its own. Throughout this book, there are a range of texts and types of text. There are different genres. Works of high and low culture. Old and new authors. Not all the lifting in this book is heavy. And not all of it is light. Some chapters are designed to be stimulating and substantive but also more accessible, like the one with the *Onion* articles. Going through the process of analytical investigation with in-reach texts is crucial. It builds confidence. It is, well, fun. And that fun is a little contagious. Suddenly language in all kinds of places becomes more interesting. Some pairs will be more of a challenge, and some texts will perhaps be quite conspicuously "a reach." That reaching is crucial. Students need to learn to deal with and transcend those initial reactions to older texts or formal texts. Too often professional conversation about reading turns to pleasing students by meeting their literacies. As a universal approach, this can only limit our students rather than help them flourish.

Many great texts knock us off balance. That is part of the pleasure of reading, its special call to our intelligence. But many students are too easily discouraged by complexity, too quick to be intimidated. We want them to be wide awake as readers, not cowed. Sometimes education that is too grimly serious about learning and standards subtly—and not so subtly—tells students: be very afraid. Instead, they should feel capable, with a healthy intellectual humility (not a surfeit of it). But tricky waters must be navigated when we lead them out to the unquiet deep. They have to learn how to handle challenging texts, and there is no one all-purpose answer to reading them successfully. Only by doing, and doing again, do students internalize a sort of readerly resourcefulness and general confidence. So challenging journeys should be a part of what students undertake, but we need to support them as they go and teach them well.

In this book, reading questions build from a very simple place. Students are continually asked to discuss their experience reading. What was their reaction? Did they run into any trouble understanding? What did they notice? These are simple questions, obvious, even. They are unintimidating, wonderfully good at getting the ball rolling. Then the questions become more specific, more focused on form and content and literary terms, and the questions extend to looking at both texts together. There are also student reading questions for independent work that ask students to look closely at texts.

Two writing assignments come with each lesson. Practitioners of literature are better readers, and better readers are better writers. The readings in this book explore genre; the assignments often ask them to play with different genres in their own writing. Usually one assignment is more analytical in focus and one is more creative. Not all of the analytical assignments are full-length essays and not all of them conform exactly to essay structure. Some assignments allow for literary response in the first person. Writing in the first person about literature can be a potent way to make a little room for that first-person singular instinct of youth but it also, importantly, makes reading a personal matter. In fact, expository form and conventions only become more interesting choices when students have a broader range of experience as writers about literature. Experience articulating ideas in a variety of modes mixes it up, makes writing more interesting, enlivening the voice of the student writer.

Discussions of reading and literacy can be not only frighteningly dry but full of doomsday scenarios. The world of education, in need of dollars and support and assistance, has its own language, and like all professional languages, this language has its place. We need to know broad trends in learning; we desperately need to know who isn't getting it and why. But how the statistics are skewing and why certain populations are troping in which directions and which standard we are meeting are all, at least in tone and feeling, nothing we should share with students, however loud these discussions are in our own lives.

Indeed, we need ourselves to stay in touch with the beauty and power of reading, so uniquely human, with its strange frequency, which links us uniquely to ourselves, to other people, to history. We need to recall something in ourselves. Where was that special place we read as children? Where was the bed, the closet, the chair? What were the loved books that we pulled around us cloaklike to live in for a while? There "lives the dearest freshness deep down things," in the words of Gerard Manley Hopkins, and we need to keep "that dearest freshness" alive in our own relationship to books—to be real guides because it really matters, still, to us, too.

So, we should bring students something rich and strange. The tragedians. The hot-for-power politicians. The president. The former slave. The poets and lyricists. The critics. The satirists, the fools, and the clowns.

TEXT PAIRS	SOCIAL STUDIES LINKS	THEMES	FOCAL POINTS	OTHER TEXTS TO TRY
SHAKESPEARE and KING	The Hundred Years War; The Civil Rights Movement	overcoming adversity; hope; national identity	persuasion, 500 years apart	Obama's 2008 Presidential Acceptance Speech; President Lyndon B. Johnson's "We Shall Overcome" Speech to Congress, 1965
OBAMA and - SCHWARZENEGGER	political party conventions	political rhetoric; campaign strategies	formula writing across party lines	Obama's 2008 Acceptance Speech; McCain's 2008 Acceptance Speech
DE GOUGES and TRUTH	feminism; enlightenment	human rights; suffrage; slavery and feminism	written versus spoken words; high and low diction	Gloria Steinem's *Outrageous Acts and Every Day Rebellions*; Betty Friedan's *The Feminine Mystique*
BUSH and SONTAG and BYLES	9/11/01; American foreign policy; The Middle East	freedom of speech; democracy; critique of leaders during wartime	style: simple versus complex language	F.D.R's "I Hate War;" Lincoln's The Gettysburg Address
OWEN and REMARQUE	World War I	adult betrayal of youth in wartime	poetry versus prose	Tim O'Brien's *The Things They Carried*; Anthony Swofford's *Jarhead: A Marine's Chronicle of the Gulf War and Other Battles*; warstories.com
SWIFT and LEWIN	18th-century poverty; the Vietnam War	systemic social failure; hypocrisy	satire and social commentary	James Thurber's "The Unicorn in the Garden"
THE ONION ARTICLES	9/11/01; American pharmaceutical industry	21st-century America; America and history; pathologizing normal behavior	satire and social commentary; parody of American magazine writing	*The Onion* online; Saturday Night Live; The Daily Show with Jon Stewart
SEAVER and HERBERT	intellectual property; corporate power	ownership of language	satire in corporate debate	Matt Groening's *The Simpsons*; Greg Daniel's *The Office*
KIPLING and JOHNSON	America in the Philippines; racism	colonialism and racism	poetry and politics: imitation of form	Joseph Conrad's *Heart of Darkness*
YOUNG and SKYNYRD and ZEVON	the American South	the Civil War legacy: Southern history	radio, music, and public debate	Woody Guthrie's *This Land Is Your Land* in response to Irving Berlin's *God Bless America*
JAMES and LAMOTT	the contemporary literary world	jealousy	mock epic poetry and contemporary prose	Alexander Pope's *The Dunciad*; Stephen King's *On Writing, A Memoir of the Craft*
PAMUK and MITCHELL	The Ottoman Empire; old New York	urban portraiture; aging citizens and the past	descriptive technique	Virginia Woolf's essay *The London Scene*
TAN and RODRIGUEZ	immigration and education policy in late 20th-century America	immigrants and English	personal experience with political conclusions	Sherman Alexie's essay "Superman and Me"
SANDERS and UNSIGNED ARTICLE ON ALCHOLISM	alcohol abuse in American culture	drinking	personal narrative versus medical writing for lay reader	Dick Lourie's poem "Forgiving Our Fathers"
SENECA and DIDION	illness and culture	learning to cope with illness	the personal essay, old and new	Susan Sontag's essays *Illness as Metaphor* and *AIDS and Its Metaphors*

NEW TEXT PAIR	NEW FOCUS
King and Obama	American dreamers: African-Americans speaking forty years apart
Shakespeare and Owen	signing up: the call to fight
Sontag and Unsigned *Onion*	9–11-01 commentary
Sontag, Lewin, and Owen	war critique
King and Johnson	American racism
King, Skynyrd, Young	the American South: George Wallace
Lamott and Sanders	personal experiences and lessons learned
Lewin and Bush	America's military
King and Tan	American diversity
Tan and Truth	varieties of English
Rodriguez and Sanders	parents
King, Kipling, Johnson	the legacy of racism
Rodriguez and Obama	American diversity
Rodriguez, Tan, Schwarzenegger	the immigrant experience

PART **1**

PERSUASION POLITICS

DR. MARTIN LUTHER KING JR.
"I Have a Dream"

FORM: *Address to National Rally*
DATE: 1963

WILLIAM SHAKESPEARE
"St. Crispin's Day Speech"

FORM: *Battle Speech from* Henry V *(fictionalized version of historical event)*
DATE: 1599

NOTE ON TEACHING

On the Internet, audio versions of these speeches are available at americanrhetoric.com, and you might also consider showing video versions. It is especially instructive to listen to the "I Have a Dream" speech, which allows us to better experience a historic text in its historic context. And it allows us to see—and hear—how a speech can be written almost like a musical score to have crescendos of emotion and meaning. In the case of *Henry V*, Kenneth Branagh delivered the most recent definitive performance of the "St. Crispin's Day Speech" on film; there is as well the influential, earlier Laurence Olivier production.

THE INTERSECTION

These iconic speeches form something of an epicenter for the study of persuasive language. They are wondrously powerful, written to be spoken, and, for all their complexity, in reach for most readers. Further, abundant employment of device in both make their paired study an excellent introduction to rhetoric.

Your students might wonder—what could sixteenth-century blank verse have in common with the speeches of a twentieth-century American civil rights leader? Obvious differences abound, and yet this pairing is remarkable because it shows students that people throughout the centuries have riffled in the same bag of tricks to make their case to others, and further, that scholars, writers, and speakers are great *readers* and pay homage to earlier wordsmiths. I lead this book with this pair to launch the idea you'll see pop up over and over again: Writers talk to each other across time. There are no strange bedfellows after all.

There is another interesting point of connection between these writers, albeit an indirect one. King's many allusions to the works of William Shakespeare in his writings and speeches suggest a sharp awareness of Shakespeare's oeuvre. Indeed, the civil rights leader maneuvers in ways both explicit and implicit that echo Elizabethan rhetoric, a tradition with a long reach. For example, he plays with the opening line of Richard III in his line "the winter of our legitimate discontent." Of course, King's use of rhetoric has multiple origins. Certainly as a clergyman he would be exposed to rhetoric as part of his education, and seminary study includes homiletics, which is focused on sermon writing and delivery.

▶ POINTS FOR DISCUSSION: *"I Have a Dream"*

HALLMARKS *alliteration, allusiveness, anaphora, conceit*

FORM AND CONTENT After reading aloud and/or playing a tape of the speech, give students a moment to reflect. (How they respond will vary, of course, and hearing it is far more affecting than reading it. King's voice is a remarkable, nearly musical instrument.) Ask, "What do you think?" Spend a few minutes allowing students to share reactions. What do they think King wanted his audience to feel at the end of the speech? What can students glean about the historical moment?

TONE AND AUDIENCE Ask students to think about the setting of this speech—and to imagine a crowd of a quarter of a million. Who was there? Is King only speaking to the African Americans? Are there any moments when he seems to be speaking more to America in general? What evidence is there that he addresses a broader audience than the one before him? (You might direct them to the lines about America receiving a rude awakening if things remain "business as usual.") What is his tone there? Is it threatening in any sense? Is there a sense of "or else"? What other notes does he strike as he both challenges his audience to action and inspires hope?

FOCAL POINT: ALLUSIVENESS This text's numerous allusions form an intriguing aggregate. Group students in twos or threes and ask them to comb through the speech, looking for allusions. If something seems to them like a reference but they cannot place it, ask them to write it down anyway. You might ask them to track down allusions that night on the Internet, depending on your students' access to the Web. They can simply Google a phrase, placing it in quotes, or you can help them with identification later. They should learn the idea that it doesn't cost anything to take a note to follow up on later.

List on the board all the references King makes, going from group to group gathering their findings (try to get at least one from each study section). Then ask students to consider the significance of King's allusions. What kinds of allusions does he make? Why does he make references of such breadth? His references are from all realms of culture, from both written and oral traditions. He moves, quite at liberty, from Shakespearean drama to political documents to Negro spirituals. What do these references suggest about how he envisions his audience? Is he speaking just to the demonstrators? How does he see them? How does he want his audience(s) to see him?

> **Allusions:** *the Emancipation Proclamation, the Bible (Psalm 30, Amos, Isaiah), the Gettysburg Address, the U.S. Constitution, the Declaration of Independence, William Shakespeare's Richard III, "My Country 'Tis of Thee," and the Negro spiritual "Free at Last."*

Finally, ask them to look specifically at the end of the speech where King links "My Country 'Tis of Thee" and "Free at Last." He moves from the urgent call for freedom to ring, quoting "My Country 'Tis of Thee," to envisioning it happening, and shifts finally to the Negro spirtual "Free at Last" and comes triumphantly to the climax of his speech, "Free at last! Free at last! / Thank God Almighty, we are free at last!" What is the significance of linking songs from these worlds of national song and Negro spiritual together in this context? And finally, what do students make of the use of the present tense in the last line? In what sense, were these protesters already free?

▶ POINTS FOR DISCUSSION: *"St. Crispin's Day Speech"*

HALLMARKS *long sentences, periodic sentences, enjambment*

FORM AND CONTENT In this speech, an English king asks his troops to carry on even though they are outnumbered five to one. His troops have been on an extended campaign and are reluctant to meet their enemy under such depleted conditions. To prepare students to read this speech, ask them how they think they might be feeling if they were going into battle with the odds five to one against them. How might they view their leader? Contextualizing the speech makes it easier to understand. Its form, a call to arms, is designed to move its audience from uncertainty to confidence. How does the king make them a "band of brothers"? Indeed, what is the effect of such a phrase? Why is he creating a sense of filial relation (and obligation)?

Shakespeare is thought here to exaggerate the odds against the English, thereby heightening their valor and lending to their victory on a field at Agincourt a sense that it was not just remarkable but miraculous and God-appointed.

TONE AND AUDIENCE In the case of drama, audience is an explicit matter. There is a dramatic audience for the speech, Henry's men, as well as the English theatregoing audience of the Elizabethan period. How much does this speech flatter the English? Does it seem nationalistic? What is the king's tone when his talk turns to England and Englishmen? How does he suggest a sense of the loyalty of the English? Why will Englishmen "hold their manhoods cheap" in line 53? What does this suggest about Englishmen?

FOCAL POINT: TEXT AND SUBTEXT This speech provides excellent ground for studying text and subtext. What are the explicit statements and what is implied? Direct students' attention to the lines where Henry offers any doubters what is, at least on the face of it, an easy out.

They should consider why, in the first place, Henry V suggests to his already depleted troops that they go home if that have "no stomach to the fight"? Why does he say such a thing? He says he will give them money and secure travel (a made passport). It sounds quite enlightened and liberating: there is no threat, it would seem, of dishonorable discharge endangering one's postbattle reputation. Does he intend, in fact, for them to go? Would they want to leave? How would one likely feel in acceptance of this offer?

▶ **POINTS FOR DISCUSSION:** *Connecting the Authors*

As is true of all the text pairs in this book—and all the discussion questions I put forth—the ultimate goal here is to help students *enjoy* these works. In the questions that follow, there are no entirely correct answers; they are framed to get students to share responses and opinions and back up their ideas with the text. Ask, "What would you say is the intention of each speech? Are the goals the same? Different? Which speaker has the more complex audience?"

One of these speeches is historic and one is, in a sense, historical fiction. At the height of the civil rights movement, the "I Have a Dream" speech was delivered in 1963 at the Lincoln Memorial before a quarter of a million people. In Dr. King's speech we have a historic document of certain authenticity, because it was taped. King is trying to make history with this speech, and to change history for African Americans. Shakespeare, on the other hand, uses history to write a work of dramatic fiction; the speech of the English King is utterly invented, though the battle at Agincourt is not.

How clear and direct do students find each speaker to be in his intentions? Do they find one writer more manipulative than the other? More persuasive? Which writer makes more use of rhetorical device? Which writer is sparer? Is one of these speakers making a more explicit effort to appear rational? In different ways, these speeches are poetic. How important is that poetic quality to their persuasiveness?

FOCAL POINT: PREDICTIVENESS Both of these speeches operate in a predictive mode. King asserts to the demonstrators that their march will go down in history. Most certainly, it did. Shakespeare's King Henry, at length, projects that Crispin's Day will become a new touchstone in English culture, and because they do win, his lines ring true both within their fictive world and beyond it. "Crispin's Day" is a beloved speech, a model of English courage and loyalty. Ask students to look through both speeches for the use of the future tense. What is the special power of projecting into the future at a time of crisis? Is it a form of encouragement? A projection of survival? What does an emphasis on the future suggest about a present situation? (Surely, that the present is something to overcome, as, for example, the song "We Shall Overcome" suggests.)

DR. MARTIN LUTHER KING JR. ~ *"I Have a Dream"*

1. Why do you think Martin Luther King Jr. makes such use of the repetition of images and sounds? What is the effect?

2. This speech is delivered by a Protestant clergyman. Does it seem sermonlike to you? How is it different from a lecture?

3. In line 79 Martin Luther King says, "You have been the veterans of creative suffering." What do you take that to mean? How can suffering be creative? What are they creating?

4. How does King both reassure and ignite the protesters?

5. Where do you think the speech comes to its climax? Where is its mountaintop?

6. What, in a couple of sentences, would you say is King's dream? Restate it in your own words.

WILLIAM SHAKESPEARE ~ *"St. Crispin's Day Speech"*

There is an extraordinary range of references to this speech. A recent Stephen Ambrose book and HBO miniseries, *Band of Brothers*, took its title from it. In the movie *Renaissance Man*, one of the characters quotes it. There are numerous stories of it being read to teams before significant games.

1. When an actor looks at a long speech in a play, he often considers the motivations for the speech as a way to think about its meaning. Play the actor and think about why Henry says what he says. What are his motivations?

2. At lines 49–50, Henry says, "be he ne'er so vile, / This day shall gentle his condition." Why does he promise to make even the lowest of his soldiers gentlemen?

3. What do you think Shakespeare's attitude is toward the warrior king as he portrays him? Is he creating an admirable character?

4. There is an obvious moment of conversion at the end of this speech. In fact, Westmoreland, some lines later, wishes ". . . Would you and I alone, / without more help, could fight this royal battle." Why does the speech have this effect? And, if you read between the lines, is there anything manipulative or questionable about this speech?

5. This speech, which is well beloved, is often quoted. Coaches, politicians, and screenwriters make much use of it. On TV and in movies, many a prebattle speech, if not most of them, has been quite shamelessly lifted from Shakespeare. Why do you think that is?

SPOTLIGHT ON RHETORIC: ANAPHORA

Barack Obama, on accepting the Democratic nomination for the President of the United States, made elaborate use of King's repetition of "Now is the time." Obama's historic speech was delivered on August 28, 2008, forty-five years to the day after King's "I Have a Dream" speech on August 28, 1963. He is the first African-American to receive the nomination for the presidency.

Anaphora is the repetition of words, phrases, or clauses in successive lines, stanzas, or paragraphs. The use of anaphora in the "I Have a Dream" speech is especially notable. The purposes of such repetition are manifold. Obviously, it creates emphasis. It creates something to remember and know. It can become a kind of verbal drumbeat running through a piece. Anaphora can work at times a bit like theme and variation: here are all the ways I have a dream—here are all its aspects. Further, the repeated phrase serves to unify as well. And a beautiful phrase can run waterlike through a piece. We see anaphora in prose as well as poetry (for example, in Walt Whitman's 1855 "Song of Myself").

In the "I Have a Dream" speech, King also makes use of conceit. A *conceit* is an extended metaphor. Conceits crystallize and develop an idea in memorable terms. King develops the image of the "blank check," perhaps commenting on money-minded America. These are quite practical terms, familiar to everyone, that make very memorable the idea that the policies for blacks were bankrupt morally but also unfair, and not just unfair, but against a founding precept of the Constitution: all men are created equal.

FIND IT

Find examples of three or more of these devices, underlining them and noting in the margin where they appear.

1. alliteration
2. allusion
3. anaphora
4. imperative
5. polysyndeton

PERSUASIVE WRITING

Write a persuasive speech in which you make ample use of anaphora, using the "I Have a Dream" speech as a model. Imagine an audience; identify what you wish to persuade them to do. Let a phrase or phrases recur insistently throughout your speech. Your speech could address a topic of national or global importance, but it could discuss something smaller and more local, too. Or you might simply write a persuasive speech that attempts to sell something. Pay attention, too, to the strengths of your argument. Persuade with the sound of your language but also persuade with logic.

ESSAY TOPICS

"The climax of oratory is reached by a rapid succession of waves of sound and vivid pictures. The audience is delighted by the changing scenes presented to their imagination. Their ear is tickled by the rhythm of the language. The enthusiasm rises. A series of facts is brought forward, all pointing in a common direction. The end appears in view before it is reached. The crowd anticipates the conclusion and the last words fall amid a thunder of assent." (Winston Churchill, *The Scaffolding of Rhetoric*)

1. In the "I Have a Dream" speech, Martin Luther King Jr. references songs. In an essay of four or five paragraphs, answer the following questions: Why does he allude to songs and why does he allude to the songs that he does? How common were they then, would you guess? Look closely at how he uses them in his speech. What would the speech be like without them? Is there, in fact, something songlike about his own speech?

2. In an essay of four to five paragraphs, answer this question: How does Henry V build an argument that leads the former doubter, Westmoreland, to say he wishes he and Henry alone could fight the French at Agincourt? Consider the king's tone, his argument, his imagery, and all he says that wins the hearts of his men and steadies them in a dark hour. Before you begin writing this essay, go through the text and take notes directly on it. Underline crucial lines and write a list of all the persuasive things he says. Be sure to quote from the text to prove your points.

Dr. Martin Luther King Jr. · *"I Have a Dream"*

1929–1968
BORN ATLANTA, GEORGIA, U.S.A.

I am happy to join with you today in what will go down in history as the greatest demonstration for freedom in the history of our nation.

Five score years ago, a great American, in whose symbolic shadow we stand today, signed the Emancipation Proclamation. This momentous

5   decree came as a great beacon light of hope to millions of Negro slaves who had been seared in the flames of withering injustice. It came as a joyous daybreak to end the long night of their captivity.

But one hundred years later, the Negro still is not free. One hundred years later, the life of the Negro is still sadly crippled by the manacles of segrega-

10 tion and the chains of discrimination. One hundred years later, the Negro lives on a lonely island of poverty in the midst of a vast ocean of material prosperity. One hundred years later, the Negro is still languished in the corners of American society and finds himself an exile in his own land. And so we've come here today to dramatize a shameful condition.

15 In a sense we've come to our nation's capital to cash a check. When the architects of our republic wrote the magnificent words of the Constitution and the Declaration of Independence, they were signing a *promissory note* to which every American was to fall heir. This note was a promise that all men, yes, black men as well as white men, would be guaranteed the

20 "unalienable Rights" of "Life, Liberty and the pursuit of Happiness." It is obvious today that America has defaulted on this promissory note, insofar as her citizens of color are concerned. Instead of honoring this sacred obligation, America has given the Negro people a bad check, a check which has come back marked "insufficient funds."

25 But we refuse to believe that the bank of justice is bankrupt. We refuse to believe that there are insufficient funds in the great vaults of opportunity of this nation. And so, we've come to cash this check, a check that will give us upon demand the riches of freedom and the security of justice.

We have also come to this hallowed spot to remind America of the fierce

30 urgency of Now. This is no time to engage in the luxury of cooling off or to take the tranquilizing drug of gradualism. Now is the time to make real the promises of democracy. Now is the time to rise from the dark and desolate valley of segregation to the sunlit path of racial justice. Now is the time to lift our nation from the quicksands of racial injustice to the solid rock of

35 brotherhood. Now is the time to make justice a reality for all of God's children.

promissory note—
written promise to pay a sum
of money

continued on following page

40

It would be fatal for the nation to overlook the urgency of the moment. This sweltering summer of the Negro's legitimate discontent will not pass until there is an invigorating autumn of freedom and equality. Nineteen sixty-three is not an end, but a beginning. And those who hope that the Negro needed to blow off steam and will now be content will have a rude awakening if the nation returns to business as usual. And there will be neither rest nor tranquility in America until the Negro is granted his citizenship rights. The whirlwinds of revolt will continue to shake the foundations of

45

our nation until the bright day of justice emerges.

But there is something that I must say to my people, who stand on the warm threshold which leads into the palace of justice: In the process of gaining our rightful place, we must not be guilty of wrongful deeds. Let us not seek to satisfy our thirst for freedom by drinking from the cup of bitter-

50

ness and hatred. We must forever conduct our struggle on the high plane of dignity and discipline. We must not allow our creative protest to degenerate into physical violence. Again and again, we must rise to the majestic heights of meeting physical force with soul force.

The marvelous new militancy which has engulfed the Negro community

55

must not lead us to a distrust of all white people, for many of our white brothers, as evidenced by their presence here today, have come to realize that their destiny is tied up with our destiny. And they have come to realize that their freedom is inextricably bound to our freedom.

We cannot walk alone.

60

And as we walk, we must make the pledge that we shall always march ahead.

We cannot turn back.

There are those who are asking the devotees of civil rights, "When will you be satisfied?" We can never be satisfied as long as the Negro is the victim

65

of the unspeakable horrors of police brutality. We can never be satisfied as long as our bodies, heavy with the fatigue of travel, cannot gain lodging in the motels of the highways and the hotels of the cities. We cannot be satisfied as long as the Negro's basic mobility is from a smaller ghetto to a larger one. We can never be satisfied as long as our children are stripped

70

of their self-hood and robbed of their dignity by a sign stating: "For Whites Only." We cannot be satisfied as long as a Negro in Mississippi cannot vote and a Negro in New York believes he has nothing for which to vote. No, no, we are not satisfied, and we will not be satisfied until "justice rolls down like waters, and righteousness like a mighty stream."

75 I am not unmindful that some of you have come here out of great trials and tribulations. Some of you have come fresh from narrow jail cells. And some of you have come from areas where your quest—quest for freedom left you battered by the storms of persecution and staggered by the winds of police brutality. You have been the veterans of creative suffering. Con-

80 tinue to work with the faith that unearned suffering is redemptive. Go back to Mississippi, go back to Alabama, go back to South Carolina, go back to Georgia, go back to Louisiana, go back to the slums and ghettos of our northern cities, knowing that somehow this situation can and will be changed.

85 Let us not wallow in the valley of despair, I say to you today, my friends.

And so even though we face the difficulties of today and tomorrow, I still have a dream. It is a dream deeply rooted in the American dream.

I have a dream that one day this nation will rise up and live out the true meaning of its creed: "We hold these truths to be self-evident, that all men

90 are created equal."

I have a dream that one day on the red hills of Georgia, the sons of former slaves and the sons of former slave owners will be able to sit down together at the table of brotherhood.

I have a dream that one day even the state of Mississippi, a state sweltering

95 with the heat of injustice, sweltering with the heat of oppression, will be transformed into an oasis of freedom and justice.

I have a dream that my four little children will one day live in a nation where they will not be judged by the color of their skin but by the content of their character.

100 I have a *dream* today!

I have a dream that one day, down in Alabama, with its vicious racists, with its governor having his lips dripping with the words of *interposition* and *nullification*—one day right there in Alabama little black boys and black girls will be able to join hands with little white boys and white girls as sis-

105 ters and brothers.

I have a *dream* today!

I have a dream that one day every valley shall be exalted, and every hill and mountain shall be made low, the rough places will be made plain, and the crooked places will be made straight, "and the glory of the Lord shall be

110 revealed and all flesh shall see it together."

continued on following page

This is our hope, and this is the faith that I go back to the South with.

With this faith, we will be able to hew out of the mountain of despair a stone of hope. With this faith, we will be able to transform the jangling discords of our nation into a beautiful symphony of brotherhood. With

115 this faith, we will be able to work together, to pray together, to struggle together, to go to jail together, to stand up for freedom together, knowing that we will be free one day.

And this will be the day—this will be the day when all of God's children will be able to sing with new meaning:

120 *My country 'tis of thee, sweet land of liberty, of thee I sing.*
Land where my fathers died, land of the Pilgrim's pride,
From every mountainside, let freedom ring!

And if America is to be a great nation, this must become true.

And so let freedom ring from the prodigious hilltops of New Hampshire.

125 Let freedom ring from the mighty mountains of New York.

Let freedom ring from the heightening Alleghenies of Pennsylvania.

Let freedom ring from the snowcapped Rockies of Colorado.

Let freedom ring from the curvaceous slopes of California.

But not only that:

130 Let freedom ring from Stone Mountain of Georgia.

Let freedom ring from Lookout Mountain of Tennessee.

Let freedom ring from every hill and molehill of Mississippi.

From every mountainside, let freedom ring.

And when this happens, when we allow freedom to ring, when we let it

135 ring from every village and every hamlet, from every state and every city, we will be able to speed up that day when *all* of God's children, black men and white men, Jews and Gentiles, Protestants and Catholics, will be able to join hands and sing in the words of the old Negro spiritual:

Free at last! Free at last!
140 *Thank God Almighty, we are free at last!*

WILLIAM SHAKESPEARE ⤳ *"St. Crispin's Day Speech"*

1564–1616
BORN ENGLAND

Enter the KING

WESTMORELAND: O that we now had here
    But one ten thousand of those men in England
    That do no work to-day!

5   KING: What's he that wishes so?
    My cousin Westmoreland? No, my fair cousin;
    If we are mark'd to die, we are *enow*
    To do our country loss; and if to live,
    The fewer men, the greater share of honour.
10   God's will! I pray thee, wish not one man more.
    By Jove, I am not covetous for gold,
    Nor care I who doth feed upon my cost;
    It *yearns* me not if men my garments wear;
    Such outward things dwell not in my desires.
15   But if it be a sin to covet honour,
    I am the most offending soul alive.
    No, faith, my *coz*, wish not a man from England.
    God's peace! I would not lose so great an honour
    As one man more methinks would *share* from me
20   For the best hope I have. O, do not wish one more!
    Rather proclaim it, Westmoreland, through my host,
    That he which hath no stomach to this fight,
    Let him depart; his passport shall be made,
    And *crowns for convoy* put into his purse;
25   We would not die in that man's company
    That fears his fellowship to die with us.
    This day is call'd the *Feast of Crispian*.
    He that outlives this day, and comes safe home,
    Will stand a tip-toe when this day is nam'd,
30   And rouse him at the name of Crispian.
    He that shall live this day, and see old age,
    Will yearly on the *vigil* feast his neighbours,
    And say "To-morrow is Saint Crispian."
    Then will he strip his sleeve and show his scars,
35   And say "These wounds I had on Crispian's day."
    Old men forget; yet all shall be forgot,
    But he'll remember, with advantages,

enow—
enough

yearns—
grieves

coz—
cousin

share—
take away

crowns for convoy—
travel money

Feast of Crispian—
Oct. 25 is observed in honor of martyred brothers Crispin and Crispianus

vigil—
eve of Crispin's Day

continued on following page

What feats he did that day. Then shall our names,
Familiar in his mouth as household words—

40   Harry the King, Bedford and Exeter,
Warwick and Talbot, Salisbury and Gloucester—
Be in their flowing cups freshly rememb'red.
This story shall the good man teach his son;
And Crispin Crispian shall ne'er go by,

45   From this day to the ending of the world,
But we in it shall be remembered—
We few, we happy few, we band of brothers;
For he to-day that sheds his blood with me

vile—
low born
Shall be my brother; be he ne'er so *vile*,

gentle his condition—
elevate him to gentleman
status

50   This day shall *gentle his condition*;
And gentlemen in England now-a-bed
Shall think themselves accurs'd they were not here,
And hold their manhoods cheap whiles any speaks
That fought with us upon Saint Crispin's day.

BARACK OBAMA
Keynote Address at the Democratic Convention

FORM: *Convention Address*
DATE: 2004

ARNOLD SCHWARZENEGGER
Keynote Address at the Republican Convention

FORM: *Convention Address*
DATE: 2004

THE INTERSECTION

What could be more emblematic of American presidential politics than the party convention? Balloons, banners, delegates, politicians all briefly occupy one highly heated space. Study of these keynote addresses invites students to explore aspects of campaign rhetoric and to begin to identify its conventions. Arnold Schwarzenegger, movie star turned politician, works to both promote and defend the incumbent, President George Bush, while Barack Obama, then relatively unknown, seeks to advance the Democratic candidate, John Kerry. Between these two speeches, there are intriguing differences, yet their similarities indicate the playbook of the speechwriter. The idea of writing by formula raises interesting, possibly uncomfortable questions: What does it say about us? Are our responses so predictable that they can be scripted? And simply because something is scripted, is it therefore by definition insincere?

These and other political speeches are easily located online at americanrhetoric.com. This excellent, easy-to-use website provides a massive speech bank, audio and video clips, an extensive list of terms, and a quiz to test your knowledge of rhetorical forms.

NOTE ON CONTROVERSIAL SUBJECTS

Many teachers find themselves at some point navigating the tricky waters of politics, and we each find our own way. For myself, with this discussion, I try to urge a dispassionate exchange of ideas about what is said and why. When it comes to revealing my own politics, I have made different choices with different groups of students. At times, it has seemed important to confess my bias; at other times, it has seemed better not to in order to be as inclusive as possible and to promote a balanced, analytical discussion. This latter strategy can be especially important when a student viewpoint in the minority is in danger of being quieted by the majority viewpoint (especially if I share it).

▶ POINTS FOR DISCUSSION: *Keynote Address at the Democratic Convention*

HALLMARKS *anaphora, narrative autobiography, parallel structure, direct address*

FORM AND CONTENT Before students read these speeches, I ask them to think about the purposes of a convention keynote. Why is such an address given? What sort of challenges would a speaker to a large audience face? Would the audience expect rhetorical complexity? Or simplicity? Have they ever had to listen to a long speech? Has their attention ever wavered? If so, why? I don't like to tell them too much in advance, but framing their reading with general questions can get students into a more alert analytical mode.

TONE AND AUDIENCE The word *hope* recurs in Obama's speech. Is *hopeful* indeed an apt word for the tone here? If students concur, ask them to identify what language and which passages underscore hopefulness. What might the emphasis on hope suggest about how Obama perceives his audience's state of mind?

FOCAL POINT: TEXT AND SUBTEXT This speech provides fertile ground for exploring text and subtext. What would students say are the overt subjects of this speech—that is, its stated subjects or "text"? What, on the other hand, does it *imply*? Does the speech have one goal only, or is there an implied subtext? How clearly do students come away with a sense of the tenets of the Democratic party? If one of the goals of this speech is to promote John Kerry, how well does Obama do this? In the student questions on page 18, they are asked who is more memorable to them after reading this speech, Obama or Kerry? You can extend this discussion by asking: In fact, is Obama delivering his first speech for his own run for the presidency in 2008? Does the balance of promotion even tip in his own favor over John Kerry?

Barack Obama's 2008 presidential bid has yielded many other notable speeches and dazzling examples of his gift for writing and use of rhetoric. Have your students visit YouTube to see some of them, and devise assignments that compel students to respond to them on personal and analytical levels. Another interesting tack for discussion and assignments: Conduct Internet searches to find all the heated discussion in print and on radio in 2008 about rhetoric, which Obama's candidacy ignited. For example, his Democratic opponent Hillary Clinton, concerned with Obama's rising popularity and wins in the primaries, declared that words won't get the job done, it's actions and experience that count. She swiped at his speeches by likening them to "celestial choirs." Political pundits defending Obama pointed to Winston Churchill as an example of someone whose gift for words inspired action. What's your students' view? Are words flowery, manipulative tools used by those who won't necessarily "get the job done"? Or can they be the telltale signs of someone highly capable of moving people to action? (The speeches of Martin Luther King Jr. would be interesting to bring in to this discussion.) Finally, as you explore the genre of speeches, make students aware of the role of speechwriters.

▶ **POINTS FOR DISCUSSION:** *Keynote Address at the Republican Convention*

HALLMARKS *ad-libbing, anaphora, narrative autobiography, direct address, parallel structure*

FORM AND CONTENT An address to a convention held on behalf of an incumbent president has distinct goals. The incumbent is a known, and a known often requires defense. How vigorously defensive of the Bush legacy does Schwarzenegger seem to be? How would students identify the purposes of the speech? Is it more about being a Republican, or about standing beside the record of George Bush in a time of war, just three years after September 11th?

TONE AND AUDIENCE The tone of Schwarzenegger's speech is of particular interest. What feeling do students come away with as they consider his words? What does he make them feel about being American? What does he suggest are the differences between Democrats and Republicans? Is he extending the arm of friendship to Democrats in any way? Does he seem defiant? Angry? Is he making a call to arms? Is he exuberant?

FOCAL POINT: SPEAKER'S PERSONA AND DICTION How does Schwarzenegger want us to see him? What face does he put on in his speech? What does he suggest about himself? How often does he reference his movie career, either directly or indirectly? Why does he do this? Does he reference his governorship as often as his movie career? How formal is Schwarzenegger's language? How is his identity underscored by the type of language he uses? Is his language more, or less, formal than Obama's?

▶ Points for Discussion: *Connecting the Authors*

Ask students to try to put their political opinions aside for the moment, however ridiculous that may be. Ask them to try to respond at first in a purely personal way. Which speaker do they prefer? Who seems more credible? More likeable? More intelligent? Then broaden your discussion to more political considerations. Who do they think exhibits the traits of a leader? Why? (You can encourage a dispassionate conversation by offering a couple of conspicuously balanced remarks about what you like and dislike in both speeches.) Finally, does either speech seem to persuade them mightily on behalf of the presidential candidate being introduced? Or, at the end of the day, do they feel that this is simply a situation of preaching to delegates, who have long since been converted?

FOCAL POINT: RESPONSIVENESS IN SPEAKING Ask students to place the two transcripts of speeches before them. First, make them aware that these are indeed transcripts rather than copies of the prepared speeches and ask them what the difference is. Which one of these speakers seems to ad-lib more? Where, in the language of the speakers, do they see indications of the audience response? Which speaker seems to deviate from his speech more in response to the crowd? Does one of them, as a result, seem more confident in some ways?

BARACK OBAMA ~ *Keynote Address at the Democratic Convention, 2004*

1. What was your reaction to this speech? Did you like it? Were you moved by his words of hope? What didn't you like about it?

2. What are Obama's main themes? Are there any flaws in his argument? What are they?

3. How formal does Obama's diction seem to you? Does he use many big words? Does he seem to "dumb down" his speech in any way?

4. How partisan is Obama's speech? How much does he attempt to discredit Republicans and elevate Democrats?

5. Look carefully at Barack Obama's personal narrative: He nowhere mentions that his parents divorced when he was two, though elsewhere he speaks of it freely. Why do you think he omitted that detail? What does he emphasize in his story about himself?

6. Arguably any story we tell about ourselves will be, for conscious and unconscious reasons, selective in its details. Would you characterize Obama's omission as untruthful? Is it an unimportant omission? Or a crucial one?

ARNOLD SCHWARZENEGGER ~ *Keynote Address at the Republican Convention, 2004*

1. What was your reaction to this speech? Did you like it? Were you moved by his words of hope? What didn't you like about it?

2. What are Schwarzenegger's main themes? Are there any flaws in his argument? What are they?

3. How much does Schwarzenegger use humor here?

4. What was your reaction to his now oft-quoted line, "Don't be economic girlie men"? Did you think it was funny or offensive?

5. Schwarzenegger is not a native speaker of English, as he makes clear in his speech. Can you find evidence of this in the way he speaks?

6. What does Schwarzenegger's speech tell you about how he views what it is to be American?

SPOTLIGHT ON RHETORIC: DICTION

"The unreflecting often imagine that the effects of oratory are produced by the use of long words. The error of this idea will appear from what has been written. The shorter words of a language are usually the more ancient. Their meaning is more ingrained in the national character and they appeal with greater force to simple understandings than words recently introduced from the Latin and the Greek. All the speeches of great English rhetoricians—except when addressing highly cultured audiences—display an uniform preference for short, homely words of common usage—so long as such words can fully express their thoughts and feelings." (Winston Churchill, *The Scaffolding of Rhetoric*)

The term *diction* refers to the sorts of words that characterize a passage or indeed an entire work. Some writers are famous for using certain kinds of words: Gerard Manley Hopkins is known for his notable use of words of Anglo-Saxon origin, for example. Some writers, indeed some speakers, gravitate towards more elevated language and polysyllables. The question of diction sometimes is more relevant with works loudly dominated by a certain type of word.

In politics diction shifts according to audience. A speaker may use informal, slangy words sometimes but be enormously elegant and formal on other occasions. Both Obama and Schwarzenegger gravitate towards simple words because they are speaking to a very general audience.

FIND IT

Find examples of three or more of these devices, underlining them and noting in the margin where they appear.

1. anaphora
2. if—then clauses
3. the imperative
4. parallel phrasing
5. personal narrative

ANALYTICAL WRITING

Rhetoric

Read over the three quotations below. In light of the keynote speeches you have just studied, which definition best captures how rhetoric was used by Obama and Schwarzenegger? Be sure to make it clear to the reader whether you are discussing one or both of these speeches and make your opinion clear. For example, one might say something like "No speechmaker better demonstrates Kenneth Burke's assertion that rhetoric is 'the manipulation of men's beliefs for political ends' than Barak Obama."

Plato called rhetoric the "art of enchanting the soul."

Kenneth Burke said that "[t]he most characteristic concern of rhetoric [is] the manipulation of men's beliefs for political ends . . ."

John Locke declared rhetoric a "powerful instrument of error and deceit."

SPEECH WRITING

Yours Is the National Story: Write Your Own Convention Address

In the speeches we studied here, we saw something of a pattern:

- an opening series of thank-yous

- an invocation of the speaker's political position (governor; state legislator) and reference to why he is speaking

- a recitation of personal narrative

- party tenets; the virtues of the presidential candidate

- direct address to "America" and rousing finish

You will write only one part of this speech, the personal narrative. Take your own story, whatever it may be, and cast it in terms of your nation's idealized version of itself. Make your story fit into your vision of the quintessential national myth. For these two American speakers, they establish themselves as classic Americans, though in the not-too-distant past, their stories might not have worked so well (with an Austrian-born citizen on the one hand, and a biracial American on the other). You are what is wonderful about America (or wherever you live).

Tell your story so that it might be read aloud. Be sure to script in direct address to your audience: "Ladies and Gentlemen, tonight I come . . ." and "My Fellow Americans" and "Friends" and "Fellow Republicans/Democrats."

BARACK OBAMA ⁓ *Keynote Address at the Democratic National Convention, 2004*

1961–
BORN UNITED STATES

Thank you so much. Thank you. Thank you. Thank you so much. Thank you so much. Thank you. Thank you. Thank you, Dick Durbin. You make us all proud.

5 On behalf of the great state of Illinois, crossroads of a nation, Land of Lincoln, let me express my deepest gratitude for the privilege of addressing this convention.

Tonight is a particular honor for me because, let's face it, my presence on this stage is pretty unlikely. My father was a foreign student, born and raised in a small village in Kenya. He grew up herding goats, went to school 10 in a tin-roof shack. His father—my grandfather—was a cook, a domestic servant to the British.

But my grandfather had larger dreams for his son. Through hard work and perseverance my father got a scholarship to study in a magical place, America, that shone as a beacon of freedom and opportunity to so many who 15 had come before.

While studying here, my father met my mother. She was born in a town on the other side of the world, in Kansas. Her father worked on oil rigs and farms through most of the Depression. The day after Pearl Harbor my grandfather signed up for duty; joined Patton's army, marched across 20 Europe. Back home, my grandmother raised a baby and went to work on a bomber assembly line. After the war, they studied on the G.I. Bill, bought a house through F.H.A., and later moved west all the way to Hawaii in search of opportunity.

And they, too, had big dreams for their daughter. A common dream, born 25 of two continents.

My parents shared not only an improbable love, they shared an abiding faith in the possibilities of this nation. They would give me an African name, Barack, or "blessed," believing that in a tolerant America your name is no barrier to success. They imagined—They imagined me going to the best 30 schools in the land, even though they weren't rich, because in a generous America you don't have to be rich to achieve your potential.

They're both passed away now. And yet, I know that on this night they look down on me with great pride.

continued on following page

35 They stand here—And I stand here today, grateful for the diversity of my heritage, aware that my parents' dreams live on in my two precious daughters. I stand here knowing that my story is part of the larger American story, that I owe a debt to all of those who came before me, and that, in no other country on earth, is my story even possible.

40 Tonight, we gather to affirm the greatness of our nation—not because of the height of our skyscrapers, or the power of our military, or the size of our economy. Our pride is based on a very simple premise, summed up in a declaration made over two hundred years ago:

We hold these truths to be self-evident, that all men are created equal, that they are endowed by their Creator with certain inalienable rights, that
45 *among these are Life, Liberty and the pursuit of Happiness.*

That is the true genius of America, a faith—a faith in simple dreams, an insistence on small miracles; that we can tuck in our children at night and know that they are fed and clothed and safe from harm; that we can say what we think, write what we think, without hearing a sudden knock on
50 the door; that we can have an idea and start our own business without paying a bribe; that we can participate in the political process without fear of retribution; and that our votes will be counted—at least most of the time.

This year, in this election we are called to reaffirm our values and our
55 commitments, to hold them against a hard reality and see how we're measuring up to the legacy of our forbearers and the promise of future generations.

And fellow Americans, Democrats, Republicans, Independents, I say to you tonight: We have more work to do—more work to do for the workers I met
60 in Galesburg, Illinois, who are losing their union jobs at the Maytag plant that's moving to Mexico, and now are having to compete with their own children for jobs that pay seven bucks an hour; more to do for the father that I met who was losing his job and choking back the tears, wondering how he would pay $4,500 a month for the drugs his son needs without the
65 health benefits that he counted on; more to do for the young woman in east St. Louis, and thousands more like her, who has the grades, has the drive, has the will, but doesn't have the money, to go to college.

Now, don't get me wrong. The people I meet—in small towns and big cities, in diners and office parks—they don't expect government to solve all
70 their problems. They know they have to work hard to get ahead, and they want to. Go into the *collar counties* around Chicago, and people will tell you they don't want their tax money wasted by a welfare agency or by the

collar counties—
five counties surrounding Chicago

Pentagon. Go in—Go into any inner city neighborhood, and folks will tell you that government alone can't teach our kids to learn; they know that
75   parents have to teach, that children can't achieve unless we raise their expectations and turn off the television sets and eradicate the slander that says a black youth with a book is acting white. They know those things.

People don't expect—People don't expect government to solve all their problems. But they sense, deep in their bones, that with just a slight
80   change in priorities, we can make sure that every child in America has a decent shot at life, and that the doors of opportunity remain open to all.

They know we can do better. And they want that choice.

In this election, we offer that choice. Our party has chosen a man to lead us who embodies the best this country has to offer. And that man is John
85   Kerry.

John Kerry understands the ideals of community, faith, and service because they've defined his life. From his heroic service to Vietnam, to his years as a prosecutor and lieutenant governor, through two decades in the United States Senate, he's devoted himself to this country. Again and again, we've
90   seen him make tough choices when easier ones were available.

His values and his record affirm what is best in us. John Kerry believes in an America where hard work is rewarded; so instead of offering tax breaks to companies shipping jobs overseas, he offers them to companies creating jobs here at home.

95   John Kerry believes in an America where all Americans can afford the same health coverage our politicians in Washington have for themselves.

John Kerry believes in energy independence, so we aren't held hostage to the profits of oil companies, or the sabotage of foreign oil fields.

John Kerry believes in the Constitutional freedoms that have made our
100   country the envy of the world, and he will never sacrifice our basic liberties, nor use faith as a wedge to divide us.

And John Kerry believes that in a dangerous world war must be an option sometimes, but it should never be the first option.

You know, a while back—awhile back I met a young man named Seamus
105   in a V.F.W. Hall in East Moline, Illinois. He was a good-looking kid—six two, six three, clear eyed, with an easy smile. He told me he'd joined the Marines and was heading to Iraq the following week. And as I listened to him explain why he'd enlisted, the absolute faith he had in our country and

continued on following page

110 its leaders, his devotion to duty and service, I thought this young man was all that any of us might ever hope for in a child.

But then I asked myself, "Are we serving Seamus as well as he is serving us?"

I thought of the 900 men and women—sons and daughters, husbands and wives, friends and neighbors, who won't be returning to their own home-
115 towns. I thought of the families I've met who were struggling to get by without a loved one's full income, or whose loved ones had returned with a limb missing or nerves shattered, but still lacked long-term health benefits because they were Reservists.

When we send our young men and women into harm's way, we have a solemn obligation not to fudge the numbers or shade the truth about why
120 they're going, to care for their families while they are gone, to tend to the soldiers upon their return, and to never ever go to war without enough troops to win the war, secure the peace, and earn the respect of the world.

Now—now let me be clear. We have real enemies in the world. These enemies must be found. They must be pursued. And they must be defeated.
125 John Kerry knows this. And just as Lieutenant Kerry did not hesitate to risk his life to protect the men who served with him in Vietnam, President Kerry will not hesitate one moment to use our military might to keep America safe and secure.

John Kerry believes in America. And he knows that it's not enough for just
130 some of us to prosper—for alongside our famous individualism, there's another ingredient in the American saga, a belief that we're all connected as one people. If there is a child on the south side of Chicago who can't read, that matters to me, even if it's not my child. If there is a senior citizen somewhere who can't pay for their prescription drugs, and having to choose
135 between medicine and rent, that makes my life poorer, even if it's not my grandparent. If there's an Arab-American family being rounded up without benefit of an attorney or due process, that threatens my civil liberties.

It is that fundamental belief—it is that fundamental belief: I am my brother's keeper, I am my sister's keeper that makes this country work. It's
140 what allows us to pursue our individual dreams and yet still come together as one American family.

E pluribus unum: "Out of many, one."

Now even as we speak, there are those who are preparing to divide us—
the spin masters, the negative peddlers who embrace the politics of "any-
145 thing goes." Well, I say to them tonight, there is not a liberal America and a conservative America—there is the United States of America. There is not

a Black America and a White America and Latino America and Asian America—there's the United States of America.

150 In the end—in the end—in the end, that's what this election is about. Do we participate in a politics of cynicism or do we participate in a politics of hope?

John Kerry calls on us to hope. John Edwards calls on us to hope.

I'm not talking about blind optimism here—the almost willful ignorance that thinks unemployment will go away if we just don't think about it, or
155 the health care crisis will solve itself if we just ignore it. That's not what I'm talking about. I'm talking about something more substantial. It's the hope of slaves sitting around a fire singing freedom songs; the hope of immigrants setting out for distant shores; the hope of a young naval lieutenant bravely patrolling the *Mekong Delta*; the hope of a millworker's son who
160 dares to defy the odds; the hope of a skinny kid with a funny name who believes that America has a place for him, too.

Mekong Delta—
region in Southwestern
Vietnam where Mekong
River empties

Hope—hope in the face of difficulty. Hope in the face of uncertainty. The audacity of hope!

165 In the end, that is God's greatest gift to us, the bedrock of this nation. A belief in things not seen. A belief that there are better days ahead.

I believe that we can give our middle class relief and provide working families with a a road to opportunity.

I believe we can provide jobs to the jobless, homes to the homeless, and reclaim young people in cities across America from violence and despair.

170 I believe that we have a righteous wind at our backs and that as we stand on the crossroads of history, we can make the right choices, and meet the challenges that face us.

America! Tonight, if you feel the same energy that I do, if you feel the same urgency that I do, if you feel the same passion that I do, if you feel the
175 same hopefulness that I do—if we do what we must do, then I have no doubt that all across the country, from Florida to Oregon, from Washington to Maine, the people will rise up in November, and John Kerry will be sworn in as president, John Edwards will be sworn in as vice president, and this country will reclaim its promise, and out of this long political darkness
180 a brighter day will come.

Thank you very much everybody. God bless you. Thank you.

Arnold Schwarzenegger

Keynote Address at the Republican National Convention, 2004

1947–
BORN AUSTRIA

Thank you very much. Thank you. What a greeting. What a greeting. Wow!

This—This is like winning an Oscar. As if I would know! Speaking of acting, one of my movies was called *True Lies*. And that's what the Democrats should have called their convention.

You know, on the way up here to the podium, a gentleman came up to me and said, "Governor, you are as good a politician as you were an actor." What a cheap shot. Cannot believe it.

Anyway, my fellow Americans, this is an amazing moment for me. To think that a once scrawny boy from Austria could grow up to become governor of the state of California and then stand here—and stand here in Madison Square Garden and speak on behalf of the President of the United States. That is an immigrant's dream! It's the American dream.

You know, I was born in Europe and I've traveled all over the world, and I can tell you that there is no place, no country, that is more compassionate, more generous, more accepting, and more welcoming than the United States of America.

As long as I live—as long as I live, I will never forget the day twenty-one years ago when I raised my right hand and I took the oath of citizenship. You know how proud I was? I was so proud that I walked around with the American flag around my shoulder all day long.

Tonight, I want to talk to you about why I'm even more proud to be an American—why I am proud to be a Republican, and why I believe that this country is in good hands.

When I was a boy, the Soviets occupied part of Austria. I saw their tanks in the streets. I saw communism with my own eyes. I remember the fear we had when we had to cross into the Soviet sector. Growing up, we were told, "Don't look the soldiers in the eye. Just look straight ahead." It was common belief that the Soviet soldiers could take a man out of his own car and ship him back to the Soviet Union as slave labor.

Now my family didn't have a car—but one day we were in my uncle's car. It was near dark as we came to the Soviet checkpoint. I was a little boy. I was not an action hero back then. But I remember—I remember

35 how scared I was that the soldiers would pull my father or my uncle out of the car and I would never see them again. My family and so many others lived in fear of the Soviet boot. Today, the world no longer fears the Soviet Union and it is because of the United States of America!

As a kid—as a kid I saw socialist—the socialist country that Austria
40 became after the Soviets left. Now don't misunderstand me: I love Austria and I love the Austrian people. But I always knew that America was the place for me. In school, when the teacher would talk about America, I would daydream about coming here. I would daydream about living here. I would sit there and watch for hours American movies,
45 transfixed by my heroes, like John Wayne. Everything about America— everything about America seemed so big to me, so open, so possible.

I finally arrived here in 1968. What a special day it was. I remember I arrived here with empty pockets, but full of dreams, full of determination, full of desire. The presidential campaign was in full swing. I
50 remember watching the Nixon and Humphrey presidential race on TV. A friend of mine who spoke German and English translated for me. I heard Humphrey saying things that sounded like socialism, which I had just left. But then I heard Nixon speak. Then I heard Nixon speak. He was talking about free enterprise, getting the government off your
55 back, lowering the taxes, and strengthening the military.

Listening to Nixon speak sounded more like a breath of fresh air. I said to my friend, I said, "What party is he?" My friend said, "He's a Republican." I said, "Then I am a Republican." And I have been a Republican ever since! And trust me—and trust me in my wife's family, that's no
60 small achievement. But I am proud to be with the party of Abraham Lincoln, the party of Teddy Roosevelt, the party of Ronald Reagan, and the party of George W. Bush!

To my fellow immigrants listening tonight, I want you to know how welcome you are in this party. We Republicans admire your ambition.
65 We encourage your dreams. We believe in your future. And one thing I learned about America is that if you work hard and if you play by the rules, this country is truly open to you. You can achieve anything.

Everything I have—my career, my success, my family—I owe to America.

70 In this country, it doesn't make any difference where you were born. It doesn't make any difference who your parents were. It doesn't make

continued on following page

any difference if you're like me and you couldn't even speak English until you were in your twenties.

America gave me opportunities and my immigrant dreams came true. I
75 want other people to get the same chances I did, the same opportunities. And I believe they can. That's why I believe in this country. That's why I believe in this party, and that's why I believe in this president.

Now, many of you out there tonight are "Republican" like me—in your hearts and in your belief. Maybe you're from Guatemala. Maybe you're
80 from the Philippines. Maybe you're from Europe or the Ivory Coast. Maybe you live in Ohio, Pennsylvania, or New Mexico. And maybe— and maybe, just maybe, you don't agree with this party on every single issue. I say to you tonight that I believe that's not only okay, but that's what's great about this country. Here—here we can respectfully
85 disagree and still be patriotic, still be American, and still be good Republicans.

My fellow immigrants, my fellow Americans, how do you know if you are a Republican? Well, I['ll] tell you how.

If you believe that government should be accountable to the people,
90 not the people to the government, then you are a Republican.

If you believe that a person should be treated as an individual, not as a member of an interest group, then you are a Republican.

If you believe that your family knows how to spend your money better than the government does, then you are a Republican.

95 If you believe—if you believe that our educational system should be held accountable for the progress of our children, then you are a Republican.

If you believe—if you believe that this country, not the United Nations, is the best hope for democracy, then you are a Republican.

100 And ladies and gentlemen—and ladies and gentlemen, if you believe that we must be fierce and relentless and terminate terrorism, then you are a Republican!

Now there's another way you can tell you're [a] Republican. You have faith in free enterprise, faith in the resourcefulness of the American
105 people, and faith in the U.S. economy. And to those critics who are so pessimistic about our economy, I say: "Don't be economic girlie men!"

The U.S.—the U.S. economy remains the envy of the world. We have the highest economic growth of any of the world's major industrialized

110 nations. Don't you remember the pessimism of twenty years ago when the critics said that Japan and Germany are overtaking the U.S.? Ridiculous!

Now they say that India and China are overtaking us. Now don't you believe it. We may hit a few bumps—but America always moves ahead. That's what Americans do.

115 We move prosperity ahead—we move prosperity ahead. We move freedom ahead. And we move people ahead. And under President Bush and Vice President Cheney, America's economy is moving ahead in spite of the recession they inherited and in spite of the attack on our homeland.

120 Now—now the other party says that we are two Americas. Don't you believe that either. I have visited our troops in Iraq, Kuwait, Bosnia, Germany and all over the world. I've visited our troops in California, where they train before they go overseas. I have visited our military hospitals. And I tell you this: that our men and women in uniform do
125 not believe there are two Americas. They believe there's one America and they are fighting for it!

We are one America—we are one America and President Bush is defending it with all his heart and soul.

That's what I admire most about the president: He is a man of persever-
130 ance. He's a man of inner strength. He's a leader who doesn't flinch, who doesn't waiver, and does not back down.

My fellow Americans—my fellow Americans, make no mistake about it: Terrorism is more insidious than communism, because it yearns to destroy not just the individual, but the entire international order. The
135 president did not go into Iraq because the polls told him it was popular. As a matter of fact, the polls said just the opposite. But leadership isn't about polls. It's about ma—it's about making decisions you think are right and then standing behind those decisions. That's why America is safer with George W. Bush as president.

140 He knows—he knows you don't reason with terrorists. You defeat them. He knows you can't reason with people blinded by hate. You see, they hate the power of the individual. They hate the progress of women. They hate the religious freedom of others. And they hate the liberating breeze of democracy. But ladies and gentlemen, their hate is no match
145 for America's decency.

continued on following page

We are—we are the America that sends out the Peace Corps volunteers to teach our village children. We are the America that sends out the missionaries and doctors to raise up the poor and the sick. We are the America that gives more than any other country to fight AIDS in Africa
150 and the developing world. And we are—and we are the America that fights not for imperialism but for human rights and democracy.

You know, when the Germans brought down the Berlin Wall, America's determination helped wield the sledgehammers. And when the lone, young Chinese man stood in front of those tanks in Tiananmen Square,
155 America stood with him. And when Nelson Mandela smiled in election victory after all those years in prison, America celebrated, too.

We are still the lamp lighting the world, especially [for] those who struggle. No matter in what labor camp they slave, no matter in what injustice they're trapped, they hear our call; they see our light; and
160 they feel the pull of our freedom.

They come here as I did because they believe. They believe in us. They come because their hearts say to them, as mine did, "If only I can get to America." You know, someone once wrote: "There are those who say that freedom is nothing but a dream." They are right. It's the American
165 dream.

No matter the nationality, no matter the religion, no matter the ethnic background, America brings out the best in people. And as governor—as governor of the great state of California, I see the best in Americans every day—I see the best in Americans every day—our police, our fire-
170 fighters, our nurses, doctors, and teachers, our parents.

And what about the extraordinary men and women who have volunteered to fight for the United States of America. I have such great respect for them and their heroic families.

Let me tell you about a sacrifice and the commitment that I have seen
175 firsthand. In one of the military hospitals I visited, I met a young guy who was in bad shape. He'd lost a leg, he had a hole through his stomach, and his shoulder had been shot through, and the list goes on and on and on.

I could tell that there was no way he could ever return to combat. But
180 when I asked him, "When do you think you'll get out of the hospital?" He said to me, "Sir, in three weeks." And you know what he said to me then? He said he was going to get a new leg, and then he was going to get some therapy, and then he was going to go back to Iraq and fight

185 alongside his buddies. And you know what he said to me then? You know what he said to me then? He said, "Arnold, I'll be back!"

Well, ladies and gentlemen—ladies and gentlemen, America is back. Back from the attack on our homeland, back from the attack on our economy, and back from the attack on our way of life. We are back because of the perseverance, character, and leadership of the forty-

190 third president of the United States, George W. Bush!

My fellow Americans, I want you to know that I believe with all my heart that America remains "the great idea" that inspires the world. It is a privilege to be born here. It is an honor to become a citizen here. It is a gift to raise your family here, to vote here, and to live here.

195 Our president, George W. Bush, has worked hard to protect and preserve the American dream for all of us.

And that's why I say, send him back to Washington for four more years!

Four more years! Four more years! Four more years! Four more years! For more years!

200 Thank you, America. Thank you and God bless you all. Thank you. Thank you.

OLYMPE DE GOUGES
The Rights of Women
FORM: *Political Pamphlet*
DATE: 1791

SOJOUNER TRUTH
"Ain't I a Woman?"
FORM: *Speech*
DATE: 1854

THE INTERSECTION

Eighteenth- and nineteenth-century France and America were aflame with Enlightenment ideas. At the heart of their revolutions and political controversies and finally their political documents were world-changing, incendiary ideas. These ideas were catching. Assertions of the rights of man, for instance, seemed to proliferate fertile, disquieting questions. All men are created equal. Very good. What defines a man? Who should vote? Are not slaves men? And what about women? Should they not, too, enjoy the rights due to citizens? If countries extended suffrage to a greater pool of men, then why should the right not be extended to include women? In this period, feminism as a movement began in earnest. In texts born of this period, two women, a French playwright and an African American abolitionist, wove arguments in very different ways yet made the same essential assertion: Women should have the same rights as men.

In her pamphlet *The Rights of Women*, French woman Olympe de Gouges directly echoes the form of a document central to the French Revolution, the Declaration of the Rights of Man, written in 1789. Radical in this and all else, she soon found herself guillotined during the Reign of Terror. Some sixty-two years later in America, a former slave, Sojourner Truth, also addresses the rights of women, coming at the topic dually armed for argument with her experience as a slave and a woman. In fully dialectical English, inflected with the Dutch of her former masters, her speech is one of the pithiest, most forceful arguments ever levied against the justifications for the subjugation of women.

▶ POINTS FOR DISCUSSION: The Rights of Women

HALLMARKS *aphorisms, argumentation, constitutional form (prefatory remarks in direct address, declarative statements of principles)*

FORM AND CONTENT Olympe de Gouges quite directly uses the form and ideas of the Declaration of Rights of Man, which was considered a cornerstone text for the French Revolution. It was published in pamphlet format, which was quite common to the eighteenth century. Ask students to describe what sort of document this seems to be. What do they make of the use of articles to delineate points? Why do makers of political documents do this? What is the purpose of making each point discrete and easy to refer to? Point out to students that de Gouges' articles directly correlate to the French Declaration of Human Rights but with

HISTORICAL NOTE

Teaching core texts of early feminism provides an occasion to consider how the quest for equal rights emerges out of the context of Enlightenment ideas. In our own lifetimes it's easy to equate feminism primarily with the women's movement of the 1960s and early 1970s and not fully trace its ideas back farther. De Gouges reminds us otherwise. Even today, there is no global consensus about the role of women in society, and in America, feminism as a concept or rallying cry seems to come in and out of focus, depending on events. With the perspective of time and in light of recent history, Americans have become newly conscious of the status of women in our country. And when events call our attention to how women are treated elsewhere, we see the status accorded women in our society in a new light. So questions arise with new force: Why are women subjugated to men in some societies? What is the origin of that impulse? Is it driven by religion? Economics? *Is* there a biological component? Why should the subjugation of women be repelled?

modifications based on the rights of women: "Woman is born free and lives equal to man in her rights." Why do students think she so directly worked from the Declaration, rather than coming up with articles conceived on their own? Is she solely paying respect to that document? Or is this strategic?

What would students say is her intention in this document? In some sense this is a call to arms: Were students moved by what she says? Can they relate to it at all? What do her comments suggest about the status of women in French society? What about her use of language? How formal is it? (It's more grand than formal.) How complex? How is she asserting "full possession" of her intellectual faculties in the way she writes?

TONE AND AUDIENCE De Gouges addresses both the men and women of revolutionary France in this speech. Significantly, though, at line 118 in her Postscript she says, "Oh women, women! When will you cease to be blind? What advantage have you received from the Revolution?" Ask students, "What is de Gouges' attitude toward women here? What is her attitude toward men? How much anger do you sense? Does it seem warranted?"

"I shall never cease to say it, the problem is laid down, and it must be solved. She who bears half the burden ought to have half the right. Half of the human race is deprived of equality; it must be given to them. This will be one of the grand glories of our grand century. Let the right of woman counterbalance the right of man—that is to say, let the laws be placed in conformity with the morals and manners of the country." (French author Victor Hugo, 1875, in The New York Times)

France was one of the last Continental powers to grant women the right to vote. Many countries rather quickly granted the vote after the First World War but France did not until 1944. Switzerland did not give women the right to vote until 1971 and in 1984 Lichtenstein enfranchised women.

FOCAL POINT: LANGUAGE AND AUTHORITY In this document, de Gouges uses the language of authority, speaking declaratively, speaking in the imperative, speaking aphoristically, speaking for all French women. She argues persuasively that the sexes in the animal kingdom everywhere "cooperate in harmonious togetherness in this immortal masterpiece." What happens everywhere, what all women demand are "truths," she fully claims to be entitled to define and articulate. How do students react to this? How does de Gouges' use of language compare to the opening of the Declaration of Independence: "We hold these truths to be self-evident, that all men are created equal, that they are endowed by their Creator with certain unalienable Rights, that among these are Life, Liberty and the pursuit of Happiness"? Does her way of speaking seem quite in line with this American document from 1776? Are we simply seeing here all the hallmarks of eighteenth-century revolutionary rhetoric?

▶ **POINTS FOR DISCUSSION:** *"Ain't I a Woman?"*

HALLMARKS *anaphora, argumentation, biblical allusion, dialect, direct address*

FORM AND CONTENT Sojourner Truth gave this speech at the Women's Rights Convention in Akron, Ohio, in 1854. In it she argues against the notion that women are inferior, citing all the work she did as a slave and repeatedly asking "Ain't I a Woman?" The context was a meeting about the rights of women, and she rose to

Woman?" The context was a meeting about the rights of women, and she rose to counter various arguments that had been made on the floor: most clearly that women needed special treatment due to their fragility, that they were intellectually lesser, and that Christ was not a woman and therefore women were inferior. Referencing her own experience—which was hard to argue with—and confidently citing the Bible, she proceeded to dismantle arguments made before her. What sorts of things appear to have been said before she speaks? Ask students what her counterarguments are. How persuasive do they find them? Why has this speech remained so popular?

TONE AND AUDIENCE From the moment Truth uttered her first words to the crowd in Akron, her language asserts the superiority and sway of a mother's tongue. She took the stage amid booing and hissing, which she briskly labeled "a racket." She referred to the audience as children. Ask students to look closely at the opening paragraph: How does she speak to them? Ask students to circle word choices that stand out to them. How else does Truth make her opponents look small? It's astounding how her word choices all feed her intent to diminish her opponents' force. At line 18 she refers to the argument about intellect as "mean." In another she refers to "that little man in black there." Guide students to examine Truth's tone early on, for example, when she says "the white men will be in a fix pretty soon." What is she suggesting about white men? Why will they be in a fix? After her speech, activist Lucy Gage reported that "Hundreds rushed up to shake hands with her, and congratulate the glorious old mother." Is there anything else motherlike about her speech, apart from her calling her audience children?

FOCAL POINT: DIALECTIC

Sojourner Truth's English was distinctive. She spoke with a Dutch accent because her first owners were Dutch settlers in New York. She was not literate, and yet she was well versed in the Bible and became a preacher, accustomed to public speaking. Ask students, "Do you like her way of speaking? Do you know anyone who speaks this way? What is the effect of hearing such truths from a former slave? What is the rhetorical power of dialect? Does it have a sort of author-

Sojourner Truth was a remarkable woman in every way. Indeed she was a formidable-looking woman, nearly six feet tall. She was nobody to trifle with: When on one occasion she was accused of being a man, she bared her breasts to indicate that she was not. She had mothered children, endured and escaped slavery, experienced religious revelation, worked as a preacher, lived in a commune, and met the likes of Frederick Douglass and Presidents Abraham Lincoln and Ulysses S. Grant. She recruited black soldiers for the Union Army. She had numerous friends and patrons, many of them white, who supported her work, which was extraordinary in its reach and tirelessness. Hers is truly a remarkable story.

ity? Does it seem more authentic? More true? Why?" Basically it was not a choice for Truth to speak this way; this was how she spoke. But the white activists for women's rights who gave her the rostrum *did* make a choice. What do students make of that? Considering her speech in all its aspects, why does it make sense that she gained a forum for her ideas?

With the Internet, not to mention simple video, historical memory works differently than it used to. In the past, we were dependent on the highly colored, wonderfully rich, utterly fallible reminiscences. Here we have women's rights leader Frances Gage recalling Sojourner Truth's speech:

> *The leaders of the movement trembled on seeing a tall, gaunt black woman in a gray dress and white turban, surmounted with an uncouth sun-bonnet, march deliberately into the church, walk with the air of a queen up the aisle, and take her seat upon the pulpit steps. A buzz of disapprobation was heard all over the house, and there fell on the listening ear, "An abolition affair!" "Woman's rights and niggers!" "I told you so!" "Go it, darkey!" I chanced on that occasion to wear my first laurels in public life as president of the meeting. At my request order was restored, and the business of the Convention went on.*

After the speech Gage recalled that:

> *Amid roars of applause, she returned to her corner, leaving more than one of us with streaming eyes, and hearts beating with gratitude. She had taken us up in her strong arms and carried us safely over the slough of difficulty turning the whole tide in our favor. I have never in my life seen anything like the magical influence that subdued the mobbish spirit of the day, and turned the sneers and jeers of an excited crowd into notes of respect and admiration. Hundreds rushed up to shake hands with her, and congratulate the glorious old mother, and bid her God-speed on her mission of "testifyin' agin concerning the wickedness of this 'ere people."* (Frances Gage, 1889, *in* The History of Women's Suffrage, *coauthored with Elizabeth Cady Stanton*)

◗ POINTS FOR DISCUSSION: *Connecting the Authors*

Ask your students to look at the two speeches and consider first their differences. One is highly written, shaped in the language of a foundational Republican document; the other is oral, formed in part at least reactively: Truth is speaking in response to specific comments made at the Akron convention. One is written in highly polished language, asserting intellectual authority with highly literate, politically informed language. The other is spoken in confident, dialectical English with economy of expression: What's there is choice. Ask them to consider the differences between speeches and political documents. What is the power of a speech? What can happen in such a context that cannot with a written document? What is the appeal of polished writing? What is the appeal of dialectical, familiar speech? And, for all their differences, what ideas do these two women share?

FOCAL POINT: RHETORIC Both of these writers make use of rhetorical questions. In a rhetorical question, the speaker poses a question for which no answer is expected or desired. Ask your students to go through both texts and underline them. What is their force and importance in these speeches? Why do these writers use rhetorical questions instead of assertions? Why doesn't Truth say, "See, I am a woman and I can do all these things." What does her repeated question underscore? How does it create tone? The repeated question conveys impatience: how absurd it all seems as she stands before them there.

To link this text pair to contemporary women's roles and issues, it might be interesting to scan the cover lines of current women's magazines for rhetorical questions. And further, you might encourage a rollicking class discussion of whether women have come a long way, baby. Obviously there are countless ways to link this text pair to the speeches, writings, and careers of prominent contemporary women in politics.

OLYMPE DE GOUGES ∾ The Rights of Women

1. This document opens with a rhetorical question: "Man, are you capable of being just?" What is the effect? Why does the speaker begin provocatively?

2. De Gouges says that man "wants to command as a despot a sex which is in full possession of its intellectual faculties." In this period of Revolutionary France, an implication of despotism was highly charged. Why does she use the word *despot* here?

3. Rather famously, de Gouges wrote in Article 10 that because women have the right to mount the scaffold (for execution) "she must equally have the right to mount the rostrum." A *rostrum* is a platform for public oration. What do you think she means here?

4. In the Postscript, de Gouges addresses her sex: "Woman, wake up; the tocsin of reason is being heard throughout the whole universe; discover your rights. The powerful empire of truth is no longer surrounded by prejudice, fanaticism, supersition, and lies." When she says "discover your rights," what does she suggest about rights? Do they exist because they are articulated in a document? Or are they, does she imply, naturally existing?

SOJOURNER TRUTH ∾ *"Ain't I a Woman?"*

"If Sojourner Truth seems somewhat larger than life, it is because she was." (Ira Berlin, *The New York Times*, 1996)

1. How does Truth speak to her audience? What kind of language does she use?

2. What lines does she say that specifically counter the idea that women are fragile?

3. What is the impact of her repeated rhetorical question "Ain't I a Woman?"

4. To whom is she alluding when she says, "If the first woman God ever made was strong enough to turn the world upside down all alone, these women ought to be able to turn it back, and get it right side up again!"

SPOTLIGHT ON RHETORIC: THE IMPERATIVE

The imperative or command form of the verb is employed in all sorts of situations. The use of the imperative is often quite benign and even bland in everyday life. Everybody uses the imperative, from babies pointing to boxes of cookies ("Open") to teachers giving homework ("Read Chapter 10").

Within the context of argumentation, the imperative has a different force and often conveys an authoritative tone. De Gouges commands us "Observe the Creator in his wisdom." Sojourner Truth tells us "Look at me! Look at my arm!" In literature and in speeches, the conspicuous presence of the imperative is often highly suggestive and deserves close consideration.

FIND IT

Find examples of three or more of these devices, underlining them and noting in the margin where they appear.

1. alliteration

2. allusion

3. anaphora

4. aphoristic sentences

5. apostrophe

POINT OF VIEW

Write from the point of view of the opposite sex. This need not be an entire story, just an entire page in which you narrate events from the other point of view. Do everything in your power to avoid over-the-top clichés such as "I chipped a nail and almost started to cry" (the vanity-obsessed woman) or "I turned off the phone when I saw her name come up on caller ID" (the callous, self-absorbed man). Just create the plausible, simple human thoughts of your character and make their gender believable. In order to do this, you do need to imagine a specific individual.

BUILDING AN ARGUMENT

The push for women's rights and the vote for women emerged within the context of ever-broadening terms of suffrage for American voters. At first in America, only white, male landowners could vote. Then, after the Civil War, the Thirteenth Amendment accorded voting rights to all men over twenty-one, regardless of race, and the Nineteenth Amendment made voting legal for women. The Twenty-sixth Amendment was passed in 1971, granting all citizens over the age of 18 the right to vote. One argument in favor of lowering the voting age in 1971 was that if you were old enough to be drafted to fight and possibly die in the Vietnam War, then you were old enough to be able to vote (the logic of which is fairly unimpeachable). Think hard. How might one justify lowering the voting age?

Write an argument either for or against lowering the voting age to sixteen. Be sure to argue carefully in defense of your points. If you argue in favor, what supports your position? Why are sixteen year olds up to the task of voting? If against, what factors line up against their suffrage?

Before you start to write, consider what kind of piece you want to write. You could write a personal essay, but you could use a different form, too, such as a speech, a manifesto, or a chatty editorial for a youth-oriented magazine.

Be sure to suit your words to your audience: Speak appropriately. If slang is right for your audience, then use it. Consider whom you are trying to persuade. Other teenagers? Legislators? The general public? What will appeal?

Olympe de Gouges ～ The Rights of Women

1748–1793
born France

Man, are you capable of being just? It is a woman who poses the question; you will not deprive her of that right at least. Tell me, what gives you sovereign empire to oppress my sex? Your strength? Your talents? Observe the Creator in his wisdom; survey in all her grandeur that nature with whom

5 you seem to want to be in harmony, and give me, if you dare, an example of this tyrannical empire. Go back to animals, consult the elements, study plants, finally glance at all the modifications of organic matter, and surrender to the evidence when I offer you the means; search, probe, and distinguish, if you can, the sexes in the administration of nature. Everywhere you

10 will find them mingled; everywhere they cooperate in harmonious togetherness in this immortal masterpiece.

Man alone has raised his exceptional circumstances to a principle. Bizarre, blind, bloated with science and degenerated—in a century of enlightenment and wisdom—into the crassest ignorance, he wants to command as

15 a despot a sex which is in full possession of its intellectual faculties; he pretends to enjoy the Revolution and to claim his rights to equality in order to say nothing more about it.

Declaration of the Rights of Women and the Female Citizen

Mothers, daughters, sisters and representatives of the nation demand to be

20 constituted into a national assembly. Believing that ignorance, omission, or scorn for the rights of woman are the only causes of public misfortunes and of the corruption of governments, the women have resolved to set forth in a solemn declaration the natural, inalienable, and sacred rights of woman in order that this declaration, constantly exposed before all the

25 members of the society, will ceaselessly remind them of their rights and duties; in order that the authoritative acts of women and the authoritative acts of men may be at any moment compared with and respectful of the purpose of all political institutions; and in order that citizens' demands, henceforth based on simple and incontestable principles, will always sup-

30 port the constitution, good morals, and the happiness of all. Consequently, the sex that is as superior in beauty as it is in courage during the suffering of maternity recognized and declares in the presence and under the auspices of the Supreme Being, the following Rights of Woman and of Female Citizens.

continued on following page

Article 1

35 Woman is born free and lives equal to man in her rights. Social distinctions can be based only on the common utility.

Article 2

The purpose of any political association is the conservation of the natural
40 and imprescriptible rights of woman and man; these rights are liberty, property, security, and especially resistance to oppression.

Article 3

The principle of all sovereignty rests essentially with the nation, which is nothing but the union of woman and man; no body and no individual can
45 exercise any authority which does not come expressly from it [the nation].

Article 4

Liberty and justice consist of restoring all that belongs to others; thus, the only limits on the exercise of the natural rights of woman are perpetual male tyranny; these limits are to be reformed by the laws of nature and
50 reason.

Article 5

proscribe—
outlaw

Laws of nature and reason *proscribe* all acts harmful to society; everything which is not prohibited by these wise and divine laws cannot be prevented,

constrained—
forced

and no one can be *constrained* to do what they do not command.

55 ### Article 6

The laws must be the expression of the general will; all female and male citizens must contribute either personally or through their representatives to its formation; it must be the same for all: male and female citizens, being equal in the eyes of the law, must be equally admitted to all honors,
60 positions, and public employment according to their capacity and without other distinctions besides those of their virtues and talents.

Article 7

No woman is an exception: she is accused, arrested, and detained in cases determined by law. Women, like men, obey this rigorous law.

65 ### Article 8

The law must establish only those penalties that are strictly and obviously necessary, and no one can be punished except by virtue of a law estab-

promulgated—
proclaimed public

lished and *promulgated* prior to the crime and legally applicable to women.

Article 9

70 Once any woman is declared guilty, complete rigor is [to be] exercised by the law.

Article 10

scaffold—
platform for hanging or beheading

rostrum—
stage for public speaking

No one is to be disquieted for his very basic opinions; woman has the right to mount the *scaffold*; she must equally have the right to mount the 75 *rostrum*, provided that her demonstrations do not disturb the legally established public order.

Article 11

The free communication of thoughts and opinions is one of the most precious rights of woman, since the liberty assures the recognition of children 80 by their fathers. Any female citizen thus may say freely, I am the mother of a child which belongs to you, without being forced by a barbarous prejudice to hide the truth; [an exception may be made] to respond to the abuse of this liberty in cases determined by the law.

Article 12

85 The guarantee of the rights of woman and the female citizen implies a major benefit; this guarantee must be instituted for the advantage of all, and not for the particular benefit of those to whom it is entrusted.

Article 13

For the support of the public force and the expenses of administration, the 90 contributions of woman and man are equal; she share all the duties and all the painful tasks; therefore, she must have the same share in the distribution of positions, employments, offices, honors and jobs.

Article 14

Female and male citizens have the right to verify, either by themselves or 95 through their representatives, the necessity of the public contribution. This can only apply to women if they are granted an equal share, not only of wealth, but also of public administration, and in the determination of the proportion, the base, the collection, and the duration of the tax.

Article 15

100 The collectivity of women, joined for tax purposed to the aggregate of men, has the right to demand an accounting of his administration from any public agent.

continued on following page

Article 16

null—
invalid

105 No society has a constitution without the guarantee of the rights and the separation of powers; the constitution is *null* if the majority of individuals comprising the nation have not cooperated in drafting it.

Article 17

Property belongs to both sexes whether united or separate; for each it is an inviolable and sacred right; no on can be deprived of it, since it is the true
110 patrimony of nature, unless the legally determined public need obviously dictates it, and then only with a just and prior indemnity.

Postscript

tocsin—
warning bell

Woman, wake up; the *tocsin* of reason is being heard throughout the whole universe; discover your rights. The powerful empire of nature is no
115 longer surrounded by prejudice, fanaticism, superstition, and lies. The flame of truth has dispersed all the clouds of folly and usurpation. Enslaved man has multiplied his strength and needs recourse to yours to break his chains. Having become free, he has become unjust to his companion. Oh, women, women! When will you cease to be blind? What advantage have you
120 received from the Revolution? A more pronounced scorn, a more marked disdain. In the centuries of corruption you ruled only over the weakness of men. The reclamation of your patrimony, based on the wise decrees of nature—what have you to dread from such a fine undertaking? The *bon*

bon mot—
witty remark

mot of the legislator of the marriage of Cana? Do you fear that our French
125 legislators, correctors of that morality, long ensnared by political practices now out of date, will only say again to you: women, what is there in common between you and us? Everything, you will have to answer. If they persist in their weakness in putting this non sequitur in contradiction to their principles, courageously oppose the force of reason to the empty preten-
130 sions of superiority; unite yourselves beneath the standards of philosophy; deploy all the energy of your character, and you will soon see these

servile—
slave-like

haughty men, not groveling at your feet as *servile* adorers, but proud to share with you the treasures of the Supreme Being. Regardless of what barriers confront you, it is in your power to free yourselves; you have only to

tableau—
picture

135 want to. Let us pass not to the shocking *tableau* of what you have been in society; and since national education is in question at this moment, let us see whether our wise legislators will think judiciously about the education of women.

SOJOURNER TRUTH ~ *"Ain't I a Woman?"*

1797–1883
BORN UNITED STATES

Delivered 1851 at the Women's Convention in Akron, Ohio

Well, children, where there is so much racket there must be something out of kilter. I think that 'twixt the negroes of the South and the women at the North, all talking about rights, the white men will be in a fix pretty soon. But what's all this here talking about?

5 That man over there says that women need to be helped into carriages, and lifted over ditches, and to have the best place everywhere. Nobody ever helps me into carriages, or over mud-puddles, or gives me any best place! And ain't I a woman? Look at me! Look at my arm! I have ploughed and planted, and gathered into barns, and no man could head me! And ain't I a woman? I could work as much and eat as much 10 as a man—when I could get it—and bear the lash as well! And ain't I a woman? I have borne thirteen children, and seen most all sold off to slavery, and when I cried out with my mother's grief, none but Jesus heard me! And ain't I a woman?

15 Then they talk about this thing in the head; what's this they call it? [audience member suggests intellect] That's it, honey. What's that got to do with women's rights or negroes' rights? If my cup won't hold but a pint, and yours holds a quart, wouldn't you be mean not to let me have my little half measure full?

20 Then that little man in black there, he says women can't have as much rights as men, 'cause Christ wasn't a woman! Where did your Christ come from? Where did your Christ come from? From God and a woman! Man had nothing to do with Him.

If the first woman God ever made was strong enough to turn the world 25 upside down all alone, these women together ought to be able to turn it back, and get it right side up again! And now they is asking to do it, the men better let them.

Obliged to you for hearing me, and now old Sojourner ain't got nothing more to say.

PART **2**

WARTIME

President George W. Bush — Presidential Remarks, Barksdale Air Force Base, September 11, 2001
Presidential Address to the Nation, September 12, 2001

Susan Sontag — Editorial, *The New Yorker*, September 24, 2001
Melissa Byles — "Open Letter to Susan Sontag"

Wilfred Owen — "Dulce et Decorum Est"
Erich Maria Remarque — Excerpt from the Novel *All Quiet on the Western Front*

PRESIDENT GEORGE W. BUSH
Presidential Remarks, Barksdale Air Force Base

FORM: *Speech*
DATE: 1:04 P.M., September 11, 2001

SUSAN SONTAG
The New Yorker: The Talk of the Town

FORM: *Editorial*
DATE: September 24, 2001

PRESIDENT GEORGE W. BUSH
Presidential Address to the Nation

FORM: *Speech*
DATE: September 12, 2001

MELISSA BYLES
"Open Letter to Susan Sontag"

FORM: *Letter*
DATE: 2001

THE INTERSECTION

An American president speaks under profound duress in these first two selections. The first are remarks made in the early afternoon of September 11th, and the second piece is the transcript of his second formal address to the nation after the attacks, on September 12th. These are historic utterances, born of a devastating moment in American history, in world history. Some days later, in an edition of *The New Yorker* devoted to the attacks, American intellectual Susan Sontag published a blistering critique of the language used to discuss the attacks, taking particular issue (quite famously) with the use of the word *cowards* to describe hijackers "willing to die themselves in order to kill others." In the final selection, Melissa Byles takes aim at Sontag for her emphasis on language and, more generally, for intellectualizing a tragic event.

CAUTIONARY NOTE Talking about September 11th in the classroom requires forethought. Politics are involved, and not only that: Some years later, it still can resonate as a traumatic event not only for students but for teachers. This lesson has the potential to be a challenging and important investigation into national conversation at a time of crisis; indeed, our ability to speak openly is an expression of our democratic entitlement to free speech. Encourage students to feel free to speak their minds but to base their observations on this reading of these texts rather than any preconceived ideas they quite naturally might have. Try to keep this lesson from becoming a forum for political grandstanding.

SEQUENCING NOTE

Because there are four texts involved in this lesson, you may want to spread them over a few days, assigning first the president's remarks and speech, discussing them the next day, and then assigning the next two pieces the next night. Giving time to the president's speeches gives students appropriate, respectful space for careful reading, which paves the way for a more serious, credible assessment of the commentary on the language of September 11th.

The president's speeches may be heard and watched online. There are audio, video, and transcript sources available on the White House's website and at americanrhetoric.com. Many of the president's major addresses can be listened to in Spanish at whitehouse.gov. Note that some transcripts do not convey the speech as actually spoken. For instance, the president falters a few times in his Barksdale remarks, just as one might be expected to, but a transcript does not always reflect such. In other words, from source to source, standards and practices for editing transcripts vary. You might clarify for your students the difference between a copy of a written speech and a transcript, which may include all the ad libs and repetitions of the speech as actually delivered.

Should you have a student directly affected by the attacks, which will remain possible for some time, you might preview this lesson with parents, teachers, administrators, or the student to evaluate its viability. It is not out of the question that a student who suffered a loss might be supported by this lesson, just as books about death can sometimes help a student who has lost a loved one grieve, making them feel less alone with their tragedy. Johnny Carson used to say of Abraham Lincoln's death that he couldn't tell jokes about it. "Too soon," he'd quip. But it might be too soon for *you* to bring the eleventh to the classroom, and you do have to take your own temperature. Can you calmly lead a discussion on this topic?

▶ **POINTS FOR DISCUSSION:** *Remarks by President upon Arrival at Barksdale Air Force Base* and *Address to the Nation from Cabinet Room*

HALLMARKS *simplicity of syntax and diction, parallel phrasing, anaphora*

FORM AND CONTENT After reading the president's speech at Barksdale together, ask students if they see evidence of the on-the-fly situation in which these remarks were delivered and no doubt composed. Ask what they make of his opening lines "Freedom itself was attacked this morning by a faceless coward. And freedom will be defended." How does that strike them as a speech opener? Clearly the word *freedom* is emphasized, but does it strike them as somewhat abrupt? Why does he say that "we have taken the necessary security precautions to continue the functions of your government"? What does this suggest about his view of the intention of the attacks? Note that by this time, at 1:04 P.M., all three attacks had occurred. What does it suggest that Bush speaks of defending freedom? (Is he already viewing this as war and as well signaling that the United States will strike back once the enemy is known? Is he trying to assure citizens that their armed forces will defend them against subsequent attacks?) What do they make of his use of a more truncated closing, "God bless," rather than the traditional "May God bless America"?

The student questions compel them to think about why the president gave the second speech at the Cabinet Room, and not the Oval Office again, as he did the first night. Ask them, "Why might he have delivered his address at the Oval Office first?" The first night, his location spoke volumes: After the evacuation of the White House, we have this very day retaken our rightful place. The second night, his choice emphasized proper counsel, prompt action, and military preparedness. And on some level, the Cabinet Room symbolically reminds us of his cabinet and the chain of command (the first five in line after the president: the vice president, the Speaker of the House, the speaker pro tempore of the Senate, the secretary of state, the secretary of treasury).

Working as a class, list on the board what you deem the purpose of each paragraph in the cabinet speech—doing this makes the development of Bush's discussion explicit. How much of this speech is devoted to hard facts? Where are they? Toward the end of the speech, Bush relays that he has authorized emergency funds. Why does he do this? Remind them that conditions remained chaotic the next day. Other than that, are there many facts relayed? What is he telling America about its enemy? About the days to come? Is he suggesting American military action by calling the terrorist attacks acts of war?

TONE AND AUDIENCE At first blush, identifying the audience of the Cabinet Room speech is somewhat easy: It is America. What is the president trying to say to citizens? What sort of tone is he trying to strike? How much is he trying to console? His speech the previous night had quoted Psalms and asked for prayers for those who lost loved ones and for the nation. How is this speech different? How does he create a tone of firm resolve to prevail? Ask students what they noticed about his language. In particular, what is their reaction to his repetition of "This enemy" and "This is an enemy"? This use of the rhetorical device anaphora is also used in Martin Luther King Jr.'s "I Have a Dream" speech. What is its impact? What does it contribute to the feeling of this speech? How is its use different here?

In another way, Bush's speech is directed toward a global audience. Which lines seem broader in their focus? What does he signal to the friends of America? What does he signal to its enemies?

FOCAL POINT: STYLE AND DICTION The language of the Cabinet Room speech tends to be simple, direct, and in places stirring. In syntax, the president seldom varies his pattern, his sentences opening with a subject–verb pattern with independent clauses. The sentences are neither long nor complicated, and they march with a linear movement from speech beginning to speech end. There is a strong sense of drive in the speech. Ask students to describe the president's sentences: Help them to notice the simplicity of the sentences and to speculate on its purpose. This is obviously a choice, this level of simplicity. What is its purpose? For one thing, the simplicity facilitates ease of understanding. But attune them as well to the feeling it creates of clear, unambiguous direction. We will not stop. Our task is clear and simple; our danger is present and clear. No dependent clauses start any of the sentences. There are no contingent statements, no if–then clauses. This rhetorical choice, which exudes certitude, is meant to persuade Americans and the world of his—and our—resolve and our readiness.

Further, ask students to notice how complex his vocabulary choices are—or rather, how simple. Here we see Bush electing simplicity and clarity over subtlety and complication. In anticipation of reading the Sontag piece, ask students to discuss the president's depiction of this event as a battle between good and evil. The questions on page 53 invite them to consider this point, and it bears classroom discussion, too. What sense does that statement have? What are the problems with depicting the conflict in such terms? Is America only good? Are the terrorists only evil? Do they believe that evil exists? What about his characterization of the terrorists as *cowards* and *cowardly* in the Barksdale remarks? Do they understand what he means?

▶ POINTS FOR DISCUSSION: *Editorial,* The New Yorker

HALLMARKS *editorial remark using critical terms, rhetorical questions, allusion*

FORM AND CONTENT This piece appeared together with reflections from other writers such as John Updike as comments in the Talk of the Town section of *The New Yorker*. It provided one of the first broad critical statements about the rhetoric of September 11th. I intentionally list many questions so you'll have ample entry points to discuss this difficult subject. Generally, it works well to try to get your students to refrain from judgment at first and work dispassionately to examine what Sontag is saying and how she says it. (Knowing the political context prior to 9/11 is helpful). First, what does she object to exactly? Why does she say that you cannot call the hijackers cowards? In what sense is that true? Why is the post–9/11 rhetoric "unworthy of a mature democracy"? Why does she think politicians are trying to infantalize the public? Is it unfair for her to attack remarks made just hours after the event? Are you offended? On her side? Somewhere in between? Point out the way Sontag talks about grieving: Does she speak enough and respectfully enough about the dead? Is she being intentionally provocative? (She strongly implies, for example, that the Bush Administration speaks like the Soviet Party Congress, with its "self-congratulatory bromides.") When you look at the ending, does Sontag explain what America has to be in clear, linear, direct terms, or does she include this line more to encourage us to think about America? Why does she say that this was not Pearl Harbor? What is the difference? What does she suggest about why language matters so much? Sontag emphasizes how language can not only distract us from the truth but cloak the truth. If the hijackers are cowards, if they are evildoers, we are, by extension, brave and good people. Why did the attacks happen? Oversimplification leads us away from considering true historic, social, and political causes and solutions in tune with them.

TONE AND AUDIENCE *The New Yorker* readership is the audience for this comment. How would students describe Sontag's tone? Sorrow? Outrage? Ask them to name some of the words that best communicate her point of view. How formal is this writing? What do they make of the atypical structure of the first sentence, especially the pair of adjectives that seem to dangle at sentence end, a bit like notes. The rhetoric is "startling, depressing." Does that sound unusual to them? Is it typical English? What is the effect? Who does she mean by "the voices licensed to follow the event"? Do they find her tone refreshingly straightforward and honest? Difficult but appropriatly challenging? Abrasive? Offensive? Is she countering what she thinks of as concealing, manipulative rhetoric with candor and frankness, valuing them in themselves? Even if it offends others? Are there worse things than causing offense?

> *On September 17, 2001, Bill Maher also commented on the president's use of the word* cowardly *for the hijackers on his show* Politically Incorrect. *He said, "We have been the cowards, lobbing cruise missiles from 2,000 miles away. That's cowardly. Staying in the airplane when it hits the building, say what you want about it, it's not cowardly." Maher was fired for this remark.*

FOCAL POINT: RHETORICAL QUESTIONS Rhetorical questions are questions posed for which no answer is expected. Indeed, the question posed usually makes or strongly implies an assertion. Sontag writes, "How many citizens are aware of the ongoing American bombing of Iraq?" Clearly, the answer she intends is utterly clear: very few are aware. Ask students to consider her use of rhetorical questions. How is posing a question different from making a direct assertion? She could simply have said, "Very few citizens are aware of the ongoing bombing." What's the difference? How do rhetorical questions help to convey her outrage? Her bewilderment? Do they suggest a feeling of isolation?

▶ POINTS FOR DISCUSSION: *"Open Letter to Susan Sontag"*

HALLMARKS *open letter in direct address*

FORM AND CONTENT Melissa Byles attacks Sontag's critique of the improper use of the word *cowardly*, the timing of her analysis, and more generally her intellectual stance. What is your students' reaction to this letter? What is her main point about Sontag's analysis of courage and cowardice? What is she implying about Sontag's focus on words over images? What is she implying about Sontag's critique of language? Why does she accuse Sontag of a lack of intellectual rigor? Do your students agree with Byles' assessment that it is unfair to critique Bush for things said immediately following the attacks?

TONE AND AUDIENCE The audience for this piece is, of course, Susan Sontag, and her readers, too, no doubt. Sontag's remarks were objected to widely. What is Byles' tone? What about her opening line? What is its tone? Is it sincerely polite and deferential? If not, why is she being sarcastic in her tone? Is she implying that Sontag expects deference?

▶ POINTS FOR DISCUSSION: *Connecting the Authors*

Political rhetoric is at the center of this controversy. One of Sontag's central complaints is that the rhetoric of September 11th is manipulative, designed to deceive and infantilize the public, and her attack on the word *coward* illustrates her point. She calls the rhetoric of politicians and media commentators "sanctimonious, reality-concealing rhetoric."

Ask your students to place Bush's speeches and Sontag's letter before them on the table. Now that they have considered all the points of view, ask them to think about Sontag's critique of Bush. Do they think it has merit? Why? Why not? You might ask one of your students to read his speech aloud. Is Bush in fact too simple in his language? Or is that simplicity necessary in a diverse democracy? Does he (and his speech writers) underestimate the American people? Or does he take correct measure?

FOCAL POINT: THE POWER OF LANGUAGE This one word, *coward*, launched a thousand and one comments and reflections regarding September 11th. Bush used the word *coward* for terrorists on other occasions as well. For their challenges to the president's use of the term, Susan Sontag was castigated broadly and Bill Maher was fired from ABC. Talking heads everywhere weighed in. Why is it that this word *coward* for terrorists emerged as such a tender point? And what do students make of how the use of one word can start a fire?

> *The* 9/11 Commission Report *is a powerful investigation into and analysis of the events surrounding the attacks. Its writing, rational, economical, and movingly clear, exemplifies the modern prose style so indelibly articulated in Strunk and White's* The Elements of Style.

SEPTEMBER 11TH TIME LINE: FOUR FLIGHTS USED AS BOMBS
(BASED ON *THE 9/11 COMMISSION REPORT*)

8:46:40 A.M.	American Airlines Flight 11 hits 1 WTC (North Tower)
9:03:11 A.M.	United Airlines Flight 175 hits 2 WTC (South Tower)
9:05 A.M.	President Bush notified of attacks while reading to students at Booker Elementary School, Sarasota, Florida
9:30 A.M.	President Bush briefly addresses nation from Booker Elementary about two airplanes attacking the country in "an apparent terrorist attack"
9:37:46 A.M.	American Airlines Flight 77 crashes into the Pentagon
9:37 A.M.	Vice President Dick Cheney ordered to underground bunker in White House
9:45 A.M.	White House evacuated with an order from the Secret Service "to run"
9:54 A.M.	Air Force One departs Sarasota with no clear destination, intending to get "up in the air—as fast and as high as possible—and then decide where to go" (9/11 report). The president is advised by the Secret Service and Vice President Dick Cheney not to return to Washington due to its instability.
9:57 A.M.	Passenger assault on hijackers of Flight 93, headed toward White House or Capitol Building
10:03:11 A.M.	On the verge of a successful passenger insurrection, Flight 93 hijackers intentionally crash into a field in Shanksville, Pennsylvania
1:04 P.M.	President Bush speaks at Barksdale Air Force Base
1:48 P.M.	Air Force One with president departs for Omaha, Nebraska
6:54 P.M.	President Bush arrives at White House
8:30 P.M.	President Bush gives first formal address to the nation after the attacks from Oval Office

PRESIDENT GEORGE W. BUSH ∿ *Presidential Remarks, Barksdale Air Force Base, September 11, 2001*

1. Read President Bush's brief speech carefully and then look closely at your September 11th time line. It occurred at 1:04 P.M. on September 11th in Barksdale, Louisiana, as he was traveling back to Washington. He had first and last spoken early in the attacks, at 9:30 A.M. in Sarasota, Florida, saying that the nation had suffered a terrorist attack. Since that time, both the north and south towers of the World Trade Center had collapsed, the Pentagon had been attacked and part of it had collapsed, and a hijacked plane had crashed in Pennsylvania. The White House had been evacuated, and New York and Washington were now walking home in the smoke made that morning. What would you say is his intention in this speech? What is he trying to convey to the American people?

2. Would you say that his remarks are meant to threaten those responsible for the attacks?

3. When President Bush uses the phrase *cowardly acts* to describe the terrorists, what do you think he means by that?

4. Do you note any words or phrases that the president repeats here?

5. What other observations do you have, based on the timing of these remarks? Why do you think he made a point of addressing the American people midday? What does it imply?

PRESIDENT GEORGE W. BUSH ∿ *Presidential Address to the Nation, September 12, 2001*

1. This national address was the President's fourth public appearance since the start of the attacks on September 11th. There were the two brief sets of remarks, and an address from the Oval Office on the night of the 11th. The speech you read was delivered from the Cabinet Room. The cabinet is constituted of Bush's top advisors from all governmental sectors and includes the vice president and the heads of fifteen executive departments, including the secretaries of state, defense, and transportation. Why do you think he chose to deliver his speech from this venue rather than once again from the Oval Office? What is the significance of these locations?

2. Read the first sentence of Bush's speech quite carefully. What does his first statement emphasize?

3. What do you suspect is the significance of the president calling the attacks *acts of war*?

4. How does he characterize "the enemy"?

5. The president forecasts that "[t]his will be a monumental struggle of good versus evil, but good will prevail." What is your reaction to the language of good and evil? Does it seem religious to you? Too simple? Simply correct?

SUSAN SONTAG   *Editorial,* **The New Yorker,** *September 24, 2001*

1. What would you say is in general the point of Sontag's critique of the language used for the attacks?

2. In lines 2–3, she says that "self-righteous drivel and outright deceptions" are being "peddled by public figures and TV commentators." What is her tone there?

3. Who does she mean by "the voices licensed to follow the event"?

4. What do you think she means in line 31 when she calls this language "unworthy of a mature democracy"? What, instead, would she like to see?

5. In line 36 Sontag enjoins the American populace: "let's not be stupid together." How in her view are Americans being stupid?

MELISSA BYLES   *"Open Letter to Susan Sontag"*

1. What is Melissa Byles' general critique of Susan Sontag's discussion?

2. How does she depict Sontag in her opening paragraph?

3. What is Byles' attitude toward Sontag's critique of the rhetoric on September 11th?

4. In the last line of her editorial, Byles suggests that Sontag will be more persuasive when her views are presented with "less intellectual arrogance." Considering Sontag's piece in general, what would you say Byles considers particularly arrogant?

5. Were you at any point confused by Byles' letter? Did it seem to make references outside the circumference of your knowledge?

continued on following page

SPOTLIGHT ON RHETORIC: SYMBOLISM AND METONYMY

"The subtlest change in New York is something people don't like to speak much about but that is in everyone's mind. The city, for the first time in its long history, is destructible. A single flight of planes no bigger than a wedge of geese can quickly end this island fantasy, burn the towers, crumble the bridges, turn the underground passages into lethal chambers, cremate the millions. The intimation of mortality is part of New York now: in the sound of jets overhead, in the black headlines of the latest edition. All dwellers in cities must live with the stubborn fact of annihilation; in New York the fact is somewhat more concentrated because of the concentration of the city itself, and because, of all targets, New York has a certain clear priority. In the mind of whatever perverted dreamer who might loose the lightening, New York must hold a steady, irresistible charm." (E. B. White, *Here Is New York*, 1948)

The *Concise Oxford Dictionary of Literary Terms* defines a *symbol* as "in the simplest sense, anything that stands for or represents something else beyond it—usually an idea conventionally associated with it. Objects like flags and crosses can function symbolically." Within works of literature, symbols emerge to give life to some aspect of a work, like the albatross in "The Rime of the Ancient Mariner" by Samuel Taylor Coleridge in 1798 in *The Lyrical Ballads*.

In life and politics, buildings and places can have symbolic value, and in conflicts, their symbolic value, wherein great meaning is attached to them, can make them targets. The World Trade Center was attacked as a symbol of American capitalism, for example. The Pentagon was attacked as a symbol of American governance and will abroad. Events can attach new significance to symbols, too. The president delivered his address on the September 11th at 8:30 P.M. from the Oval Office; there is nothing unusual about an address from this location. This is in fact conventional; the Oval Office is the symbolic heart of the presidency. However, after a day of clear and present danger to America and its government, one that included the evacuation of the White House, President Bush's speech from the Oval Office had heightened symbolic meaning: We have resumed our rightful place; the government is functioning; Washington, its seat, is secure.

Related to this sort of symbolism is the use of the figure of speech, *metonymy*. In metonymy, the name for something is replaced with the name of something associated with it. For example, Americans use the term *White House* to mean the president or the will of the president as represented by his White House staff. When we refer to *Wall Street*, we are not usually referencing a place, but an institution strongly associated with it, the seat of the American Stock Exchange. Indeed, where there is such metonymy, where a place is fused with a larger meaning, you might well wonder: Is this place a target because of what it represents?

FIND IT

Find examples of three or more of these devices, underlining them and noting in the margin where they appear.

1. alliteration
2. anaphora
3. asyndeton
4. metonymy
5. parallel structure

RESPONSE WRITING

"We came into this process with strong opinions about what would work. All of us have had to pause, reflect, and sometimes change our minds as we studied these problems and considered the views of others. We hope our report will encourage our fellow citizens to study, reflect—and act." (Thomas H. Kean, Chair, and Lee H. Hamilton, Vice Chair, in the Preface to the *9/11 Commission Report*)

In a paragraph, explain why it is important to be able to change your mind in light of the views of others. How can flexibility be an intellectual virtue rather than a weakness? What happens if someone is never influenced in light of new information?

THE BURDENS OF REALITY

In his poem "Four Quartets," T. S. Eliot wrote, "Go, go, go, said the bird: human kind / Cannot bear very much reality." In Susan Sontag's piece she says that the American public is not being asked "to bear much of the burden of reality." Write a personal essay called "The Burdens of Reality" in which you reflect on the idea that reality is burdensome. What would you say are the burdens of reality at the present moment? For the nation? For the world? Feel free to speak very personally.

Questions You Might Try to Answer: How well are we handling the burdens of knowing world events at the moment? Do we shield ourselves too much from the truth? From the news? Or do we expose ourselves too much? Is it the nature of media at the present moment that we can be overwhelmed? There is a lot of information out there, a lot of news. Are we responsible for knowing it all? What constitutes responsible behavior? Dr. Andrew Weil in his book *Spontaneous Healing* (1996) recommends going on "news fasts" to avoid becoming overwhelmed by world events. Does that make sense? Or is that self-indulgence? Are there limits to what we can bear, as T. S. Eliot's line suggests?

"Those who cannot remember the past are condemned to repeat it." (George Santayana, 1905, *The Life of Reason*)

PRESIDENT GEORGE W. BUSH

1946–
BORN UNITED STATES

Presidential Remarks, Barksdale Air Force Base, September 11, 2001

Freedom itself was attacked this morning by a faceless coward. And freedom will be defended.

I want to reassure the American people that full—the full resources of the federal government are working to assist local authorities to save lives and
5   to help the victims of these attacks. Make no mistake, the United States will hunt down and punish those responsible for these cowardly acts.

I've been in regular contact with the vice president, secretary of defense, the national security team, and my cabinet. We have taken all appropriate— appropriate security precautions to protect the American people.

10   Our military at home and around the world is on high alert status. And we have taken the necessary security precautions to continue the functions of your government.

We have been in touch with leaders of Congress and with world leaders to assure them that we will do what is—whatever is necessary to protect
15   America and Americans.

I ask the American people to join me in saying a "thanks" for all the folks who have been fighting hard to rescue our fellow citizens, and to join me in saying a prayer for the victims and their families.

The resolve of our great nation is being tested, but make no mistake. We
20   will show the world that we will pass this test.

God bless.

PRESIDENT GEORGE W. BUSH ~ *Presidential Address to the Nation, September 12, 2001*

1946–
BORN UNITED STATES

President's Address from Cabinet Room Following Cabinet Meeting, 12 September 2001

I just completed a meeting with our national security team, and we've received the latest intelligence updates. The deliberate and deadly attacks, which were carried out yesterday against our country, were more than acts of terror. They were acts of war. This will require our

5   country to unite in steadfast determination and resolve. Freedom and democracy are under attack. The American people need to know we're facing a different enemy than we have ever faced. This enemy hides in shadows and has no regard for human life. This is an enemy who preys on innocent and unsuspecting people, then runs for cover, but it won't

10 be able to run for cover forever. This is an enemy that tries to hide, but it won't be able to hide forever. This is an enemy that thinks its harbors are safe, but they won't be safe forever. This enemy attacked not just our people but all freedom-loving people everywhere in the world.

The United States of America will use all our resources to conquer this

15 enemy. We will rally the world. We will be patient. We'll be focused, and we will be steadfast in our determination. This battle will take time and resolve, but make no mistake about it, we will win. The federal government and all our agencies are conducting business, but it is not business as usual. We are operating on heightened security alert. America

20 is going forward, and as we do so, we must remain keenly aware of the threats to our country.

Those in authority should take appropriate precautions to protect our citizens. But we will not allow this enemy to win the war by changing our way of life or restricting our freedoms. This morning, I am sending

25 to Congress a request for emergency funding authority so that we are prepared to spend whatever it takes to rescue victims, to help the citizens of New York City and Washington, D.C., respond to this tragedy, and to protect our national security. I want to thank the members of Congress for their unity and support. America is united. The freedom-

30 loving nations of the world stand by our side. This will be a monumental struggle of good versus evil, but good will prevail.

Thank you very much.

SUSAN SONTAG

1933–2004
BORN UNITED STATES

Editorial, The New Yorker, September 24, 2001

The disconnect between last Tuesday's monstrous dose of reality and the self-righteous drivel and outright deceptions being peddled by public figures and TV commentators is startling, depressing. The voices licensed to follow the event seem to have joined together in a campaign to infantilize the public. Where is the acknowledgment that this was not a "cowardly" attack on "civilization" or "liberty" or "humanity" or "the free world" but an attack on the world's self-proclaimed super-power, undertaken as a consequence of specific American alliances and actions? How many citizens are aware of the ongoing American bombing of Iraq? And if the word "cowardly" is to be used, it might be more aptly applied to those who kill from beyond the range of retaliation, high in the sky, than to those willing to die themselves in order to kill others. In the matter of courage (a morally neutral virtue): whatever may be said of the perpetrators of Tuesday's slaughter, they were not cowards.

Our leaders are bent on convincing us that everything is O.K. America is not afraid. Our spirit is unbroken, although this was a day that will live in infamy and America is now at war. But everything is not O.K. And this was not Pearl Harbor. We have a robotic president who assures us that America stands tall. A wide spectrum of public figures, in and out of office, who are strongly opposed to the policies being pursued abroad by this Administration apparently feel free to say nothing more than that they stand united behind President Bush. A lot of thinking needs to be done, and perhaps is being done in Washington and elsewhere, about the ineptitude of American intelligence and counter-intelligence, about options available to American foreign policy, particularly in the Middle East, and about what constitutes a smart program of military defense. But the public is not being asked to bear much of the burden of reality. The unanimously applauded, self-congratulatory *bromides* of a Soviet Party Congress seemed contemptible. The unanimity of the *sanctimonious*, reality-concealing rhetoric spouted by American officials and media commentators in recent days seems, well, unworthy of a mature democracy.

Those in public office have let us know that they consider their task to be a manipulative one: confidence-building and grief management. Politics, the politics of a democracy—which entails disagreement, which promotes

bromides—
clichéd statements

sanctimonious—
falsely holy

BUSH

SONTAG

BYLES

35   candor—has been replaced by psychotherapy. Let's by all means grieve together. But let's not be stupid together. A few shreds of historical awareness might help us to understand what has just happened, and what may continue to happen. "Our country is strong," we are told again and again. I for one don't find this entirely consoling. Who doubts that America is

40   strong? But that's not all America has to be.

May I interpret you a little, Susan Sontag? You tell us you despise TV, you never watch it when you're at home, you don't even own a TV set, but on September 11 you were in Berlin and, like so many of us, you were glued to CNN. That's understandable. Then you became incensed.

5 Not by the images, but by the words. The terrorists who had crashed those planes were being called "cowards," their action "cowardly." A travesty of language! So right away you shot off an article to *The New Yorker*, which appeared in the September 24 issue, the one with the black-on-black subtle cover, and was translated in several foreign

10 newspapers. Your point:

"If the word 'cowardly' is to be used, it might be more aptly applied to those who kill from beyond the range of retaliation, high in the sky [i.e. American bomber pilots], than to those willing to die themselves in order to kill others. In the matter of courage (a morally neutral virtue):

15 whatever may be said of the perpetrators of Tuesday's slaughter, they were not cowards."

You made your point. But was it opportune? To blame for using the wrong words those whose job was to say something publicly about the day's events, yet who likely were stunned almost to speechlessness as

20 we all were—like blaming Bush for blurting out, at the beginning, that we wanted Osama bin Laden dead or alive—seems more than a little pedantic and censorious: it looks like a comic caricature of "the intellectual." And over and beyond the issue of timeliness, and passing over, too, your parenthetical statement that courage is a morally neutral

25 virtue (parentheses are almost invariably pregnant with hard questions): is it really true that the perpetrators of the September 11 slaughter cannot be called "cowards"? More generally, is not "cowards" an apt word for fanatics of all sorts? Obviating life's perplexing ambiguities, the difficult problems of being in the world and of living with others, in

30 the name of a simple faith in a beyond—in this particular case, a faith which promises those young men who blow themselves up for Allah eternal delights in a paradise where flow rivers of milk, wine and clarified honey, with beautiful maidens whose virginity is ever renewed, like the moon—may we not properly call such contempt for life and such

35 simple faith cowardly? I am putting this question about cowardice to you without much hope of getting an answer: "intellectuals" do not like to deal with live questions or questions about faith. Too intractable.

Am I being unfair in calling you an intellectual between quotes? Yet
I think it's justified. . . . You appear to have no doubts about what's right
40 and what's wrong. . . . Well then, what's wrong with saying occasionally,
"I don't know," or, "I'm not sure"? Even from a purely rhetorical perspective, it would be a smart move. Your chief argument—which is
your fellow dissenters' chief argument as well—that our country is
afflicted with imperial arrogance, would thereby gain in dignity, and it
45 will become more persuasive once it is presented with less intellectual
arrogance.

WILFRED OWEN
"Dulce et Decorum Est"
FORM: *Poem*
DATE: 1919

ERICH MARIA REMARQUE
Excerpt from the Novel *All Quiet on the Western Front*
FORM: *Novel*
DATE: 1929

THE INTERSECTION

Here emerge critiques of military recruitment during World War I. Both selections assert forcefully—and famously—that adults manipulated the young into enlisting, invoking a sense of duty to the Fatherland in tender, callow minds. Intriguingly, enemies agree here: We have between them English and German perspectives. Instead of nationality, these works call to mind another timeless, altogether transnational constituency of wartime. Youth.

For further background, the BBC has an excellent site devoted to World War I: www.bbc.co.uk/ history/worldwars/wwone/. There is also a very fine film of All Quiet on the Western Front, *which was a 1930 Academy Award winner.*

HISTORICAL NOTE

These works are important touchstones for the World War I period. Also known as The Great War, World War I opened the twentieth century on a dark note. The cost in terms of military and civilian lives was a tragic immensity. It was a grueling, frightening war, with the stalled action on the western front, the horrors of trench warfare and gas, and the emergence of new technologies in the field, such as the use of airplanes in bombardments. And there was a sense that the world was changing, and not necessarily for the better. In *The Great War and Modern Memory*, Paul Fussell (1975) credits the war, in its tragic absurdity and waste, with the emphasis on irony in the twentieth century. There was scant sense of achievement at war's end, for all its fourteen million dead.

▶ **POINTS FOR DISCUSSION:** *"Dulce et Decorum Est"*

HALLMARKS *didactic mode, mixed diction (high and low), dramatic imagery (similes, metaphors), formal play poetically*

FORM AND CONTENT This poem suggests traditional forms without exactly conforming to one. Its rhyme scheme and use of iambic pentameter, however irregular and rough, recall a sonnet. The sonnet, in its Elizabethan orderliness, is the formal gesture of a departed world, which is significant. Share with students the Shakespearean sonnet "When in Disgrace with Fortune in Men's Eyes." They can quite quickly see the orderliness of that form, its strict length (fourteen lines) and rhyme scheme (three quatrains with a closing couplet, abab cdcd efef gg). Ask them to label the end rhymes of both poems. Then ask them to look at lines 13 and 14 in "Dulce." If it were a sonnet, in lines 13 and 14 we would expect closure in the form of a closing couplet. What, instead does Wilfred Owen discuss there? The poem, rather than moving to its moment of lucid closure, goes on just as the traumatic memories do. What is the effect? Guide students to see that form is mimicking content.

There is another form suggested in the final stanza of "Dulce," the *envoi*, which is a final stanza that instructively addresses a real or fictional someone, often about the previous stanzas of the poem. Geoffrey Chaucer wrote an envoi to King Richard II at the end of "Lak of Stedfastnesse." In the closing couplet, Chaucer advises his king in bold imperatives: "Dred God, do law, love trouthe and worthinesse / And wed thy folk again to stedfastnesse."

TONE AND AUDIENCE This poem has lost its original dedication to Jessie Pope, an English poet who wrote jingoistic verses that appalled Owen with their cheap patriotism. Ask students to consider the effect of that dropped audience. How would the dedication affect our reading of who the *you* of the poem is? Without it, who does that *you* become? Is it more, or less, universal without that dedication? What is the speaker's attitude toward *you*? What sort of tone does he strike? (Using an if–then clause, he creates a strongly instructive tone and a corrective one, characterizing adults as speaking superficially, with "high zest.")

FOCAL POINT: METER The meter of "Dulce" is as interesting as its form. Instead of sticking to strict iambic pentameter, the poet plays with both line length and rhythm. Iambic pentameter, the dominant meter in English poetry, was favored by dramatists because it was thought to be closest to natural speech. Iambic pentameter is five metrical feet of two syllables, with the first syllable unstressed and the second one stressed. It can sound quite natural. Here are three colloquial lines in iambic pentameter that you might share with students:

> Your cell phone is about to lose its charge.

> My brother said he'd drive us to the dance.

> I'll meet you at the diner after school.

The spondee is a metrical foot associated with shock and grief. For example, Ophelia utters "O Woe is me . . ." when she begins to absorb Hamlet's state of mind and her loss of him.

Owen subverts the easy cadence of iambic pentameter. Sometimes he creates a "reversed foot," like the opening of line 10, which opens with the trochee "Fitting." A *trochee* is a stressed syllable followed by an unstressed one. Sometimes he changes the iamb to the strongest possible meter, the spondee, which is two stressed syllables in a row, like in line 9: "Gas! GAS!" Can the students find other spondees and trochees? What is their effect? How do they contribute to our sense of what is being described? How do they make us aware of their unnatural, exhausted movement?

> Trochees: "Fitting"; "Dim, though"

> Spondees: "Knock-kneed"; "Quick, boys!"

Not everyone admired Wilfred Owen's work. Irish poet William Butler Yeats did not include him in the Oxford Book of Modern of Modern Verse, 1892–1935, *which angered critics. In a 1936 letter to Dorothy Wellesley, Yeats wrote that he considered Owen "unworthy of the poets' corner of a country newspaper." Yeats went on to sharpen his complaint: "He is all blood, dirt and sucked sugar stick . . . he calls poets 'bards,' a girl a 'maid,' and talks about 'Titanic wars.'"*

▶ **POINTS FOR DISCUSSION:** All Quiet on the Western Front

HALLMARK *first-person plural narrative*

FORM AND CONTENT In this opening section of the novel (the first ten or so pages of Chapter 1), the author uses the narrator to establish the context: a group of German soldiers five miles away from the front lines. The narrator, by explaining the perspective of the young soldiers, not only sets the scene but unveils important themes about World War I: The soldiers are young, hungry, accustomed to witnessing death and injury, and disillusioned. You might read aloud several pages and then ask students, "What do you notice?" After students share their responses, lead them to consider the kind of narration at work here. Is it highly narrative writing, in which we are in the throes of a fictional moment? In fact, the narration is in a more general, abstract mode; although we have the specifics of character, the excitement about double food rations, and the "wonderfully care-free" afternoon, on close inspection of the language, students will notice the author painting a lot of general truths about war and the collective *we* of all soldiers. Why might the author choose to do this at the beginning of a novel?

TONE AND AUDIENCE Ask students, "Who is the audience for this narrative? An insider, fully familiar with the soldier's perspective? And what is the tone? Is it self-pitying? Sentimental? Unsentimental?" Point out to students that before the war, these soldiers were clearly exposed to high-flung rhetoric about the Fatherland. They have been awakened to the reality, which is different. Challenge students to find sentences or passages that express disillusionment. Does the writing have a realistic or no-nonsense tone? Are there moments that are funny? (In line 45, "He sits down to eat as thin as a grasshopper and gets up as big as a bug in the family way" is one such moment.) Can a moment be both funny and profoundly serious? You might read aloud to students lines 98–101, when the commander comments, " 'Yes, we did have losses yesterday.' He glanced into the dixie. 'The beans look good.' Ginger nodded. 'Cooked with meat and fat.' " What does that exchange say about war? (Heavy loss of comrades is discussed as being on par with beans.)

FOCAL POINT: USE OF PRONOUN Ask students to look for the dominant pronoun in the passage. How many times does it [*we*] occur? What does its dominance suggest about the author's intentions? How would it be different if the author were only emphasizing his narrator's perspective through use of the first person and instead of *we*, the word *I*?

▶ **POINTS FOR DISCUSSION:** *Connecting the Authors*

Once students have read both of these pieces, ask them to reflect on their experiences. Which selection is more challenging to read? Did they find one more shocking than the other? More appealing? What do they make of the similarity of perspective? What does it suggest that soldiers on opposite sides emerged with congruent perspectives? Both authors fought in the war: Does it make the writing more credible? More persuasive?

> Owen and Remarque both wrote from personal experience. While Remarque survived the war, eventually emigrating to America, Owen died in the Battle of the Sambre, a week before the end of the war. Most of his war poetry, including "Dulce," was published posthumously.

FOCAL POINT: THEME Ask students to note any similarities in theme that they see. Both directly reference a classical conception of the Fatherland. What do they take that to mean? What attitude do the authors share toward the adults that pushed them into service? Further, what is the impact of citing a classical author or classical ideas as the justification for anything? Why do people do that? What are we really saying when we point to a classical precedent? Is it simply that we are saying, "Look, here's an old idea so it must be true"? Or are we saying, "Look, a fancy, top-drawer classical writer said this, so it must be true? He, and not I (alive in the sordid, cheap present), knows the truth"?

Reading Questions FOR STUDENTS

WILFRED OWEN ~ *"Dulce et Decorum Est"*

1. An important first analytical question for this or any poem is: Does this poem tell a story? Is it a narrative poem? Or is it more lyric, attempting to create a more unified image or idea or feeling? What would you say this poem is, narrative or lyric?

2. Focus for a moment on the first stanza. Who is speaking? What exactly is being described by the poetic narrator?

3. Why do think there is a new stanza at "Gas! GAS!"? He could easily have run them together. Why didn't he?

4. How does the mode of the poem change in the last stanza? What pronoun newly appears in that stanza? Why?

5. The grammar of that stanza is governed by what we call an "if–then" clause. How many "if" clauses are there? What is the point of the "then" clause?

6. The title of this poem is a shortening of a classical maxim coined by Horace in his *Odes*. In the closing couplet, Owen cites the line in full. It means, "It is sweet and fitting to die for the Fatherland." What is the effect of shortening the length of the lines in the title to "Dulce et Decorum Est" or "Sweet and Fitting It Is"?

ERICH MARIA REMARQUE ~ **All Quiet on the Western Front**

1. What sort of picture does the author paint of the difference between life before the war and during the war for these young men?

2. What is the tone of the opening paragraphs of this book?

3. What is the author's attitude toward the classical conception of the Fatherland?

4. Based on what you have read thus far, would you suspect that this is a prowar or antiwar novel? Or neither?

5. Look at the passage that comprises lines 157–67. What do you make of all the details of nature? Do you think the author is convey-ing the soldiers' state as being truly carefree? Are we to take the narrator at his words or are we supposed to also notice a darker undercurrent beneath the bucolic images of butterflies and wind tossed hair? Are we to believe that the bumblebees' buzz really cov-ered the soldiers' awareness of the sounds of battle?

6. The original title of this book in German (*Im Westen nichts Neues*) meant literally "nothing new in the West." What do you make of the title change for the English translation? What is the difference between the two titles?

continued on following page

SPOTLIGHT ON RHETORIC: DICTION

Diction is "characteristic word choice" or the type of words that are generally used in a piece of writing or a section of writing. In "Dulce et Decorum Est," there is something of a shift in diction in the last stanza to more formal language. On a piece of paper create two columns of words and phrases with the headings "Low" and "High." *High* diction is more formal and may sound more old-fashioned and archaic. The term *low* is used for words that are more informal and colloquial. Below these column headings list the words that fit "High" and "Low." Why do you think the writing becomes more formal in that final stanza?

FIND IT

In Wilfred Owen's poem, find examples of three or more of these devices, underlining them and noting in the margin where they appear.

1. alliteration

2. conditional statements

3. imperative

4. simile

"I decline to accept the end of man. It is easy enough to say that man is immortal simply because he will endure: that when the last ding-dong of doom has clanged and faded from the last worthless rock hanging tideless in the last red and dying evening, that even then there will still be one more sound: that of his puny inexhaustible voice, still talking. I refuse to accept this. I believe that man will not merely endure: he will prevail. He is immortal, not because he alone among creatures has an inexhaustible voice, but because he has a soul, a spirit capable of compassion and sacrifice and endurance. The poet's, the writer's, duty is to write about these things. It is his privilege to help man endure by lifting his heart, by reminding him of the courage and honor and hope and pride and compassion and pity and sacrifice which have been the glory of his past. The poet's voice need not merely be the record of man, it can be one of the props, the pillars to help him endure and prevail." (William Faulkner, acceptance speech for the Nobel Prize for Literature, December 10, 1950)

Author's Intentions

Didacticism and Propaganda: A Distinction to Consider

According to the *Oxford Concise Dictionary of Literary Terms* (1990), *didacticism* is something instructive, designed to impart information, advice, or some doctrine, morality, or philosophy. In *propaganda*, people write to enlist people in some religious or political cause. Propaganda is generally held in low esteem in the literary world, as work that typically resorts to cheap tricks, falsities, and exaggerations to make its point.

Are either of these works didactic? If so, is their didacticism justified? To take it one step further: Are either of these works propaganda? Write a composition in which you explain why you think what you think. Ask your instructor if he or she wants a formal essay response or a more informal, page-long discussion.

On Being Young

SUBJECT What is it like to be young today? Write very specifically about what it is like to be young right now given everything you can think of: the state of the country, the economy, the use of technology, the environment, the world. Adults often speak nostalgically of youth as an easy, golden time. Is it easy to be young? Why? Why not? And, from time immemorial, some adults speak slightingly of youth. "Kids today" are always more spoiled or entitled or ruder or lazier than they used to be. What is the truth of the matter as you see it? Speak freely and confidently. You are young. Most certainly, you know something very real about this subject. Try to be specific. Don't just generalize. Why do you think what you think?

FORM Write your discussion in a series of paragraphs that all begin with a phrase, like "To be young is to . . . ," or with a question, like "What is it like to be young?" Follow this with some aspect of being young. These sections can allow you to pursue different aspects of your experience, and with this format you don't have to unify the paragraphs by creating transitions. The lead-in will create continuity.

WILFRED OWEN ~ *"Dulce et Decorum Est"*

1893–1918
BORN UNITED KINGDOM

Bent double, like old beggars under sacks,
Knock-kneed, coughing like hags, we cursed through sludge,
Till on the haunting flares we turned our backs
And towards our distant rest began to trudge.
5   Men marched asleep. Many had lost their boots
But limped on, blood-shod. All went lame; all blind;
Drunk with fatigue; deaf even to the hoots
Of disappointed shells that dropped behind.

Gas! GAS! Quick, boys!— An ecstasy of fumbling,
10   Fitting the clumsy helmets just in time;
But someone still was yelling out and stumbling
And flound'ring like a man in fire or *lime* . . .
Dim, through the misty panes and thick green light
As under a green sea, I saw him drowning.

15   In all my dreams, before my helpless sight,
He plunges at me, guttering, choking, drowning.

If in some smothering dreams you too could pace
Behind the wagon that we flung him in,
And watch the white eyes writhing in his face,
20   His hanging face, like a devil's sick of sin;
If you could hear, at every jolt, the blood
Come gargling from the froth-corrupted lungs,
Obscene as cancer, bitter as the cud
Of vile, incurable sores on innocent tongues,—
25   My friend, you would not tell with such high zest
To children ardent for some desperate glory,
The old Lie: Dulce et decorum est
Pro patria mori.

lime—
caustic substance

Erich Maria Remarque ✍ *Excerpt from the Novel*
All Quiet on the Western Front

1898–1970
BORN GERMANY

We are at rest five miles behind the front. Yesterday we were relieved,
and now our bellies are full of beef and haricot beans. We are satisfied
and at peace. Each man has another mess-tin full for the evening; and,
what is more, there is a double ration of sausage and bread. That puts
a man in fine trim. We have not had such luck as this for a long time.
The cook with his carroty head is begging us to eat; he beckons with
his ladle to everyone that passes, and spoons him out a great dollop.
He does not see how he can empty his stewpot in time for coffee.
Tjaden and Muller have produced washbasins and had them filled up
to the brim with a reserve. In Tjaden this is voracity; in Muller it is fore-
sight. Where Tjaden puts it all is a mystery, for he always will be thin as
a rake.

What's more important still is the issue of a double ration of smokes.
Ten cigars, twenty cigarettes, and two quids of chew per man; now that
is decent. I have exchanged my chewing tobacco with Katczinsky for
his cigarettes; which means I have forty altogether. That's enough for
a day.

It is true we have no right to this windfall. The Prussian is not so generous. We have only a miscalculation to thank for it.

Fourteen days ago we had to go up and relieve the front line. It was
fairly quiet on our sector, so the quartermaster who remained in the
rear had requisitioned the usual quantity of rations and provided for
the full company of one hundred and fifty men. But on the last day an
astonishing number of English heavies opened up on us with high-
explosive, drumming ceaselessly on our position, so that we suffered
severely and came back only eighty strong.

Last night we moved back and settled down to get a good sleep for
once: Katczinsky is right when he says it would not be such a bad war
if only we could get a little more sleep. In line we have had next to
none, and fourteen days is a long time at one stretch.

It was noon before the first of us crawled out of the quarters. Half an
hour later every man had his mess-tin and we gathered at the cook-
house, which smelt greasy and nourishing. At the head of the queue
of course were the hungriest—little Albert Kropp, the clearest thinker

continued on following page

35   among us and therefore only a lance-corporal; Muller, who still carries his school textbooks with him, dreams of examinations, and during a bombardment mutters propositions in physics; Leer, who wears a full beard and has a preference for the girls from the officers' brothels. He swears they are obliged by an army order to wear silk chemises

40   and to bathe before entertaining guests from the rank of captain and upwards. And as the fourth, myself, Paul Baumer. All four are nineteen years of age, and all four joined up from the same class as volunteers for the war.

Close behind us were the four friends: Tjaden, a skinny locksmith of

45   our own age, the biggest eater of the company. He sits down to eat as thin as a grasshopper and gets up as big as a bug in the family way; Haie Westhus, of the same age, a peat-digger, who can easily hold a ration loaf in his hand and say: Guess what I've got in my fist; then Detering, a peasant, who thinks of nothing but his farm-yard and his

50   wife; and finally Stanislaus Katczinksy, the leader of our group, shrewd, cunning, and hard-bitten, forty years of age, with a face of the soil, blue eyes, bent shoulders, and a remarkable nose for dirty weather, good food, and soft jobs.

Our gang formed the head of the queue before the cook-house. We

55   were growing impatient, for the cook paid no attention to us.

Finally Katczinsky called to him: "Say, Heinrich, open up the soup-kitchen. Anyone can see the beans are done."

He shook his head sleepily: "You must all be there first." Tjaden grinned: "We are all here."

60   The sergeant-cook still took no notice. "That may do for you," he said. "But where are the others?"

pushing up daisies—
dead

"They won't be fed by you to-day. They're either in the dressing-station or *pushing up daisies*."

The cook was quite disconcerted as the facts dawned on him. He was

65   staggered. "And I have cooked for one hundred and fifty men—"

Kropp poked him in the ribs. "Then for once we'll have enough. Come on, begin!"

Suddenly a vision came over Tjaden. His sharp, mousy features began to shine, his eyes grew small with cunning, his jaws twitched, and he

70   whispered hoarsely: "Man! Then you've got bread for one hundred and fifty men too, eh?"

The sergeant-cook nodded absent-minded, and bewildered.

Tjaden seized him by the tunic. "And sausage?"

Ginger nodded again.

75 Tjaden's chaps quivered. "Tobacco too?"

"Yes, everything."

Tjaden beamed: "What a bean-feast! That's all for us! Each man gets—wait a bit—yes, practically two issues."

Then Ginger stirred himself and said: "That won't do."

80 We got excited and began to crowd around.

"Why won't that do, you old carrot?" demanded Katczkinsky.

"Eighty men can't have what is meant for a hundred and fifty."

"We'll soon show you," growled Muller.

"I don't care about the stew, but I can only issue rations for eighty
85 men," persisted Ginger.

Katczinsky got angry. "You might be generous for once. You haven't drawn food for eighty men. You've drawn it for the Second Company. Good. Let's have it then. We are the Second Company."

We began to jostle the fellow. No one felt kindly toward him, for it was
90 his fault that the food often came up to us in the line too late and cold. Under shellfire he wouldn't bring his kitchen up near enough, so that our soup-carriers had to go much farther than those of the other companies. Now Bulcke of the First Company is a much better fellow. He is as fat as a hamster in winter, but he trundles his pots when it comes to
95 that right up to the very front-line.

We were in just the right mood, and there would certainly have been a dust-up if our company commander had not appeared. He informed himself of the dispute, and only remarked: "Yes, we did have heavy losses yesterday."

100 He glanced into the dixie. "The beans look good."

Ginger nodded. "Cooked with meat and fat."

The lieutenant looked at us. He knew what we were thinking. And he knew many other things too, because he came to the company as a non-com. And was promoted from the ranks. He lifted the lid from the

continued on following page

105 dixie again and sniffed. Then passing on he said: "Bring me a plate full. Serve out all the rations. We can do with them."

Ginger looked sheepish as Tjaden danced round him.

"It doesn't cost you anything! Anyone would think the quartermaster's store belonged to him! And now get on with it, you old blubber-sticker,
110 and don't you miscount either."

"You be hanged!" spat out Ginger. When things get beyond him he throws up the sponge altogether; he just goes to pieces. And as if to show that all things were equal to him, of his own free will issued in addition half a pound of synthetic honey to each man.

115 To-day is wonderfully good. The mail has come, and almost every man has a few letters and papers. We stroll over to the meadow behind the billets. Kropp has the round lid of a margin tub under his arm.

On the right side of the meadow a large common latrine has been built, a roofed and durable construction. But that is for recruits who as yet
120 have not learned how to make the most of whatever comes their way. We want something better. Scattered about everywhere there are separate, individual boxes for the same purpose. They are square, neat boxes with wooden sides all round, and have unimpeachably satisfactory seats. On the sides are hand grips enabling one to shift
125 them about.

We move three together in a ring and sit down comfortably. And it will be two hours before we get up again.

I well remember how embarrassed we were as recruits in barracks when we had to use the general latrine. There were no doors and
130 twenty men sat side by side as in a railway carriage, so they could be reviewed all at one glance, for soldiers must always be under supervision.

Since then we have learned better than to be shy about such trifling immodesties. In time things far worse than that came easy to us.

135 Here in the open air though, the business is entirely a pleasure. I no longer understand why we should always have shied at these things before. They are, in fact, just as natural as eating and drinking. We might perhaps have paid no particular attention to them had they not figured so large in our experience, nor been such novelties to our
140 minds—in the old hands they had long been a mere matter of course.

The soldier is on friendlier terms than other men with his stomach and intestines. Three-quarters of his vocabulary is derived from these regions, and they give an intimate flavour to expressions of his greatest joy as well as of his deepest indignation. It is impossible to express

145 oneself in any other way so clearly and pithily. Our families and our teachers will be shocked when we go home, but here it is the universal language.

Enforced publicity has in our eyes restored the character of complete innocence to all these things. More than that, they are so much a mat-

150 ter of course that their comfortable performance is fully as much enjoyed as the playing of a safe top running flush. Not for nothing was the word "latrine-rumour" invented; these places are the regimental gossip-shop and common rooms.

We feel ourselves for the time being better off than in any palatial

155 white-tiled "convenience." There it can only be hygienic; here it is beautiful.

These are wonderfully care-free hours. Over us is the blue sky. On the horizon float the bright yellow, sunlit observation-balloons, and the many little white clouds of the anti-aircraft shells. Often they rise in a

160 sheaf as they follow an airman. We hear the muffled rumble of the front only as very distant thunder, bumblebees droning by quite drown it. Around us stretches the flowery meadow. The grasses sway their tall spears; the white butterflies flutter around and float on the soft warm wind of the late summer. We read letters and newspapers and smoke.

165 We take off our caps and lay them down beside us. The wind plays with our words and thoughts. The three boxes stand in the midst of the glowing, red field poppies.

skat—
card game

We set the lid of the margarine tub on our knees and so have a good table for a game of *skat*. Kropp has the cards with him. After every *mis-*

170 *ere ouverte* we have a round of nap. One could sit like this forever.

misere ouverte—
card game

The notes of an accordion float across from the billets. Often we lay aside the cards and look about us. One of us will say: "Well, boys . . ." Or "It was a near thing that time . . ." And for a moment we fall silent. There is in each of us a feeling of constraint. We are all sensible of it; it

175 needs no words to communicate it. It might easily have happened that we should not be sitting here on our boxes to-day; it came damn near to that. And so everything is new and brave, red poppies and good food, cigarettes and summer breeze . . .

PART **3**

SATIRIC PENS

JONATHAN SWIFT
"A Modest Proposal"
FORM: *Satiric Parody/Essay*
DATE: 1729

LEONARD LEWIN
Excerpt from the Book *The Report from Iron Mountain*
FORM: *Satiric Parody/nonfiction*
DATE: 1967

THE INTERSECTION

Social satire is the common cause of these two pieces. In both parodies, a bogus narrative persona advances an absurd train of logic in rational-sounding language. Sounding for all the world like a social reformer, Jonathan Swift proposes that hunger and poverty in Ireland will be greatly ameliorated if the poor sell their "yearling children" for food. And in Leonard Lewin's extended satire, a nonexistent member of a nonexistent government think tank presents findings about the harmful effects of peace breaking out. True to the spirit of satire, wit and literary prowess serve together in these examples to skewer a societal ill—inept solutions to poverty in one and the contradictory motives of the military-industrial complex in the other.

> ## POINTS FOR DISCUSSION: *"A Modest Proposal"*

HALLMARKS *Juvenalian satire, parody, invented narrative persona*

FORM AND CONTENT This satiric essay takes the form of a social reform pamphlet that, in effect, proposes mass murder—but in the most helpful and rational tone. The student questions ask them to identify the proposal and indeed to also explain their reaction. Further, lead your students to consider how the piece works. How does Swift make his proposal sound reasonable? Help them find the building argument. (He first makes the questionable assertion that children should be useful and soon begins discussing them as commodities-in-waiting, as untapped natural resources, like oil.) How do these premises line up with current assumptions about children? Do we believe that children should be useful? Do we assume that children should not burden mothers? What other assumptions does the piece seem to make? Whose welfare seems to concern the speaker most of all?

Jonathan Swift was an Irish clergyman, eventually dean of St. Patrick's Dublin, but he is best known as an author. His writings include satires, political pamphlets, longer prose works, and religious writings—he is perhaps most famous for Gulliver's Travels. *In "A Modest Proposal" he addresses Irish poverty, attacking not only the government, which was under English control, the landlords, and Irish society in general, but also the economics of the early Industrial Age in which people were viewed as commodities.*

INSTRUCTIONAL NOTE

These pieces are challenging but ultimately accessible reading that may well be best approached at first by reading them aloud in the classroom. For many students, interpretation is enhanced when the reading experience is slowed. And, equally important, they are also likely to enjoy their shock over these pieces if you start them together. Ideally, let the students discover for themselves the nature of what they are reading, but keep in mind that they may need a hint or two from you. Consider reading the first pages of "A Modest Proposal" right through to the end of the proposal paragraph, which begins "I have been assured by a very knowing American . . ." Keep in mind, too, that "A Modest Proposal" is the more transparent act of satire and thus the easier beginning as students get their feet wet with a complex literary mode.

In part, Swift mocks the rhetoric of social reform argumentation and debate; he mimics this language to an exquisite degree. Ask students to look for concrete examples of rhetorical strategies he uses to create the impression of a logically building argument. In keeping with Latin satire, the narrator dismisses in list form the actual reforms he would like to see in place. See the paragraph that begins, "Therefore let no man talk to me of other expedients . . ."

Among the many other rhetorical devices Swift uses and parodies, you might help students identify the definition of a core problem to be solved (the care and feeding of poor children), the articulation of a proposed solution, the use of statistical evidence, the enumeration of the proposal's benefits in six points, various assertions of collateral benefits to the scheme, and in the last paragraph, the claim to impartiality because the speaker cannot profit by his proposal.

TONE AND AUDIENCE The tone of "A Modest Proposal" is bivalent. On the one hand, there is the rational tone sounded by the social reformer. This is the overt voice of the essay and easily identified. On the other hand, there is the voice of the author, covertly critiquing a society that cannot provide for its populous and finds the impoverished not only an expensive nuisance but aesthetically unpleasing, uncomfortable, and "melancholy." Help students distinguish between the narrator and the writer. What is the tone of the narrator? How does Swift make him sound? And what about the author? What can they detect about his attitude toward his countrymen? The sharp wrath of his satiric project emerges in lines such as "I grant that this food will be somewhat dear, and therefore very proper for landlords, who, as they have already devoured most of the parents, will seem to have the best title to the children." What is he implying about landlords? Are landlords his only target? Does he have a single uniform target? Is societal hypocrisy about charitable concern for the poor the general target? And who would they say is the audience for this piece? A quite well-read person? The general reader?

FOCAL POINT: THE PARODIST'S POSE Swift builds his argument with numerous rhetorical devices, yet for all the devices that he employs to create the semblance of a pamphlet, at the same time, his comments also lead us to suspect that he is not in earnest (for example, when he talks about how infant skin will make "admirable gloves"). Do students think he does intend us to realize he is speaking satirically? If so, what is the effect of realizing the satiric game being played? Try to flush out any students who did take it at face value. Ask them to look again, reading a second time for any signals that the proposal is in parody. Finally, what do students think is Swift's intention in his writing? What sorts of questions about poverty does he want his reader to consider? And did they ever wonder if he is more absorbed in playing a sort of literary game than actually making a clear point?

For centuries, political pamphlets, usually ephemeral documents of a few pages, appeared amid controversies. They were often outright polemics. Today, pamphlets are more often used to disseminate more neutral information, such as medical advice or product specifications, though the polemical pamphlet does still exist, most usually in the form of propaganda.

HALLMARKS *Juvenalian satire, parody of a government study, military/governmental rhetoric*

FORM AND CONTENT *The Report from Iron Mountain* is in the form and language of a governmental report. It contains the bogus but oddly credible-sounding findings of a think tank about the possible effects of peace as well as contingency plans for peace, just as one prepares for possible emergencies. The benefits of war are treated to systematic review, and in the end, possible alternatives posited. What point do students think the author is in fact making? What does he suggest about our dependency on war? What does he suggest about the benefits nations enjoy during wartime? Why might nations be unmotivated to negotiate peace? Finally, ask students to try to define the actual position of the writer on war. Does this strike them as a prowar text, as it positions itself, or is it in fact antiwar?

When the 109-page book The Report from Iron Mountain *was published by Dial Press in 1967, the government reacted nervously. Indeed, concerns about a possible security breach reportedly ran all the way to the Oval Office—according to* U.S. News and World Report *(Nov. 20, 1967), President Lyndon Johnson "hit the roof." Finally, in 1972, Leonard Lewin confessed to his authorship in* The New York Times, *though he was from the beginning one of the suspected authors. Lewin was a freelance writer and former labor organizer. Doubts have lingered to this day, however, and some maintain that it was indeed a leaked if quasi-official document and that Lewin's confession was part of the cover-up.*

TONE AND AUDIENCE Leonard Lewin wrote *The Report from Iron Mountain* in the diction and style of a government think tank. The voice is twofold, as is typical of satiric parody. There is the narrative persona used to advance an absurd premise, in this case, the first-person plural of a group study. This creates a sort of mask for the writer. Then there is the writer himself whose views on the war prompt the satiric critique in the first place. How believable do students find the voice and language of the report? What is the effect of the first-person plural? Is it anything like the use of the royal *we*? Why is *we* used? How does it help to create the sound of a document written by a think tank . . . a group, that is. What is the tone of the writing here? How does the speaker sound? Who would they say is the audience for this piece? The general reader? Highly educated people? Note that its rather dense prose and measured governmental diction would put off many readers; it is a demanding text to read.

FOCAL POINT: THE PARODIST'S POSE AND VERISIMILITUDE The voice, style, and structure of this document seldom if ever waver; its consistency is one reason it caused confusion when it was published, in addition to the political context of its appearance. It seemed plausible. Ask students why they think it caused the confusion that it did. Why did quite a few people, even quite educated people, think it was real? What words, phrases, and rhetorical strategies give the impression of an orderly, sincere, highly reasoned work? For example, point out the sentence "It is not necessary, for the purposes of our study, to assume that a general détente of this sort will come about—and we make no such argument—but only that it may." This is only one example of the measured, distinction-making language that characterizes much of this piece. And yet look what's being posited here! *Détente* is a cause of concern rather than occasion for rejoicing. Have students enjoy the delicious frisson between tone and content. Point out in lines 32–39 the way Lewin authoritatively speaks of the initial plan for the report and how their findings prompted further study of "the real functions of war in modern societies." Through this we have a sense of real action, of a plan that had to be modified in light of real research.

Lewin subtly constructs a vital semblance of historical accuracy. What else makes the piece seem real? Given how various signals in the piece combine to make the proposal sound legitimate, ask students to consider how important language is. How susceptible are we to how things sound? How dangerous is this susceptibility? How alert are we in our everyday lives to the persuasive power of language? We think, Why would anybody make this up? It is so intricate, so reasonable, so intelligent sounding. Why aren't we more skeptical? Should we always be skeptical? Can one be too cautious? Other aspects of the form and rhetoric of a governmental document are the definition of the project, including its genesis and history, a set of findings and recommendations, the general attempt to mimic military speech and jargon, and of course all the conventions of books (like a table of contents and footnotes), and of course the book itself.

❱ Points for Discussion: *Connecting the Authors*

Ask students to put the two pieces next to each other on their desks. You might begin a comparative discussion by asking your students which they liked more and why. Was one funnier? Was either of them offensive? Does one seem more formal? Does one seem more successful as social commentary? Why do they think these authors and indeed other satirists turn to parody rather than some more overt critique of society? Why write *The Report from Iron Mountain* rather than an op-ed in *The New York Times*? What is achieved in satire that cannot be done in an editorial? Can one be more indirect in satire? More direct? How directly do these writers hit a defined target? If your students are familiar with television news satire (such as *The Daily Show* with Jon Stewart or Steve Colbert's *The Colbert Report*), it might be fun to talk about the political satire served up by these shows and compare it to Lewin and Swift. Stewart is considered by some to be the foremost satirist of our time. How does he deliver his satire? What devices does he use? What might it say about our culture that, for many people, these shows provide their daily dose of current events news?

FOCAL POINT: SATIRE Which piece made it clearer that it was a satiric parody? If students feel *The Report* is cagier about its satiric pose, do they view it as a flaw? Should Lewin have made the satiric aspect plainer? Why did he "disguise" it? Point out to them that *The Report from Iron Mountain* was long, a short book rather than a long essay, like Swift's. Does the length of the book connect to the nature of its satire? Does he need to be more covert about his ruse because his conceit is extended for an entire book?

JONATHAN SWIFT ～ *"A Modest Proposal"*

1. What in essence is the "modest proposal"? What was your reaction to it? Did you find it funny? Upsetting? Sickening?

2. What problem does the speaker purport to solve? Poverty and hunger? Or the disagreeable "melancholy" sight of poverty and the demand for charity? Whose interests are emphasized?

3. When the narrator announces his proposal, he refers to cooking methods for yearling children: "a young healthy child well nursed is at a year old a most delicious nourishing, and wholesome food, whether stewed, roasted, baked, or boiled; and I make no doubt that will equally serve in a fricassee or ragout." What is the effect of detailing cooking methods here in this sort of detail?

4. The word *breed* or *breeders* recurs in this piece. What kind of language is that? In what sorts of contexts does the word *breed* occur?

5. Does Swift make it clear that this is satire? If so, in which line or lines do you think he most overtly indicates that his meaning is not what he says it is?

6. Look at the use of statistics. Why does the narrator use them? Why, indeed, does anybody cite statistics?

7. To what end does the speaker explain at the end of the essay that he has no way to stand a profit by the scheme? What classic argument does Swift employ here (and mock)?

8. What is the satiric object here? What and whom is Swift lampooning? Government policy? Apathy toward the starving? Social reformers? The poor? The hypocrisy of its supposedly charitable Christian audience? All of these?

LEONARD LEWIN ～ **The Report from Iron Mountain**

1. What is the basic project of this think tank from Iron Mountain?

2. Why is it written in the first-person plural?

3. In Section 1, the author says that they wanted to conduct their study with "military-style objectivity." What are some words and phrases that sound particularly in line with this criterion?

4. How do you find the writing style? Is it clear? Confusing?

5. What is the attitude toward peace as the author discusses contingency planning for it? Is it in their view desirable?

6. The author says that the military tensions between America and its enemies seem "susceptible of political solution." What does that phrasing suggest about the possibility for détente (a relaxing of formally hostile relations)? Does this emphasize the differences between great nations? Or downplay them?

7. We tend, of course, to worry about war breaking out and not the reverse. What sorts of questions does Lewin engender by talking about all the benefits of war?

8. Does the author ever reveal clearly that this is a satire?

The title *The Report from Iron Mountain* is a reference to the place where the research group met, an "underground nuclear hideout."

SPOTLIGHT ON RHETORIC: PARODY AND SATIRE

Parody: A parody is a satiric, often humorous imitation of some serious piece of writing or type of piece of writing. Also known as *spoofs* or *lampoons*, they appear in other realms than literature, like the parodic skits of *Saturday Night Live*.

Types of satire: Satire occurs when a writer or comedian attacks some social problem or phenomenon. In satire, usually some form of vice, folly, or outright wrongdoing is ridiculed or lampooned. In some cases, this lampooning takes the form of parody. At its core, satiric parody is an ironic literary act; there is an essential inconsistency between what is said and what is meant.

Juvenalian satire: These satires tend to be the harshest in their condemnation. They are associated with the Roman poet Juvenal, whose first-century satires were bitter critiques of his Roman countrymen.

Horatian satire: The satires of Horace are considered gentler satires and less inclined to excoriating wit. Some lighter human folly tends to be explored in them, like in Alexander Pope's *Rape of the Lock*, in which the foolishness of high society is somewhat indulgently lampooned.

FIND IT

Find examples of three or more of these devices, underlining them and noting in the margin where they appear.

1. didacticism
2. enumeration
3. false logic
4. jargon

ESSAY OPTIONS

1. Write an analysis of either "A Modest Proposal" or *The Report from Iron Mountain* in which you answer the following question: How does the writer create the appearance of a real document? How do tone, form, and the use of various rhetorical strategies combine to create the impression of an authentic document? Before you begin to write, read through your chosen piece, noting all the places where you see sentences you may want to quote. Be sure to quote in your essay: this is the best way to support your statements. Make sure you introduce your quotation adequately and that you discuss it in particular after you quote it.

2. In the lines below, Jonathan Swift explains and defends his use of satire. Is his self-assessment valid? How does the essay seek to cure "the Vices of Mankind"? Does "A Modest Proposal" seem malicious? Does he name names? Does he keep his critique general?

"Verses on the Death of Dr. Swift"

Jonathan Swift

As with a moral View design'd
To cure the Vices of Mankind:
His vein, ironically grave,
Expos'd the Fool, and lash'd the Knave.
. . . .
Yet, Malice never was his Aim;
He lash'd the Vice but spar'd the Name.
No Individual could resent,
Where Thousands equally were meant.
His Satyr points at no Defect,
But what all Mortals may correct. . . .

(1739, ll. 313–16, 459–64)

A MOCK PROPOSAL

Write a mock proposal in the most serious language you can muster. Your proposal should be absurd, as silly as "My Cat Stoopy for President" or "Bring Back Kings to America" or "Small Children Deserve the Right to Drive."

Your piece should include a clear definition of the proposal. Consider enumerating all the reasons your proposal makes sense. What additional advantages would it have? Be sure to cite false statistics confidently. You might make ample use of phrases like, "for this reason" and "thus" and "therefore" and "for all these aforementioned reasons."

JONATHAN SWIFT 〜 *"A Modest Proposal"*

1667–1745
BORN IRELAND

For Preventing the Children of Poor People in Ireland from Being a Burden to Their Parents or Country, and for Making Them Beneficial to the Public

It is a melancholy object to those who walk through this great town or travel in the country, when they see the streets, the roads, and cabin doors, crowded with beggars of the female sex, followed by three, four, or six children, all in rags and importuning every passenger for an alms. These mothers, instead of being able to work for their honest livelihood, are forced to employ all their time in strolling to beg sustenance for their helpless infants: who as they grow up either turn thieves for want of work, or leave their dear native country to fight for the *Pretender* in Spain, or sell themselves to the Barbadoes.

Pretender—
James Stuart

I think it is agreed by all parties that this *prodigious* number of children in the arms, or on the backs, or at the heels of their mothers, and frequently of their fathers, is in the present deplorable state of the kingdom a very great additional grievance; and, therefore, whoever could find out a fair, cheap, and easy method of making these children sound, useful members of the commonwealth, would deserve so well of the public as to have his statue set up for a preserver of the nation.

prodigious—
extraordinary

But my intention is very far from being confined to provide only for the children of professed beggars; it is of a much greater extent, and shall take in the whole number of infants at a certain age who are born of parents in effect as little able to support them as those who demand our charity in the streets.

As to my own part, having turned my thoughts for many years upon this important subject, and maturely weighed the several schemes of other projectors, I have always found them grossly mistaken in the computation. It is true, a child just dropped from its *dam* may be supported by her milk for a solar year, with little other nourishment; at most not above the value of 2 shillings, which the mother may certainly get, or the value in scraps, by her lawful occupation of begging; and it is exactly at one year old that I propose to provide for them in such a manner as instead of being a charge upon their parents or the parish, or wanting food and *raiment* for the rest of their lives, they shall on the contrary contribute to the feeding, and partly to the clothing, of many thousands.

dam—
mother, usually of a domesticated animal

raiment—
clothing

5

10

15

20

25

30

continued on following page

35

There is likewise another great advantage in my scheme, that it will prevent those voluntary abortions, and that horrid practice of women murdering their bastard children, alas! too frequent among us! sacrificing the poor innocent babes I doubt more to avoid the expense than the shame, which would move tears and pity in the most savage and inhuman breast.

40

The number of souls in this kingdom being usually reckoned one million and a half, of these I calculate there may be about two hundred thousand couple whose wives are breeders; from which number I subtract thirty thousand couples who are able to maintain their own children, although I apprehend there cannot be so many, under the present distresses of the kingdom; but this being granted, there will remain an hundred and seventy thousand breeders. I again subtract fifty thousand for those women who

45

miscarry, or whose children die by accident or disease within the year. There only remains one hundred and twenty thousand children of poor parents annually born. The question therefore is, how this number shall be reared and provided for, which, as I have already said, under the present situation of affairs, is utterly impossible by all the methods hitherto pro-

50

posed. For we can neither employ them in handicraft or agriculture; we neither build houses (I mean in the country) nor cultivate land: they can very seldom pick up a livelihood by stealing, till they arrive at six years old, except where they are of towardly parts, although I confess they learn the rudiments much earlier, during which time, they can however be properly

55

looked upon only as probationers, as I have been informed by a principal gentleman in the county of *Cavan*, who protested to me that he never knew above one or two instances under the age of six, even in a part of the kingdom so renowned for the quickest proficiency in that art.

Cavan—
county in northeast Ireland

60

I am assured by our merchants, that a boy or a girl before twelve years old is no salable commodity; and even when they come to this age they will not yield above three pounds, or three pounds and half-a-crown at most on the exchange; which cannot turn to account either to the parents or kingdom, the charge of nutriment and rags having been at least four times that value.

65

I shall now therefore humbly propose my own thoughts, which I hope will not be liable to the least objection.

70

I have been assured by a very knowing American of my acquaintance in London, that a young healthy child well nursed is at a year old a most delicious, nourishing, and wholesome food, whether stewed, roasted, baked, or boiled; and I make no doubt that it will equally serve in a fricassee or a ragout.

I do therefore humbly offer it to public consideration that of the hundred and twenty thousand children already computed, twenty thousand may be reserved for breed, whereof only one-fourth part to be males; which is

75 more than we allow to sheep, black cattle or swine; and my reason is, that these children are seldom the fruits of marriage, a circumstance not much regarded by our savages, therefore one male will be sufficient to serve four females. That the remaining hundred thousand may, at a year old, be offered in the sale to the persons of quality and fortune through the king-

80 dom; always advising the mother to let them suck plentifully in the last month, so as to render them plump and fat for a good table. A child will make two dishes at an entertainment for friends; and when the family dines alone, the fore or hind quarter will make a reasonable dish, and seasoned with a little pepper or salt will be very good boiled on the fourth day,

85 especially in winter.

I have reckoned upon a medium that a child just born will weigh 12 pounds, and in a solar year, if tolerably nursed, increaseth to 28 pounds.

I grant this food will be somewhat dear, and therefore very proper for landlords, who, as they have already devoured most of the parents, seem to

90 have the best title to the children.

Infant's flesh will be in season throughout the year, but more plentiful in March, and a little before and after; for we are told by a grave author, an eminent French physician, that fish being a prolific diet, there are more children born in Roman Catholic countries about nine months after Lent

95 than at any other season; therefore, reckoning a year after Lent, the markets will be more glutted than usual, because the number of popish infants is at least three to one in this kingdom: and therefore it will have one other collateral advantage, by lessening the number of *papists* among us.

papists—
Catholics

I have already computed the charge of nursing a beggar's child (in which

100 list I reckon all cottagers, laborers, and four-fifths of the farmers) to be about two shillings per annum, rags included; and I believe no gentleman would *repine* to give ten shillings for the carcass of a good fat child, which, as I have said, will make four dishes of excellent nutritive meat, when he hath only some particular friend or his own family to dine with him. Thus

repine—
complain

105 the squire will learn to be a good landlord, and grow popular among his tenants; the mother will have eight shillings net profit, and be fit for work till she produces another child.

Those who are more thrifty (as I must confess the times require) may flay the carcass; the skin of which artificially dressed will make admirable

110 gloves for ladies, and summer boots for fine gentlemen. . . .

continued on following page

I have too long digressed, and therefore shall return to my subject. I think the advantages by the proposal which I have made are obvious and many, as well as of the highest importance. For first, as I have already observed, it would greatly lessen the number of papists, with whom we are yearly over-
115 run, being the principal breeders of the nation as well as our most danger-ous enemies; and who stay at home on purpose with a design to deliver the kingdom to the Pretender, hoping to take their advantage by the absence of so many good protestants, who have chosen rather to leave their country than stay at home and pay *tithes* against their conscience
120 to an episcopal curate.

tithes—
donation of 10 percent of
income to the church

Secondly, The poorer tenants will have something valuable of their own, which by law may be made liable to distress and help to pay their land-lord's rent, their corn and cattle being already seized, and money a thing unknown.

125 Thirdly, Whereas the maintenance of an hundred thousand children, from two years old and upward, cannot be computed at less than ten shillings a-piece per annum, the nation's stock will be thereby increased fifty thou-sand pounds per annum, beside the profit of a new dish introduced to the tables of all gentlemen of fortune in the kingdom who have any refinement
130 in taste. And the money will circulate among ourselves, the goods being entirely of our own growth and manufacture.

Fourthly, The constant breeders, beside the gain of eight shillings sterling per annum by the sale of their children, will be rid of the charge of main-taining them after the first year.

135 Fifthly, This food would likewise bring great custom to taverns; where the vintners will certainly be so prudent as to procure the best receipts for dressing it to perfection, and consequently have their houses frequented by all the fine gentlemen, who justly value themselves upon their knowl-edge in good eating: and a skilful cook, who understands how to oblige
140 his guests, will contrive to make it as expensive as they please.

Sixthly, This would be a great inducement to marriage, which all wise nations have either encouraged by rewards or enforced by laws and penal-ties. It would increase the care and tenderness of mothers toward their children, when they were sure of a settlement for life to the poor babes,
145 provided in some sort by the public, to their annual profit instead of expense. We should see an honest emulation among the married women, which of them could bring the fattest child to the market. Men would become as fond of their wives during the time of their pregnancy as they are now of their mares in foal, their cows in calf, their sows when they are

150 ready to farrow; nor offer to beat or kick them (as is too frequent a practice) for fear of a miscarriage.

propagation—
reproduction

Many other advantages might be enumerated. For instance, the addition of some thousand carcasses in our exportation of barreled beef, the *propagation* of swine's flesh, and improvement in the art of making good bacon, so
155 much wanted among us by the great destruction of pigs, too frequent at our tables; which are no way comparable in taste or magnificence to a well-grown, fat, yearling child, which roasted whole will make a considerable figure at a lord mayor's feast or any other public entertainment. But this and many others I omit, being studious of brevity. . . .

expedients—
drastic measures

160 Therefore let no man talk to me of other *expedients*: of taxing our absentees at five shillings a pound: of using neither clothes, nor household furniture, except what is of our own growth and manufacture: of utterly rejecting the materials and instruments that promote foreign luxury: of curing the expensiveness of pride, vanity, idleness, and gaming in our women: of
165 introducing a vein of parsimony, prudence and temperance: of learning to love our country, wherein we differ even from Laplanders, and the inhabitants of Topinamboo: of quitting our animosities, and factions, nor act any longer like the Jews, who were murdering one another at the very moment their city was taken: of being a little cautious not to sell our country and
170 consciences for nothing: of teaching our landlords to have at least one degree of mercy towards their tenants. Lastly, of putting a spirit of honesty, industry, and skill into our shop-keepers, who, if a resolution could now be taken to buy only our native goods, would immediately unite to cheat and exact upon us in the price, the measure and the goodness, nor could ever
175 yet be brought to make one fair proposal of just dealing, though often and earnestly invited to it. . . .

I profess, in the sincerity of my heart, that I have not the least personal interest in endeavoring to promote this necessary work, having no other motive than the public good of my country, by advancing our trade, pro-
180 viding for infants, relieving the poor, and giving some pleasure to the rich. I have no children by which I can propose to get a single penny; the youngest being nine years old, and my wife past child-bearing.

LEONARD LEWIN ❦

1916–1999
BORN UNITED STATES

Excerpt from the Book
The Report from Iron Mountain

Introduction

The report which follows summarizes the results of a two-and-half-year study of the broad problems to be anticipated in the event of a general transformation of American society to a condition lacking its most critical current characteristics: its capability and readiness to make war when doing so is judged necessary or desirable by its political leadership.

Our work has been predicated on the belief that some kind of general peace may soon be negotiable. The *de facto* admission of Communist China into the United Nations now appears to be only a few years away at most. It has become increasingly manifest that conflicts of American national interest with those of China and the Soviet Union are susceptible of political solution, despite the superficial contraindications of the current Vietnam war, of the threats of an attack on China, and of the necessarily hostile tenor of day-to-day foreign policy statements. It is also obvious differences involving other nations can be readily resolved by the three great powers whenever they arrive at a stable peace among themselves. It is not necessary, for the purposes of our study, to assume that a general *détente* of this sort will come about—and we make no such argument—but only that it may.

It is surely no exaggeration to say that a condition of general world peace would lead to changes in the social structures of the nations of the world of unparalleled and revolutionary magnitude. The economic impact of general disarmament, to name only the most obvious consequence of peace, would revise the production and distribution patterns of the globe to a degree that would make the changes of the past fifty years seem insignificant. Political, sociological, cultural, and ecological changes would be equally far-reaching. What has motivated our study of these contingencies has been the growing sense of thoughtful men in and out of government that the world is totally unprepared to meet the demands of such a situation.

We had originally planned, when our study was initiated, to address ourselves to these two broad questions and their components: What can be expected if peace comes? What should we be prepared to do

de facto—
existing without lawful authority

détente—
relaxation of strained relations

about it? But as our investigation proceeded it became apparent that certain other questions had to be faced.

What, for instance, are the real functions of war in modern societies, beyond the ostensible ones of defending and advancing the "national interests" of nations? In the absence of war, what other institutions exist or might be devised to fulfill these functions? Granting that a "peaceful" settlement of disputes is within the range of current international relationships, is the abolition of war, in the broad sense, really possible? If so, is it necessarily desirable, in terms of social stability? If not, what can be done to improve the operation of our social system in respect to its war-readiness?

The word peace, as we have used it in the following pages, describes a permanent, or quasi-permanent, condition entirely free from the national exercise, or contemplation, of any form of the organized social violence, or threat of violence, generally known as war. It implies total and general disarmament. It is not used to describe the more familiar condition of "cold war," "armed peace," or other mere respite, long or short, from armed conflict. Nor is it used simply as a synonym for the political settlement of international differences. The magnitude of modern means of mass destruction and the speed of modern communications require the unqualified working definition given above; only a generation ago such an absolute description would have seemed utopian rather than pragmatic. Today, any modification of this definition would render it almost worthless for our purpose. By the same standard, we have used the word war to apply interchangeably to conventional ("hot") war, to the general condition of war preparation or war readiness, and to the general "war system." The sense intended is made clear in context.

The first section of our Report deals with its scope and with the assumptions on which our study was based. The second considers the effects of disarmament on economy, the subject of most peace research to date. The third takes up so-called "disarmament scenarios" which have been proposed. The fourth, fifth, and sixth examine the nonmilitary functions of war and the problems they raise for a viable transition to peace; here will be found some indications of the true dimensions of the problem not previously coordinated in any other study. In the seventh section we summarize our findings, and in the eighth we set forth our recommendations for what I believe to be a practical and necessary course of action.

continued on following page

Section 1

75 ### Scope of the Study

When the special study group was established in August, l963, its members were instructed to govern their deliberations in accordance with three principal criteria. Briefly stated, they were these: 1) military-style objectivity; 2) avoidance of preconceived value assumptions; 3) inclu-
80 sion of all relevant areas of theory and data.

These guideposts are by no means as obvious as they may appear at first glance, and we believe it necessary to indicate clearly how they were to inform our work. For they express succinctly the limitations of previous "peace studies," and imply the nature of both government and
85 official dissatisfaction with these earlier efforts. It is not our intention here to minimize the significance of the work of our predecessors, or to belittle the quality of their contributions. What we have tried to do, and believe we have done, is extend their scope. We hope that our conclusions may serve in turn as a starting point for still broader and more
90 detailed examinations of every aspect of the problems of transition to peace and of the questions which must be answered before such a transition can be allowed to get under way.

THE ONION
"Talking to Your Child About the WTC Attack"

FORM: *Satiric Parody*
DATE: September 26, 2001

THE ONION
"More U.S. Children Being Diagnosed with Youthful Tendency Disorder"

FORM: *Satiric Parody*
DATE: September 27, 2000

THE INTERSECTION

The spirit of satire is alive and well in these two child-focused articles from *The Onion*, a publication devoted to parodies of current events and issues. "Talking to Your Child About the WTC Attack" is a send-up of a how-to article that provides a series of ludicrous talking points for parents. This was published September 26, 2001. "More U.S. Children Being Diagnosed with Youthful Tendency Disorder" targets the absurd modern propensity for concocting syndromes and disorders out of normal behavior. Further, it takes a shot at our desire to evade responsibility for our actions by hiding behind medical labels.

Although The Onion *is an entire newspaper devoted to parody, it's been mistaken for and cited as real news, no doubt delighting the paper's mischievously witty writers and editors. Deborah Norville of MSNBC once cited a bogus statistic about Americans and exercise from an* Onion *article entitled "Study: 58% of U.S. Exercise Televised." Overseas, where confusion might be more expected, Reuters reported (June 7, 2002) that the* Beijing Evening News *published a report based on an* Onion *article entitled "Congress Threatens to Leave D.C. Unless New Capitol Is Built," which purports that Congress wants a building with a retractable dome.*

▶ POINTS FOR DISCUSSION: *"Talking to Your Child About the WTC Attack"*

HALLMARKS *parody of self-help rhetoric (talking points, issue script), covert didacticism*

FORM AND CONTENT "Talking to Your Child" parodies the form and content of the how-to article and shoots some political darts to boot. Its writer needles us for so readily and pervasively embracing this simplistic form for dealing with complex, difficult issues, and further, it sets us up to consider if our diet of sound-bite information in American newspaper, magazine, and other media may actually play a role in the events pre– and post–9/11. Why were we so uninformed, so taken by surprise? Is our political awareness so lulled and dulled by modern media that we have become anti-intellectual? Anti-inquiry? Here, a mere three weeks after 9/11, the writer dares to poke fun at the talking heads, advising parents on how to talk about a difficult topic with children: unprecedented terrorism on our turf. In a sense, the authors are saying that the truth about our nation's role in creating the conditions for 9/11 may not be child-friendly, but by gosh we ought to reckon with those facts. In fact, the actual content of the piece and its audience is adults; it's

INSTRUCTIONAL NOTE

Should your students respond to these articles with happy interest, consider subscribing to *The Onion*, which is published weekly in print and online. You'll need to vet the articles as some can be too adult and even offensive, but when you cherry pick the pieces, this newspaper can lead to stimulating discussions exploring parody. After all, students can feel the bite of satire best when they have that firsthand understanding of the topic being skewered. It's fun and easy to augment this lesson by showing students a couple of current examples—articles in popular magazines that strike you as similar to these two parody pieces. And keep *Onion* articles in the back of your mind as a way to mix up classroom routine; a brief look at a bit of topical satire can provide comic relief—and intellectual sustenance—when everyone is weary.

something of a primer on the rise of Muslim fundamentalism and on the background of the Taliban in particular.

Begin your discussion by soliciting general reactions. Ask, "Did you find this funny? Can you identify what sort of piece is this? Is it real or is it a parody? How do we know?" Nudge students to identify the telltale signs that it's satire—for example, the talking points are ludicrous, full of vocabulary improbable for children as well as complex, not to mention crushing historical background. Would anyone actually talk to a child this way? Why not? What, in fact, does much of this article discuss? Did they find it funny? Did it go too far? Are some subjects sacrosanct? Or is the proverb true—that laughter is the best medicine?

TONE AND AUDIENCE *The Onion* articles speak to its reading audience, which is, usually, fully aware of their parodic nature. The tone of "Talking to Your Child About the WTC Attack" is shaped by the classic dual voice of parody. There is the speaker, who uses the vague psychological speech usual in some magazine writing. Then there is the satiric voice of *The Onion* writer, which moves to comedic effect, but which also lampoons. How would students describe the persona of the speaker? Does he seem to be a magazine writer? A specialist in child psychology? And then again, what about the writer? What attitude does he seem to have toward the attacks? Is a particular attitude present? What is his attitude toward his American audience? Toward the terrorists?

FOCAL POINT: COVERT DIDACTICISM This piece contains historical background to the September 11th attacks in New York City, Washington, and Pennsylvania; concrete information takes up much of the piece. What do students make of the history embedded there? Does that information strike them as having been common knowledge for its American audience? If not, what is the effect of presenting historical facts *for children* that many adults would not necessarily have known or remembered? What is the writer getting at here about the American awareness of geopolitical events that preceded September 11th? How does he use form to imply that the general understanding of the events was at a childlike level before the attacks? Note that the instructiveness of this piece is not overt; indeed its didacticism runs in a more subterranean vein.

A POINT TO CONSIDER As time goes by, more and more students will need to have the events of September 11th constructed for them by you. However, especially in the affected regions, some students may have a personal connection to September 11th and you may teach someone who experienced a direct loss in connection with the attacks. In this case, consider previewing the lesson with other colleagues, administrators, the student's family, or the student before presenting it.

▶ Points for Discussion: *"More U.S. Children Being Diagnosed with Youthful Tendency Disorder"*

HALLMARKS *parody of a health article (including psychological jargon, anecdotal storytelling, quotes from experts, and informational sidebar)*

FORM AND CONTENT "Youthful Tendency Disorder" parodies a type of article common to magazines and newspapers that provides medical or psychological information for the lay reader. As such articles often do, this piece makes heavy use of anecdotal storytelling. Its opening line begins with a dramatic pseudoanecdote: "Nicholas and Beverly Serna's daughter Caitlin was only four years old, but they already knew there was a problem." Ask students their reaction to the piece. Did any of them think it could be real? If so, why? The writer describes typical childhood play as medical symptoms. What is the writer making fun of?

TONE AND AUDIENCE Help students think through the voices of the piece. With what sort of tone does the narrative speaker discuss YTD, as it is called (also spoofingly) in the article? How serious is his tone? Then again, what about the tone of the writer of the spoof? What is his attitude toward pathologizing the normal behavior of children? Do you think he simply finds it ridiculous? Does he imply that there is any danger in the way childhood behavior is discussed today?

FOCAL POINT: VERISIMILITUDE Various elements included in this piece conspire to create the illusion of reality. This piece quotes bogus doctors from actual renowned medical institutions. There is a sidebar of "Warning Signs." How important is this illusion of reality to the success of the satire? Does the author want to fool the reader? Or ape a form for its comedic effect? Where do they see the first clear signal that this is satire?

❭ POINTS FOR DISCUSSION: *Connecting the Authors*

These pieces together create a fine context for exploring what makes something funny. What is humor about? In both of *The Onion* pieces, serious matters become fodder for comedy. What is the benefit of writing about something serious in a comic way? What's the advantage to the author? What's the payoff for the audience? What sorts of things and people tend to get parodied? Why are politicians such frequent targets? Can students make any generalizations? When reading a parody or seeing the parody of television sketch comedy, do they ever feel uncomfortable? Jokes and parodies can make us aware of impressions or thoughts we didn't know we had: we often laugh because we are caught off guard. However, the dynamics of parody are complex. Try to get students to articulate their reactions and impressions.

I do not hesitate in this discussion of humor and satire to articulate impressions in a more tentative mode. I do this because it is, in fact, slippery business trying to identify how satire works. Further, if they see you trying out ideas, this emboldens them to do the same. Not everything needs to sound perfectly formulated and officially stamped correct by the gods of academia. Indeed scholars themselves struggle to explain literature clearly and, from reference work to reference work, sometimes define its core terms inconsistently. How do students see it? Why? I keep pursuing these simple questions, and these simple questions lead students to trust themselves.

FOCAL POINT: AWARENESS OF GENRE *The Onion* is generally well known as a satiric newspaper. Satires are not always understood to be satires, but in the case of the *The Onion*, the reader most usually is aware that the context and nature of the writing is parodic. How might it affect reading if you know something is parodic? What if you do not? How might it be to see a parody in an unexpected context? Finally, to what extent do these pieces seem to be entertainment most of all?

THE ONION ➰ *"Talking to Your Child About the WTC Attack"*

1. Where in the article is the first occasion where its parodic nature becomes apparent?

2. Look at the date of the article. Why do you think there is so much historical information presented here?

3. What appeal might this article have had so soon after the attacks? How do you think you would have reacted to it? Do you think it's funny? Offensive?

4. Do you think this piece seems anti-American? Anti-Muslim? Either or neither of these? Both? Is an attitude detectable?

5. The author returns to language more common to conversations with children in the last line: "Hopefully, though, the above will serve as a start, helping your child better understand why the bad men did this terrible thing." How did that affect you? Do you have any sense of why the author possibly did that? What would the piece be like without this return to childlike terms?

THE ONION ➰ *"More U.S. Children Being Diagnosed with Youthful Tendency Disorder"*

1. What would you say is being made fun of in this article? Is there more than one target?

2. What does the author do to make the article look legitimate? Try to name at least two things that make it look like a real article.

3. Why does the mother of Caitlin say she is relieved by the diagnosis? Is the article poking fun at today's parents?

4. Why does the author turn the syndrome into an acronym?

5. How does the packaging of typical childhood behavior as an illness look to you? Do you think someone could be fooled into thinking this is a real disorder?

6. What does the author suggest here about how well adults understand children?

7. The author references a new drug for possible treatment of YTD. What would you say is the author's attitude toward medicating small children?

Spotlight on Rhetoric: Lampoon and Spoof

lampoon: a sharp satiric attack, usually directed at an individual

spoof: a form of comic parody that tends to be light in nature

Find It

Find examples of three or more of these devices, underlining them and noting in the margin where they appear.

1. anecdotal proof
2. false evidence
3. imperative
4. invented authorities
5. sidebar

THE AUTHOR'S CRAFT

In a short essay of no more than four paragraphs, answer this question: How do these *Onion* articles create an illusion of reality? What sorts of rhetorical devices, literary elements, and language do the authors use to foster this illusion? Consider discussing, either as part of your thesis or more passingly in conclusion, whether or not the authors truly intend for us to be fooled.

PARODY WRITING

Write a parody using "More U.S. Children Being Diagnosed with Youthful Tendency Disorder" as a model. Invent a medical syndrome out of what we consider normal behavior. Try to develop your piece into at least five paragraphs, but ask your teacher for specifications for presentation.

To get an idea, consider of all the various developmental stages from childhood to old age (early childhood has been taken, obviously). You might, for example, write about what you know and zero in on the habits and angst of teen years. Can you pathologize what you observe? Turn what is typical for young adults into a medical syndrome with various traits.

Think about the characteristics of the age you're writing about. You might list them for yourself before you turn them into a syndrome or disorder. Then turn them all into danger signs. Be sure to use urgent serious tones or speak hyperbolically. You might organize your discussion around two key anecdotes (invented ones, that is). Consider, too, making your opening line a single dramatic moment from one of your invented anecdotes.

Tip: Parody is, in part, an art of illusion. Consider using some of the techniques of *The Onion* articles: anecdotal storytelling, invented specialists, bogus statistics, sidebars, talking points, and photographs. However, spend a moment or two flipping through magazines. How are articles formatted? What seems typical? What seems corny? What irritates you with its foolishness? Consider taking a staged photograph to go with your article (as *The Onion* does).

On one occasion a spoof took on a life of its own. Actual psychiatrist Dr. Ivan Goldberg made up an Internet addiction disorder (IAD) as a joke. His parody arose from the idea that the term *addiction* is used too loosely and that any number of behaviors could be described as addictive if the definition of addiction is too loose. However, many see this as an actual disorder, though neither the American Medical Association nor American Psychiatric Association has accepted it. (The text is widely available on the Internet and further information worthy of pursuit is available at wikipedia.com.)

THE ONION   〜 *"Talking to Your Child About the WTC Attack"*

September 26, 2001—*The Onion* Issue 37.34

The events of Sept. 11 are extremely difficult for a child to understand. What should you tell your child when he or she asks why this happened? Obviously, there's no easy answer, but the following is a start:

Talking to Your Child About the WTC Attack

5

Sit your child down, and gently explain to him or her that the destruction of the Twin Towers was part of a Holy War, or *jihad*, against the U.S. perpetrated by a small faction of Islamic fundamentalists bent on the annihilation of Western society.

10

As your child may or may not know, much of modern Islamic fundamentalism has its roots in the writings of Sayyid Qutb, whose two-year sojourn to the U.S. in the late 1940s convinced him that Western society and non-Islamic ideologies were flawed and corrupt. Over the course of the next several decades, his writings became increasingly popular throughout the Arab world, including Afghanistan.

15

Patiently explain to your child that in 1979, the Soviet Union invaded Afghanistan, outraging the U.S. Determined to stem the tide of communism, the U.S. provided Afghanistan with military support in the form of weapons and training. Among the beneficiaries of this support were many of Qutb's radical-fundamentalist adherents. These fundamentalists eventually took over Afghanistan in the form of a group called the Taliban. Militarized and radicalized by years of war, Taliban leaders turned against the U.S., which long supported them in their fight against the occupying Soviets but eventually came to be seen as the embodiment of Western immorality.

20

25

You should also let your child know that among those supported by the Taliban is Osama bin Laden, a Saudi multi-millionaire and terrorist who for years has taken refuge in encampments in the rugged hills of Afghanistan. Like his Taliban brethren, bin Laden believes that the U.S. is guilty of apostasy and should be punished accordingly.

30

Your child will likely ask why bin Laden is so angry at the U.S. Explain to him or her that much of his anger is rooted in the fact that, during the Gulf War, the U.S. stationed troops in Saudi Arabia, the nation that is home to the Islamic holy cities of Mecca and Medina. Bin Laden was further angered by America's post-Gulf War efforts to oust Iraqi dictator Saddam Hussein by imposing an embargo against his nation.

35

continued on following page

No doubt, your child will have more questions. He or she will likely want to know what role other terrorist groups played in the attack, as well as what destabilizing effects a U.S. invasion of Afghanistan could have on the increasingly volatile political climate in Pakistan. Hopefully, though, the
40   above will serve as a start, helping your child better understand why the bad men did this terrible thing.

THE ONION ～ *"More U.S. Children Being Diagnosed with Youthful Tendency Disorder"*

September 27, 2000—*The Onion* Issue 36.34

REDLANDS, CA—Nicholas and Beverly Serna's daughter Caitlin was only four years old, but they already knew there was a problem.

5 Day after day, upon arriving home from preschool, Caitlin would retreat into a bizarre fantasy world. Sometimes, she would pretend to be people and things she was not. Other times, without warning, she would burst into nonsensical song. Some days she would run directionless through the backyard of the Sernas' comfortable Redlands home, laughing and shrieking as she chased imaginary objects.

10 When months of sessions with a local psychologist failed to yield an answer, Nicholas and Beverly took Caitlin to a prominent Los Angeles pediatric neurologist for more exhaustive testing. Finally, on Sept. 11, the Sernas received the heartbreaking news: Caitlin was among a growing legion of U.S. children suffering from Youthful Tendency Disorder.

15 "As horrible as the diagnosis was, it was a relief to finally know," said Beverly. "At least we knew we weren't bad parents. We simply had a child who was born with a medical disorder."

Onion Med Watch

Youthful Tendency Disorder (YTD), a poorly understood neurological
20 condition that afflicts an estimated 20 million U.S. children, is characterized by a variety of senseless, unproductive physical and mental exercises, often lasting hours at a time. In the thrall of YTD, sufferers run, jump, climb, twirl, shout, dance, do cartwheels, and enter unreal, unexplainable states of "make-believe."

25 "The Youthful child has a kind of love/hate relationship with reality," said Johns Hopkins University YTD expert Dr. Avi Gwertzman. "Unfit to join the adult world, they struggle to learn its mores and rules in a process that can take the entirety of their childhood. In the meantime, their emotional and perceptive problems cause them to act out in
30 unpredictable and extremely juvenile ways. It's as though they can only take so much reality; they have to 'check out,' to go Youthful for a while."

On a beautiful autumn day in Asheville, NC, six-year-old Cameron Boudreaux is swinging on a park swingset—a monotonous, back-and-

continued on following page

35 forth action that apparently gives him solace. Spotting his mother on a nearby bench, Cameron rushes eagerly to her and asks, "Guess what?" His mother responds with a friendly, "What?" With unbridled glee, Cameron shouts, "Chicken butt!"—cryptic words understood only by him—before laughing and dashing off again, leaving his mother dis-
40 traught over yet another baffling non-conversation.

"I must admit, it's been a struggle," Mary Boudreaux said. "What can I say to him when he says something like that, something that makes no sense? Or when he runs through the house yelling while I'm trying to balance the checkbook? You can't just say, 'Please, Cameron, don't have
45 a disorder for just a few minutes so I can concentrate.'"

Cameron's psychological problems run even deeper. He can name every one of his beloved, imaginary Pokemon characters, but the plain realities of the actual world he inhabits are an enigma: Ask Cameron the name of the real-life city councilman sponsoring the referendum to
50 renovate the park just across the street from his house—a park he plays in daily—and he draws a blank.

According to Dr. Dinesh Agarwal, director of child psychiatry at NYU Medical Center, such disconnectedness from reality is a coping mecha- nism for YTD sufferers. "The Youthful child is born into a world he or
55 she does not fully understand," Agarwal said. "Their brain pathways are still forming, and they need to repetitively relearn how to assimilate into society. These disassociative play-fantasies apparently help them accomplish that."

Common YTD Warning Signs

- Near-constant running, jumping, skipping
- Sudden episodes of shouting and singing
- Preferring playtime and flights of fancy to schoolwork
- Confusing self with animals and objects, including tigers, dinosaurs, and airplanes
- Conversations with "imaginary friends"
- Poor impulse-control with regard to sugared snacks

IRA C. HERBERT
"Dear Grove Press"
FORM: *Letter*
DATE: 1970

RICHARD SEAVER
"Dear Coca-Cola"
FORM: *Letter*
DATE: 1970

THE INTERSECTION

This entertaining correspondence between corporate giant Coke and Grove Press, a renowned independent publisher, affords uncommon access to the behind-closed-doors world of corporate intellectual property skirmishes. The correspondence began when The Coca-Cola company challenged Grove Press' use of the phrase "it's the real thing" in an advertisement for a book. Coke's missive earnestly entreats Grove to cease and desist from using "the real thing," and it even presumes, or pretends to presume, that Grove's compliance is a forgone conclusion. This letter is full of the expected persuasive strategies of corporate America and the legal departments that companies of certain sizes have to protect their reputations—and their profits. The reply, sly and humorous, is satiric to the core. Grove's is a cunning hit, a slingshot aimed deftly at a Goliath's overreaching concern about infringement.

These letters came to light, at least for much of the teaching public, when they appeared on the 1998 AP Examination in Language and Composition. Funny as the pair is, their rhetorical strategies create a challenge for student readers that is simultaneously amusing and educational.

NOTE ON SEQUENCING

This text set works best if you do not hand out both letters at once. First let students look at Coke's letter and its rhetorical strategies so that they may give it full consideration. Then, before they go on, ask them to think about how they might respond to Coke's claim were they on the receiving end of it.

▶ **POINTS FOR DISCUSSION:** *"Dear Grove Press"*

HALLMARKS *letter form, business rhetoric, corporate diction*

FORM AND CONTENT The intention of this letter is to achieve compliance. To that end, Herbert, a Coca-Cola executive, tries to assert proprietary claim to the phrase "it's the real thing." Persuasiveness is a core part of this letter. Read the letter out loud with your class. What do students think of the claim Coke makes? Does it seem legitimate? What would they say is Herbert's strategy overall? How does he try to make their claim sound sensible and obvious (and possibly actionable)? What did they think about Herbert's suggestion that there could be product confusion regarding sponsorship? Further, how expressly legalistic is the argument? Are any laws cited? Is there any insinuation of legal action, perhaps, in the recitation of their historic use of the phrase since World War II? Is there any part of the letter that seems particularly weak? Is there anything that doesn't make sense? (Once you read Grove Press' reply, you may or may not want to draw their attention to the fact that Seaver, in his letter, treats many of the assertions as ludicrous: that there really could be any true harm to Coke, that it will dilute their slogan's force, that they, in effect, own the phrase.) What makes this letter instructive is that there are—as is

101

true of many things in life—two ways of looking at the letter. On the one hand, it does seem unlikely that an ad for a book could in any way be confused with a famous soft drink. But on the other hand, Coca-Cola had invested millions of dollars and decades creating a trusted brand, and it's just as "American" to protect the crafted language of commerce—a slogan that has enhanced Coke's branding.

It might be fun once students have read both letters to group students on either side of the classroom; half takes Coke's side, the other half, Grove's, and they can engage in a courtroom-style debate as opposing counsels. Or you might stage this as a legitimate debate with a resolution (such as, Resolved: The expression "it's the real thing" should only be used by Coca-Cola and its subsidiaries).

TONE AND AUDIENCE The audience for this letter most assuredly was not the American reading public; it was, quite simply Grove Press in general and Richard Seaver, its executive vice president, in particular. How would students describe the tone of the letter? Is its polite formality indeed friendly? Herbert closes by saying, "We appreciate your cooperation and your assurance that you will discontinue the use of 'It's the real thing.'" What is the tone of that statement? What is the effect of assuming compliance? Why did he state it that way? Is there something aggressive or insinuating about this (along the lines of "you better comply or else")? What about the use of the first-person plural: what does he mean when he says *we*?

FOCAL POINT: ARGUING BACK Ask students to think about the argument Herbert made. Discuss with them its central point, which is that through established use their slogan should not be used because there could be confusion and dilution of slogan effectiveness through its misuse. Ask them how they would write back to Coca-Cola. What tack would they take? You might ask them as an assignment to write a letter back to Coca-Cola. This will set up the reading of Grove's response, and they will be well positioned to appreciate its sophistication and humor.

▶ **POINTS FOR DISCUSSION:** *"Dear Coca-Cola"*

HALLMARKS *letter form, business rhetoric, corporate diction, satiric strategies*

FORM AND CONTENT Richard Seaver's letter takes aim at the arguments of Coca-Cola, meeting its corporate tone in kind; it is formal and polite, too, at least on the face of it. Indeed, at certain points Seaver seems to be satirizing Herbert's letter, taking its core propositions and running with them to hilarious effect. He also interprets (or mischievously misinterprets) Coke's statement about confusion of sponsorship to mean that Coke is concerned that books and Cokes will be confused. He clearly considers Coke's concern hyperbolic, which he indicates by purporting to take it seriously (and exaggerating it to comic effect). They have instructed their salesmen to help customers who will be confused. Why does Seaver do this? What is the effect? What point is he making about Coke's claims? In fact, did Herbert actually say that such confusion was the problem? Where else does he exaggerate or alter somewhat Herbert's assertions (look at his line that uses the phrase "direct and deadly threat," for example). What other arguments, real and preposterous, does he make (that Coke may benefit from their use of the phrase, that they have had roughly comparable experience with their titles being echoed in other titles, that they were merely quoting from a review)?

TONE AND AUDIENCE Seaver's letter pokes fun with some abandon. Its audience is, of course, Ira Herbert of Coca-Cola, who was only, in fact, doing his job in the classic manner of the day. What about the satiric aspect of the letter? Is Seaver laughing at or with Herbert? Do the students think he is going too far? Or does Coke deserve its skewering, with its assertion of phrase *ownership*? Is Seaver just being a smart aleck? Or does he have some larger purpose? Why do they think Seaver makes the humorousness of his response so overt? Finally, and this is just guesswork, do students imagine that this letter was circulated among friends and colleagues before it was sent? Ask them to speculate: Do they wonder if there was another audience for Seaver's high wittiness? (But do remind them that while speculation might generate interesting questions to pursue, it is just talk.)

FOCAL POINT: RHETORIC Ask students to consider Seaver's letter as an act of persuasion. What is he trying to say to get Coke to back off? Is he using humor to try to diffuse a situation and call attention to the groundlessness of their complaints? Ask them to explore that idea. How, at the same time that he is being funny, does he work in some core ideas (that Coke does not own the phrase, that they care about the First Amendment, perhaps hinting that they will defend their use in court, as they have in other cases)? Further, ask students to consider the letter's structure. Arguably, he saves one of the most directly compelling points for last: that they were merely quoting a review of the book. Why does he do that? How does closing with that information drive home their view of Coke's claim?

Grove Press is a historic independent publisher. They hold in their backlist such luminaries as Samuel Beckett, Tom Stoppard, and Sam Shepard and such avant-garde writers as Henry Miller, William S. Burroughs, and more recently writers like Kathy Ackroyd. Cold Mountain *and* The Inheritance of Loss *are Grove titles. Throughout the 1950s and 1960s, led by publisher Barney Rossett, they were leaders in a number of censorship and freedom of speech cases involving their books (hence Seaver's wry reference to defending to the death the freedom of speech of others).*

▶ **POINTS FOR DISCUSSION:** *Connecting the Authors*

Ask students to place the letters next to each other. Which seems more formulaic? Do they imagine that the Coke letter had ever been sent in another similar context? Why is it natural that Grove's letter is longer? How does Seaver echo the tone of Herbert's letter? What sort of phrasing sounds similar?

FOCAL POINT: BUSINESS DICTION What do they make of the business tone and diction in general? What is its purpose? Ask them to look for phrasing that is meant to sound cordial and polite. Why is the mode of these letters not more personal? Why are neither of the writers being more directly angry and aggressive in their language? What is supposed to be the benefit of cordiality? What are the risks of open anger? Do they see any failures of business decorum in either letter? On the face of it, Seaver seems to make sincere propositions; like any good satirist, he is not. He has not really instructed their sales people to help customers keep Cokes and books straight. Yet his language is very polite. Is he then, in his ironic use of language, being in fact very rude?

IRA C. HERBERT ~ *"Dear Grove Press"*

1. There are six paragraphs in this letter. What would you say is the discrete point of each paragraph? Write a brief descriptive phrase for each, labeling them one through six.

2. When Herbert says "We believe you will agree" at the start of the third paragraph, how do you read his tone? What do you think he is really saying there?

3. How persuasive do you find this letter? What do you think is Herbert's approach? How is he trying to persuade Grove?

4. What is the strongest part of Herbert's argument? What is the weakest?

5. What would you say is the tone of this letter?

RICHARD SEAVER ~ *"Dear Coca-Cola"*

1. What is the purpose of Seaver's letter?

2. Where does he make assertions that seem ludicrous? Name one or two.

3. Is Seaver's letter to Coke polite?

4. Do you think Seaver implies that Grove is willing to go to court to defend itself? If so, in which lines exactly?

4. What was your reaction to the letter? Did you find it funny?

SPOTLIGHT ON RHETORIC: TEXT AND SUBTEXT

Text and *subtext* are phrases used when writing seem to have an overt meaning that has as well a less obvious, even covert meaning. When we speak of subtext, we speak of what something implies as opposed to states. These letters make heavy use of implication. For example, nowhere does either party state that they are willing to go to court, and in part this is no doubt because no one indeed ever does want to go to court. However, Coke's recitation of their history of use implies a record of ownership. Grove reminds Coke too that they have been in the courts regarding First Amendment, freedom of speech issues. Arguably there are veiled threats on both sides, though in a nascent form. Coke can prove use. Grove goes to court over the First Amendment. The text in both cases seems simply to be some invocation of company history. The subtext is a legal threat (that may or may not be sincere).

FIND IT

Find examples of these devices, underlining them and noting in the margin where they appear.

1. humor

2. hyperbole

3. verbal irony

ANALYZING THE LETTERS

Option One: Write an essay in which you take a stand on these two persuasive letters: Which one is, indeed, more persuasive and why? Coke tries to assert that they have prior claim to the phrase "it's the real thing." Grove counters that they do not own the phrase. Which one substantiates its claim better and why?

Option Two: If you were hiring one of these writers to work at your company, which one would you select? Why? Write a formal business letter to your imaginary partners explaining your decision that begins with an appropriate salutation such as "Dear Colleagues." Use these letters as a model for form. Explain your decision to them, using evidence from the letters to back up your decision. Before you start writing, try to come up with multiple reasons for your preference. You will need to come up with some bogus company names and colleagues as well an address for this assignment.

A LETTER

Letter writing as part of the literary world has a long tradition. There are the letters of classical writers such as Seneca, meant to be circulated; there are biblical epistles; there are famous correspondences, like that between Abelard and Heloise in the Middle Ages, or John and Abigail Adams in Revolutionary War period. Letters, too, have been used in novels; in fact many early novels were actually faux correspondences, like the letters between Clarissa and Lovelace in Samuel Richardson's *Clarissa* (1748). These are called "epistolary novels"; Alice Walker's *The Color Purple* (1982) is an epistolary novel. At present, letter-writing decorum is evolving in light of email and its phenomenal speed. Is it possible that our speech can become too informal? Are we Smart-Texting away the eloquence of our language? Are we losing a little more history, now, each time a computer crashes and takes its email log with it?

Write a letter to the editor on a topic of public concern that you find distressing and about which you have some suggestions to make. This may or may not be an actual letter that you send in, but go through the process of writing such a letter.

You must first pick a publication. *Rolling Stone* letters to the editor will sound different from those in *The Times Picayune* or *The Washington Post*. So, you want your letter to be appropriate, and you may well want to read some letters to see how they sound and which approaches you find most compelling. You will need to find the actual information, too, on where to send such a letter: Check the publication itself or its website.

When you write your letter, try to get to the point rather quickly. In the first sentences, we need to know the topic and your basic perspective. Limit your remarks to three or four tightly constructed paragraphs; the more concise you are, the less likely it is that an editor will cut your words to save space.

IRA C. HERBERT   *"Dear Grove Press"*

March 25, 1970

Mr. R. W. Seaver
Executive Vice President
Grove Press, Inc.
5   214 Mercer Street
New York, New York 10012

Dear Mr. Seaver:

Several people have called to our attention your advertisement for *Diary of a Harlem Schoolteacher* by Jim Haskins, which appeared in the *New York*
10   *Times* March 3, 1970. The theme of the ad is "This book is like a weapon . . . it's the real thing."

Since our company has made use of "It's the Real Thing" to advertise Coca-Cola long prior to the publication of the book, we are writing to ask you to stop using this theme or slogan in connection with the book.

15   We believe you will agree that it is undesirable for our companies to make simultaneous use of "the real thing" in connection with our respective products. There will always be the likelihood of confusion as to the source or sponsorship of the goods, and the use by such prominent companies would dilute the distinctiveness of the trade slogan and diminish its effec-
20   tiveness and value as an advertising and merchandising tool.

"It's the Real Thing" was first used in advertising for Coca-Cola over twenty-seven years ago to refer to our product. We first used it in print advertising in 1942 and extended it to outdoor advertising, including painted walls—some of which are still displayed throughout the country. The line has
25   appeared in advertising for Coca-Cola during succeeding years. For example, in 1954 we used "There's this about Coke—You Can't Beat the Real Thing" in national advertising. We resumed national use of "It's the Real Thing" in the summer of 1969 and it is our main thrust for 1970.

Please excuse my writing so fully, but I wanted to explain why we feel it
30   necessary to ask you and your associates to use another line to advertise Mr. Haskins' book.

We appreciate your cooperation and your assurance that you will discontinue the use of "It's the real thing."

Sincerely,
Ira C. Herbert
35

Mr. Ira C. Herbert
Coca-Cola USA
P.O. Drawer 1734
Atlanta, Georgia 30301

5   Dear Mr. Herbert:

Thank you for your letter of March 25th, which has just reached me, doubtless because of the mail strike.

We note with sympathy your feeling that you have a proprietary interest in the phrase "It's the real thing," and I can fully understand that the public might be confused by our use of the expression, and mistake a book by a Harlem schoolteacher for a six-pack of Coca-Cola. Accordingly, we have instructed all our salesmen to notify bookstores that whenever a customer comes in and asks for a copy of *Diary of a Harlem Schoolteacher* they should request the sales personnel to make sure that what the customer wants is the book, rather than a Coke. This, we think, should protect your interest and in no way harm ours.

We would certainly not want to dilute the distinctiveness of your trade slogan nor diminish its effectiveness as an advertising and merchandising tool, but it did occur to us that since the slogan is so closely identified with your product, those who read our ad may well tend to go out and buy a Coke rather than our book. We have discussed this problem in an executive committee meeting, and by a vote of seven to six decided that, even if this were the case, we would be happy to give Coke the residual benefit of our advertising.

Problems not unsimilar to the ones you raise in your letter have occurred to us in the past. You may recall that we published *Games People Play* which became one of the biggest nonfiction best-sellers of all time, and spawned conscious imitations (*Games Children Play*, *Games Psychiatrists Play*, *Games Ministers Play*, etc.). I am sure you will agree that this posed a far more direct and deadly threat to both the author and ourselves than our use of "It's the real thing." Further, *Games People Play* has become part of our language, and one sees it constantly in advertising, as a newspaper headline, etc. The same is true of another book which we published six or seven years ago, *One Hundred Dollar Misunderstanding*.

Given our strong sentiments concerning the First Amendment, we will defend to the death your right to use "It's the real thing" in any advertis-

ing you care to. We would hope you would do the same for us, especially when no one here or in our advertising agency, I am sorry to say,

40 realized that you owned the phrase. We were merely quoting in our ads
Peter S. Prescott's review of *Diary of a Harlem Schoolteacher* in *Look*
which begins "*Diary of a Harlem Schoolteacher* is the real thing, a short,
spare, honest book which will, I suspect, be read a generation hence as
a classic . . . ."

45   With all best wishes,

Sincerely yours,
Richard Seaver

PART **4**

TEXT TALK

RUDYARD KIPLING
"The White Man's Burden"
FORM: *Poem*
DATE: February 1899

H. T. JOHNSON
"The Black Man's Burden"
FORM: *Poem*
DATE: April 1899

HISTORICAL NOTE

The full title of Kipling's poem is "The White Man's Burden: The United States and the Philippine Islands"—it first appeared in *McClure's Magazine* in response to the American conquest of the Philippines. His poem suggests that white men have a responsibility to civilize and Christianize tribal people, thankless task though it may be. He strongly underscores a sense of duty to others. At the same time, he characterizes the "other" as uncivilized and possibly demonic. White men should bring "new-caught, sullen peoples / Half-devil and half-child" toward "the light." The phrase "white man's burden" became axiomatic nearly immediately, as Johnson's poetic response suggests. There were multiple negative responses to it by such writers as Mark Twain, who was part of the Anti-Imperialist League, and it became a catchword in political cartoons.

THE INTERSECTION

"The White Man's Burden" continues to provoke strong reactions more than one hundred years after Rudyard Kipling published it in 1899. Contemporary readers know the British author Kipling for such children's classics as *The Jungle Book* (1894), with its memorable story with Riki Tiki Tavi, but in "The White Man's Burden" we see a proponent of the imperial enterprise addressing advice to another nation, America. In the poem he urges the United States to take up fully the noble burdens of empire, which includes the idea of civilizing native populations. Three months later, African American clergyman and editor of *The Christian Recorder*, H. T. Johnson, published a response. In ironic echoes of form and content, "The Black Man's Burden" attacks Kipling's assertions and assumptions about the virtue and nobility of the imperial project and connects the situation in the Phillipines to the condition of African Americans in the wake of slavery.

The prhase "White Man's Burden" was widely embraced in popular culture and is part of common parlance even today. A year after the poem, a Pears' Soap ad read, "The first step towards lightening the White Man's Burden is through teaching the virtues of cleanliness." More recently, a 2003 title in The Christian Science Monitor *alluded to Kipling: "Should Tiger Woods Carry the Black Man's Burden?"*

▶ POINTS FOR DISCUSSION: *"The White Man's Burden"*

HALLMARKS *didactic poetry, exhortation, use of the imperative*

FORM AND CONTENT A now-famous refrain opens the seven stanzas of this iambic poem. Within the eight-line stanzas there are rhymes in lines two and four and six and eight. You might use the student questions on page 115 to open a class discussion about the meaning of the phrase. And, what are their reactions to it? What is Kipling's attitude toward native people? Were they appalled? Surprised? Was there anything redeeming about his argument? Is it well intentioned on any level? Also, direct students' attention to the use of refrain and the quality of exhortation. Ask why the line is repeated. Why exactly have so many found this to be a racist formulation? What, throughout the poem, is suggested about native peoples? Do they think it is indeed racist? What about the more benevolent undercurrents of the poem, the urging to help? Can something be both racist and well intentioned? If so, why? Does the poem question imperialism? Endorse it? It certainly underscores its challenges and costs: "Go make them with your living, / And mark them with your dead!" How does the poem indicate an assumption of empire as both a reality and necessity? Indeed, the poem refers to events that have already transpired, and in this sense it is a foregone conclusion.

TONE AND AUDIENCE This poem is clearly directed to America; its subtitle was "The United States and the Philippine Islands." Ask students about the tone of the poetic narrator. Does his advice seem friendly? Patient? Condescending? World-weary? What is his diction like? Formal? Informal? What about the use of the word *ye*? Why does he use that rather archaic sounding word? What does the line "Have done with childish days" suggest about his view of America? Originally this poem was intended for Queen Victoria's Diamond Jubilee, but that plan was scrapped. Like "Dulce et Decorum Est," the original dedication changed. Why do they think it was changed?

FOCAL POINT: ALLUSION This poem alludes to New Testament lines of Paul: "When I was a child, I spoke like a child, I thought like a child, I reasoned like a child. When I became a man, I put away childish things" (I Corinthians 13:11). What does this allusion suggest about Kipling's perspective? Does it, combined with other lines from the poem, suggest that his point of view is missionary in any regard? Does it necessarily follow? What implication does the allusion make? Through it he suggests that imperialism and the civilizing of others is the work of adults; a failure to take up the burdens of empire would be a childish act (indeed America is often considered young from the European perspective). How might a biblical allusion enhance the credibility of an argument? There is an old saying, that the "Devil knows how to cite scripture." Would students call that a fitting description of Kipling's biblical allusion? Or does that go too far because Kipling is sincere in his reference?

> According to President Theodore Roosevelt, "The White Man's Burden" was "rather poor poetry, but good sense from the expansion point of view."

▶ POINTS FOR DISCUSSION: *"The Black Man's Burden"*

HALLMARKS *direct polemical response to "The White Man's Burden," ironic echoes of Kipling in phrasing and form, alternating rhyme scheme, refrain, verbal irony*

FORM AND CONTENT H. T. Johnson's poem directly attacks Kipling's poem by using a truncated version of his poem. In it he turns Kipling's refrain on its head, saying "Pile on the Black Man's Burden." Ask students what they notice first. The poem is shorter, for one thing, and makes clear reference to Kipling's poem. What is Johnson's point? Draw students out about their reaction to the poem and in particular the reformulating of Kipling's refrain. Why do they think he makes his echo of Kipling so clear? How do their points of view differ? How does Johnson characterize tribal people? Why is his poem so much shorter in form?

TONE AND AUDIENCE Johnson's entire poem alludes to Kipling's, meanwhile addressing the white man generally and America in particular. Ask students to try to define the *ye* of Johnson's poem. To whom is it directed? Kipling? How does he characterize the *ye* of the poem? Which lines are particularly damning of the treatment of the black man? How would they describe his tone, and which lines reveal his attitude most clearly? He contrasts the armies of imperialists to the "feeble folks" armed with the technology of a different world. And at its core, the poem suggests the ludiocrous: pile more burden upon a population already staggering under the history of slavery.

FOCAL POINT: IRONY The central statement and title of this poem is ironic: The poet suggests something he does not intend. In fact, he intends quite the opposite. How does the use of irony affect the tone of the poem? Does he seem sarcastic? Bitter? Is there any place where he seems to abandon irony and to speak more directly?

▶ POINTS FOR DISCUSSION: *Connecting the Authors*

The volley exchanged between these works was only part of a larger firestorm of debate over imperialism and how technologically advanced cultures intersect with tribal cultures. Turn-of-the-century imperialism, widely chronicled in literature, was working its worst. Two great novelistic depictions of imperialism were written in retrospect. In his influential and complex novel *Heart of Darkness*, Joseph Conrad (1902) described the plunder and genocide of the Belgian Congo. Conrad's work was later challenged for its attitudes by Nigerian author Chinua Achebe. In *Things Fall Apart*, Achebe (1958) wrote about the tragic result of British intervention in Nigeria. Poetry is a somewhat different vehicle for political analysis and debate. What are the advantages of poetic form? Is it likely to reach more readers? Why do students think the phrase "the white man's burden" became an axiom? (Perhaps this is in part because it gave pithy expression at last to an idea already everywhere apparent, and it also looked with sympathy upon white imperialism, which was under some attack.)

FOCAL POINT: POETIC DEBATE (*Note:* These discussion questions will help students prepare for the essay question on the student pages.) Compare and contrast the forms of the two poems: Ask students to place them side by side on their desks. Ask them to look in particular at how Johnson echoed Kipling's form, but changed it too. How is the length of Johnson's poem different? What is the effect of his greater brevity? How does it create a powerful, memorable point? Is it, comparatively, the soul of wit? In poetic debate, why might the reacting poet write a shorter poem? (A poem in response is already referencing the ideas in the first piece; this creates a sort of economy.) Further, how is his rhyme scheme different? (Rhyme also appears more regularly in his poem; every other line rhymes.) What is the effect? How does it compare to Kipling's use of rhyme? Which use of rhyme creates a tighter, more unified quality of expression? (The rhyming every other line in Johnson's poem facilitates simplicity and unity, making what he is saying quite clear and direct.) Why might Johnson resist slavish imitation of Kipling in his response? How, in a sense, is his different form an assertion of his intellectual independence from his ideas?

Reading Questions FOR STUDENTS

RUDYARD KIPLING ~ *"The White Man's Burden"*

1. Characterize the main point of this poem in a few sentences. What is the "White Man's burden"?

2. What is your reaction the refrain "White Man's burden"? Have you heard it before?

3. The poet refers to the native people as *captives*. To whom does the line "To wait in heavy harness" refer? What does this line suggest?

4. What does the word *sullen* imply? What is Kipling saying about native people? What does his use of the word suggest about him? (Consider looking up the word *sullen*.)

5. When he speaks of bringing natives slowly to "the light," what does he mean?

6. Why does he characterize the native perspective with the phrase "Our loved Egyptian night"? Why *Egyptian*, would you suppose? With what is he associating Egypt?

7. Are his intentions to oppress native people? Is there anything benevolent about his intentions?

H. T. JOHNSON ~ *"The Black Man's Burden"*

1. The poet speaks in the imperative, like Kipling does, telling the audience to "Pile on the Black Man's Burden." Does he mean what, on face value, he says? What indeed does he mean?

2. Who is the audience for this poem? What is implied?

3. What is the poet's attitude toward the "fearless armies"? What does he suggest about them?

4. How has the "Red Man's problem" been sealed? To what is this a reference?

5. What is the tone of this poem?

6. What are the differences between this poem and Kipling's? It is considerably shorter. Does that choice work well? Why do you think he only echoes Kipling's form to a degree?

continued on following page

SPOTLIGHT ON RHETORIC: EXHORTATION

In an exhortation, the narrator speaks in direct address, urging someone to take up some laudable enterprise (laudable at least in the eyes of the poet). It is a mode of speech, often in the imperative, strongly associated with religious teaching. In "The White Man's Burden," Kipling exhorts America to take up its challenges. Other familiar statements of exhortation: "Let us now praise famous men" or "Do not go gentle into that good night" or "Turn back, O Man, forswear thy foolish ways."

FIND IT

Find examples of three or more of these devices, underlining them and noting in the margin where they appear.

1. allusion
2. exhortation
3. lofty diction
4. personification
5. refrain
6. simile

ANALYTICAL ESSAY

In "The Black Man's Burden," Johnson responds swiftly to Kipling's poem. In an essay, explain what sort of counterargument Johnson makes to Kipling. Be sure to characterize Kipling's point of view; you must do this in order to explain Johnson's response. What sorts of literary techniques does he use to respond to Kipling? Look closely at the way he plays with but also alters Kipling's form. Also, pay sharp attention to his use of irony.

POEM OF EXHORTATION

Mixing the ridiculous with the sublime for comic effect is a literary tradition. In *The Rape of the Lock,* a mock epic, Alexander Pope tells the story of a young man stealing a lock of hair from a girl. An enormously silly high-society crisis ensued. He used grand language, grandiloquent conceits, and ringingly clear heroic couplets. In another twist on the comic use of mixed modes, the Reverend Jesse Jackson once read Dr. Seuss' *Green Eggs and Ham* in stentorian, preacherly tones in a legendary appearance on *Saturday Night Live* (available on YouTube).

Write a poem of exhortation in which you speak directly to someone about what they should do. Use a refrain at the start of each stanza and try to be consistent with your line lengths.

Exhortation is generally a formal enterprise and often uttered in lofty imperatives. Accordingly, your poem may be quite serious. Try in each stanza to advance the core statement you assert in your refrain and be quite specific. Why should readers do what you exhort them to? Each stanza should assert some aspect of the reasoning behind your central poetic statement.

On the other hand, you could use this form to comic effect if you are in the mood to write something lighter or just downright light. You might, for example, exhort your friends on some inconsequential subject, all the while using high-flown rhetoric. For example: "Fail Not to Wear Deodorant or Brush Your Teeth, Lest Ye Never Date, O Young Man."

Try to write at least three stanzas.

RUDYARD KIPLING ~ *"The White Man's Burden"*

1865–1936
BORN BRITISH INDIA

Take up the White Man's burden—
Send forth the best ye breed—
Go bind your sons to exile
To serve your captives' need;
5   To wait in heavy harness
On fluttered folk and wild—
Your new-caught, sullen peoples,
Half devil and half child.

Take up the White Man's burden—
10   In patience to abide,
To veil the threat of terror
And check the show of pride;
By open speech and simple,
A hundred times made plain.
15   To seek another's profit,
And work another's gain.

Take up the White Man's burden—
The savage wars of peace—
Fill full the mouth of Famine
20   And bid the sickness cease;
And when your goal is nearest
The end for others sought,
Watch Sloth and heathen Folly
Bring all your hope to nought.

25   Take up the White Man's burden—
No tawdry rule of kings,
But toil of serf and sweeper—
The tale of common things.
The ports ye shall not enter,
30   The roads ye shall not tread,
Go make them with your living,
And mark them with your dead!

Take up the White Man's burden—
And reap his old reward:
35   The blame of those ye better,
The hate of those ye guard—

hosts—
multitudes

The cry of *hosts* ye humour
(Ah, slowly!) toward the light:—
"Why brought ye us from bondage,
40 Our loved Egyptian night?"

Take up the White Man's burden—
Ye dare not stoop to less—
Nor call too loud on Freedom
To cloak your weariness;
45 By all ye cry or whisper,
By all ye leave or do,
The silent, sullen peoples
Shall weigh your Gods and you.

Take up the White Man's burden—
50 Have done with childish days—
The lightly proffered laurel,
The easy, ungrudged praise.
Comes now, to search your manhood
Through all the thankless years,
55 Cold-edged with dear-bought wisdom,
The judgment of your peers!

H. T. JOHNSON ⟿ *"The Black Man's Burden"*

1857–UNKNOWN
BORN SOUTH CAROLINA, U.S.A.

Pile on the Black Man's Burden,
    'Tis nearest at your door;
Why heed long-bleeding Cuba,
    Or dark Hawaii's shore?
5   Hail ye your fearless armies,
    Which menace feeble folks
Who fight with clubs and arrows
    and *brook* your rifles smokes.

brook—
endure

Pile on the Black Man's Burden
10   His wail with laughter drown
You've sealed the Red Man's problem,
    And will take up the Brown,
In vain ye seek to end it,
    With bullets, blood or death—
15   Better by far defend it
    With honor's holy breath.

Pile on the Black Man's burden,
    His back is broad though sore;
What though the weight oppress him,
20   He's borne the like before.

Jim-Crow laws—
segregation laws, mostly in
the South

Your *Jim-Crow laws* and customs,
    And fiendish midnight deed,
Though winked at by the nation,
    Will some day trouble breed.

25   Pile on the Black Man's burden
    At length 'twill Heaven pierce;
Then on you or your children
    Will reign God's judgments fierce.
Your battleships and armies
30   May weaker ones appall.
But God Almighty's justice
    They'll not disturb at all.

NEIL YOUNG
"Alabama"
FORM: *Song Lyric*
DATE: 1972

LYNYRD SKYNYRD (RONNIE VAN ZANT)
"Sweet Home Alabama"
FORM: *Song Lyric*
DATE: 1974

WARREN ZEVON
"Play It All Night Long"
FORM: *Song Lyric*
DATE: 1980

NOTE

Reprinting the lyrics for these songs wasn't possible, but you should be able to locate them easily to share with your students. In addition, you can listen to the songs on the artists' CDs and find additional background about the artists on the following websites: www.lynyrdskynyrd.com; www.neilyoung.com; and www.warrenzevon.com.

SEQUENCING NOTE

First, have students consider these lyrics in the order found here, looking at their poetic and rhetorical devices. Then listen to the songs in class and consider the musical dimension, the conventions of song, and how word and note combine to create meaning and experience.

THE INTERSECTION

Public debate transpires in many contexts, not only in convention halls and within literary publications, but in clubs and on the radio. Guitars, drums, and the English language can enter the mix at times, too, generating memorable social commentary. And just as more traditional literary writers do, musicians sometimes not only sample each other's musical phrasing but reference each other's words and ideas. Unlike political debates and discussions, artistic works, be they songs or poems, linger in the public consciousness, talking to each other over long arcs of time. Some lyric phrases, quoted in conversation, are quite nearly axiomatic, like Bob Dylan's "The times they are a changing." An occasion prompts us to reference a song, just as we might quote Emerson's "A foolish consistency is the hobgoblin of little minds."

In this trio of texts, we look at music from the 1970s and early 1980s. It was 1972 when Neil Young, writing about Southern racism, included "Southern Man" and "Alabama" in solo-album breakaways from Crosby, Stills, Nash & Young. In response, in 1974 Lynyrd Skynyrd released "Sweet Home Alabama" by Ronnie Van Zant, which speaks in direct address to Neil Young in one verse and generally comments on his songs about Alabama. Interestingly, this exchange between musical groups has been, if pointed, generally respectful; the musicians have been known to play each other's songs and wear each other's T-shirts on stage. Finally, in 1980, Warren Zevon wrote the lesser-known "Play It All Night Long." Its chorus directly and its title more implicitly reference "Sweet Home Alabama."

▶ **POINTS FOR DISCUSSION:** *"Alabama"*

HALLMARKS *chorus, allusion, metaphor, apostrophe, imperative*

FORM AND CONTENT Use the student questions on page 126 as a starting point for exploring "Alabama"'s form and content. Students will need to do brief Internet-based research on the state of Alabama and George Wallace in the 1960s and

Neil Young's two songs spoke about Alabama's associations with its slavery past, its entrenched "plantation era" segregationist policies, and its Governor George Wallace, best known for his resistance to the Reverend Martin Luther King Jr. and the civil rights movement. Wallace was elected governor of Alabama on four occasions (1962, 1970, 1974, 1982) and ran unsuccessfully for president on four occasions, including in 1972, the year Young released "Alabama." An early public statement, made in 1963, reveals Wallace's stance on integration and typical characterization of civil rights activists: "The president [Kennedy] wants us to surrender this state to Martin Luther King Jr. and his group of pro-Communists who have instituted these demonstrations" (*The New York Times*, May 8, 1963). You may need to provide background for students on the civil rights movement and segregation. Listen to a recording of any one of Martin Luther King Jr.'s speeches as a way of building background and showing students the musiclike power of King's voice, words, delivery, and passion. A recording of the "I Have a Dream" speech can be found at americanrhetoric.com.

1970s; please modify this instruction if necessary. Ask your class what they found out. Do their findings connect in any way to the songs? What was your students' reaction to the lyrics? How do they interpret the chorus? What about the reference to the weight on the shoulders of Alabamans? Does that, in fact, sound sympathetic? Is the speaker wholly condemning? How would they define his attitude? What about the image of the Cadillac? Is it metaphoric? (If they struggle with this question, ask them to think literally about it first, and then to extrapolate its larger meaning.) Ask them to look specifically at the lines "Your Cadillac has got a wheel in the ditch / And a wheel on the track." Finally, did they find all of the lines clear?

TONE AND AUDIENCE How would students describe the tone of these lyrics? Is it mournful? Angry? Critical? How does Young use his allusion to the Negro spiritual about death, "Swing Low Sweet Chariot"? (For another look at allusion to spirituals, see the discussion of the "I Have a Dream" speech on page 3.) Young changes the line from "Swing Low Sweet Chariot / Coming for to Carry Me Home" to "Swing low Alabama." What is the effect? What about the repeated "Oh Alabama"? What does the word *Oh* call to mind? How is *Oh* used in poetry, for example? And what about the audience of this song? (It speaks in direct address to the people of Alabama.) Are they his only audience? What about the attitude of the speaker? Does he seem arrogant? Harsh? Humble but critical?

> There are numerous ways to access recordings of these songs, including buying them as singles from various online stores or seeing if versions are available for free play on the official websites of the artists. You might want to look at a YouTube performance with your class. However, standards and practices for Internet use in the classroom are evolving in the courts as of this writing. Most schools outline Internet use in light of current law. But consider explaining to your students your source for the music and its lawfulness; this might be an opportunity for discussion about the ethical use of artistic content on the Internet.

▶ **POINTS FOR DISCUSSION:** *"Sweet Home Alabama"*

HALLMARKS *anaphora, allusion, apostrophe, interrogative mode, colloquial diction*

FORM AND CONTENT "Sweet Home Alabama" has remained in significant rotation on radio stations, especially in the South. Released in 1974, it is a response to two of Neil Young's also heavily played songs, "Southern Man" and "Alabama." Ask students to try to define the subject of these lyrics. How does Van Zant talk about Alabama? What does it emphasize? What do they think he means when he misses "Alabamy once again / And I think it's a sin, yes." Is this a confessional moment? Why does he open with it? Does that line suggest ambivalence? What about the use of *Alabamy* over *Alabama*? What is the difference? Which has more regional color? What does the writer suggest in the lines about the governor, especially the phrase "Now we all did what we could do." What do they take this to mean? What about the reference to Watergate? What do they think he means when the speaker asks (Neil Young) if his conscience

> Core members of the band Lynyrd Skynrd, including "Sweet Home Alabama" lyricist Ronnie Van Zant, died in a plane crash on October 22, 1977, in Gillburg, Mississippi, due to a fueling miscalculation.

bothered him? Is he suggesting that there is something self-righteous about Neil Young's songs? Finally, what do they make of the line about the governor being "true" toward the close of the piece? How clear is the song? Do they find any part of it cryptic? Does it make any references they didn't get? How might they follow up on unclear references on the Internet?

The band Lynyrd Skynyrd has played on stages draped with Confederate flags. Although in the past the late Ronnie Van Zant distanced the band from the flag of the Confederacy, the official band website as of this writing sells jackets with the flag on the back and the flag appears on one album cover. You might want to discuss the band's association with the Confederate flag. How do students react to that? Further, this is an opportunity to discuss how symbols work. Are they flexible? Can or should the Confederate flag have legitimacy in the view of the students? Is it a part of the Southern past that should be acknowledged? Are there dangers associated with excising important symbols of the past? What are the dangers of rehabilitating a symbol associated with slavery? Consider asking students to look at the band's website for references to the Confederate flag: www.lynyrdskynyrd.com.

TONE AND AUDIENCE How would students characterize the tone of this piece? Is it nostalgic? Sad? Upbeat? Angry? Critical but friendly? Who would they guess is its audience? Neil Young? Alabama? Southerners? America? What does the language suggest and where does it suggest it? Why is Alabama missed? Why might they call it a sin? How does colloquial diction affect the tone of the piece? Does it make it seem more accessible?

▶ POINTS FOR DISCUSSION: *"Play It All Night Long"*

HALLMARKS *colloquial diction, narrative detail, alliteration, imperative*

FORM AND CONTENT "Play It All Night Long," released in 1980, is profoundly anti-romantic about country living and implies the blue skies of "Sweet Home Alabama" are something of a delusional lie. From a literary standpoint, "Play It All Night Long" is quite poetic in its use of language, with its complex metrics and subtleties of rhyme, assonance, and alliteration. However, of the songs discussed here, it is the least well known (though Warren Zevon is renowned for "Werewolves of London" and "Excitable Boy"). Ask students about their reaction to this song. Did they like it? What about its imagery? Which lines struck them most of all? What does Zevon suggest in his lines about turning the speakers up full blast? How can music be used to drown out the misery of present circumstances? And even lull people into passivity? How does "Sweet Home Alabama" contrast with country life as Zevon depicts it? What about the choral line "Play that dead band's song." What was their reaction to this line (knowing that Lynyrd Skynyrd suffered a tragic plane crash)? How do they interpret that line? How does it relate to and contribute to the tone of the rest of the chorus?

Warren Zevon's lyrics may be considered too gritty for some classroom situations. Naturally enough highly colloquial, even vulgar language, can command student interest and, as a collateral benefit, build camaraderie, but teaching situations vary considerably. "Play It All Night Long" will not be considered suitable in some schools (in which case simply omit the song in this lesson).

TONE AND AUDIENCE What is the tone of "Play It All Night Long"? Which lines most clearly convey its despair and anger? Would they say this song is hopeless? This is clearly, at least in part, a song about a song. Like all of these songs, it was released nationwide, contributing to the exchange between Neil Young and then Ronnie Van Zant. Does this song seem to address Lynyrd Skynyrd? Americans? People who like "Sweet Home Alabama"? People sentimental about country living and/or the South? All or none of these? Is the language of this song as colloquial as Lynyrd Skynyrd's?

◗ POINTS FOR DISCUSSION: *Connecting the Authors*

Ask students to place the lyric sheets in front of them. Considering them together as a group, what do they notice? How do they feel about "Sweet Home Alabama"? Do they have sympathy for its point of view? Are there any lyrics they like especially well here? Or dislike? Does any one or more of these writers seem especially literary or poetic in his sensibility? Did any of these lyrics seem upsetting? Disturbing? Which lyrics seemed the most complex and poetic? Are any of them familiar with these songs? If not, what do they guess about the music?

Lyrics are often anthologized, yet while we often see "Western Wind" in literature collections, we seldom encounter contemporary songs. Study of lyrics can provide rich but accessible occasion for critical thinking, Internet-based research, and consideration of genre. Reading lyrics invites students to consider the force of language where they don't expect to: on their own terrain. It hits the iPod generation where they live.

Ask students, "What issues, debates, or controversies are addressed in songs today?" (like the lyrics to "Don't Snitch," Mac Dre). Consider asking them to present examples; ask them to teach you. Invite them to bring in work that generates discussions about meaning and taste. Who today writes great lyrics? What makes them great? Whose lyrics are banal, formulaic concoctions? Get them articulating what they think and why they think it; let them be the experts and you the learner. They love this!

FOCAL POINT: LYRICS AND THE MUSIC Before you play these songs for them, you might put on the board or project on your screen some of the terms for musical discussion presented in the writing assignment at the end of this lesson. While the students have the lyrics before them on their desks, play each of these songs in turn. Ask them to take any notes on the music as they listen, and consider playing each song more than once. Pause between each song and pursue some or all of the following questions: What do they notice? How do language and music combine to create the tone and quality of the music? What instruments do they notice? Which song seems most up-tempo? Which seems slowest? Most plaintive? Saddest? Happiest? Does any one of them seem particularly pleasing melodically? Does one seem dissonant in any sense? Did they dislike any of these songs?

After you have played all the songs, try to generate a discussion of them as a set. Do any of the lyrics stand on their own as poetry? Or do they all require their music for their full expression? Did anybody prefer reading the lyrics? Why do they think music is as powerful as it is? Millions have heard these songs, especially the first two. Why has that happened? (This is a popular form. Poetry is not as influential or popular a form today as once it was. Why not, do they think?)

Finally, the history of racism and slavery is not the exclusive burden of the South. Slavery is part of American history. What, you might ask students, do these songs teach us about America?

The reading questions for students invite them to consider how easy it is for us to love a song and feel we know its meaning—even when we don't. Ronald Reagan's 1984 presidential campaign famously mentioned Bruce Springsteen's "Born in the U.S.A." as a patriotic, feel-good song. It was just the opposite: Springsteen intended it as a critique of America's poor treatment of Vietnam vets, and it's one of the most misinterpreted songs ever. A TV commercial for a tropical resort used the refrain "Lust for Life" by Iggy Pop, but the song is actually about drug abuse. What does this suggest about the power of music to kind of trump the meaning of the lyrics?

YOUNG

LYNYRD SKYNYRD

ZEVON

NEIL YOUNG ～ *"Alabama"*

1. What, in general, would you say is the point of this song?

2. What poetic devices do you see in use in this song?

3. What sorts of associations do you have with banjos? Is the lyricist playing with those associations?

4. Young alludes to a line from a Robert Burns' poem, "To a Mouse," which is, roughly translated, "the best laid schemes of mice and men oft go awry." What do you make of Young's use of that line? What do you make of his use of the word *devil* there?

5. Young makes an allusion to "Swing Low Sweet Chariot," a Negro spiritual. How does he use it here? What is the effect of his rephrasing?

6. Interpret the image of the Cadillac in the chorus. Why does he use it? What does it mean? Is it a metaphor?

7. Why do you think Young ends his song in the interrogative mode (the "interrogative" is the technical term for in the form of a question)?

"The Civil War can still be lost." (Barbara Fields, historian, 1990)

8. On the Internet look up several-time governor of Alabama, George Wallace. What was his history? What were his views on desegregation? Neil Young wrote this song in 1972: What was George Wallace doing in that year? What was happening in Alabama at that time?

RONNIE VAN ZANT FOR LYNYRD SKYNYRD ～ *"Sweet Home Alabama"*

1. What would you say is the major theme or point of this song? How is it a response to "Alabama" (as well as "Southern Man")?

2. Where and why does Van Zant use anaphora?

3. How would you describe the diction of this song? Colloquial? How regional is its coloring? Are there any particularly Southern words or phrases used? If so, which ones?

4. Who would you say is the audience of this poem? What can you tell about the lyricist's desire to defend Alabama and the South in general from Neil Young's portrait of it?

5. Who is the *you* of the song? Is there more than one *you*?

6. How do you interpret the verse that begins "In Birmingham they love the governor"? Do you have any questions about its meaning?

7. Do you detect ambivalent or mixed feelings about Alabama?

WARREN ZEVON 〜 *"Play It All Night Long"*

"I believe Warren Zevon is the only man in the history of human communication to use the word 'brucellosis' in a song." (David Letterman)

1. Characterize the subject of this song. What is its attitude toward "Sweet Home Alabama"?

2. What sort of imagery dominates here? What sort of language?

3. How would you describe the line "Sweat, piss, jizz and blood." What is its effect? Do you detect any poetic device in it?

4. Try to scan the metrics of the first and second verses. There is a preponderance of trochees. What is the effect of so many metrical feet that begin with a stressed syllable?

5. We seem to hear the outlines of a vaguely defined family narrative. How does Zevon use this to structure the song?

6. What is the attitude toward "country living"?

SPOTLIGHT ON RHETORIC: LYRICS AND MELODY

These songs all fall under the rubric of popular music—music that is widely available to all and in form and content accessible to a broad audience. We seldom think of popular music in terms of its rhetoric, but consider that these songs all make some point and attempt to validate their points of view through language as well as music. And music can certainly be part of persuasion. Consider, how do these songs make you feel? Do songs ever sweep you away? Zevon very nearly refers to "Sweet Home Alabama" as a drug people use to distract them from their surroundings. Why is it that music can be so intoxicating? Can it be too seductive? Can people sing lyrics they don't think about because the music sweeps them away? Is that dangerous? Insignificant?

FIND IT

Find examples of three or more of these devices, underlining them and noting in the margin where they appear.

1. anaphora
2. apostrophe
3. colloquial diction
4. metaphor
5. simile

MUSICAL ANALYSIS

How do language and music combine in these songs to create their tone? In a series of three paragraphs, discuss how the imagery and phrasing of these songs combine to create their mood. Title each paragraph with the title of the song, and then open your paragraph with a topic sentence about the tone and mood of the song. Feel free to use the first person and to be somewhat informal in your language, but do pay attention to paragraphing structure. Develop your topic sentence in the paragraph, and in the body of the paragraph explain as specifically as possible how elements combine to create the mood of the song. Be sure to close with a concluding sentence; we shouldn't feel that your discussion stopped midstream.

You may or may not have experience with the language of music and conventions of song. Do not fret about sounding technical. It is perfectly okay to refer to "when the drums enter." Just try to be clear. Think about the sorts of instruments used and the quality they create and even their historic associations (like with the banjo).

Focus most of all on trying to express what you hear and how you hear it. However, here are some musical terms and adjectives to keep handy while you write.

Musical Terms
bridge
chorus
crescendo
decrescendo
harmony
instrumentation
introduction
major/minor mood
meter
pitch
tempo
verse

Adjectives
dense/sparse
fast/slow
happy/sad
hard/soft
loose/structured
loud/quiet
melodic/dissonance

WRITING SONG LYRICS

Write lyrics to a song about something about which you feel strongly. This could be a cause or a person; it could even be in response to another song or one of the songs in this study. Note that the writers of these songs use language in compelling, often quite poetic ways. When you write, attend closely to creating vivid verses that create mood. You might include similes, metaphors, and alliteration. Somehow . . . through lyrical imagery . . . through hints of narrative . . . make your point of view clear.

Option One: Use the music of another song: yours will be "sung to the tune of." In this case, become as familiar as possible with your model, including how many times the song repeats its chorus.

Option Two: You compose music and lyrics for the above assignment and either perform it or record it for classroom presentation.

CLIVE JAMES
"The Book of My Enemy Has Been Remaindered"

FORM: *Poem*
DATE: 1993

ANNE LAMOTT
"Jealousy," Excerpt from the Book *Bird By Bird: Some Instructions on Writing and Life*

FORM: *Personal Essay*
DATE: 1994

PUBLICATION NOTE

Clive James clearly hit a nerve with "The Book of My Enemy Has Been Remaindered." After it appeared in *Sunday Times Magazine*, it became an Internet hit. In part because of its success on the Internet, James titled his 2003 collection of poems *The Book of My Enemy*.

THE INTERSECTION

In "The Book of My Enemy Has Been Remaindered," Clive James writes about a lesser human emotion, jealousy. A victory poem in mock-epic style, this small comic masterpiece trumpets the failure of a literary enemy. In "Jealousy," Anne Lamott uses the personal essay to ruminate on this strain of jealousy so insidious for authors—literary jealousy. Lamott's is more of a discursive exploration of emotion than stylish crystallization of it. This is another example of one author "replying" to another; Lamott celebrates the liberating humor of James' poem.

> Remaindering *occurs when a publishing house takes the overstock of books that have not sold and sells them at deep discount to "the kind of bookshop where remaindering occurs," as James so wittily describes.*

▶ **POINTS FOR DISCUSSION:** *"The Book of My Enemy Has Been Remaindered"*

HALLMARKS *mixed diction (classical and colloquial), mock-epic language*

FORM AND CONTENT James achieves his comic effect through the brilliant intersection of classical language, imagery, and syntax with contemporary words and phrases that are lacking in grandeur. The arcs of thought within his poem often take wing with high-flown language. He then lands on some damningly everyday word or phrase when he moves to characterize the work of his enemy. In the first stanza, for example, he begins with his refrain "The book of my enemy has been remaindered / And I am pleased" and then ends "here is that book / Among those ranks and banks of duds, / Those ponderous and seemingly irreducible cairns / Of complete stiffs."

Before you discuss the poem or even have someone read it aloud, be sure students know the crucial term *remaindering* (see callout above). After someone reads aloud, ask students for their reaction, and be prepared for their not knowing what to make of it necessarily, since they may at first simply react to its high rhetoric. You may need to help them understand it. Explain that there are poems that are "occasional," that is, written for a certain type of event (or even a certain event very specifically). Explain that this poem uses a classical form. There are wedding poems (epithalamia), poems written on the death of someone (elegies). Dedicatory poems. What kind of poem is it? Why is it funny that this is a victory poem?

What about its form? What was their reaction to James' poetic stance of unabashed gloating over another's fall? How does the poet speak of the author whose work has been remaindered? Were they shocked? Gratified? Could they relate to it? Further, alliterative phrases like "Barbara Windsor's Book of Boobs" are more ludicrous when spoken. Where are there other examples of comic alliteration? Should all poems ideally be read aloud? How does hearing the language help with our understanding and appreciation?

TONE AND AUDIENCE The exultant attitude of the poetic speaker is everywhere evident in the poem, but do press students to express for themselves how they see the tone of the poem. Ask students to identify the lines that convey the speaker's mood. When he says "And I am pleased" and "And I rejoice," how does he sound? Do they think it sounds archaic? Kingly? Biblical? Why is it funny?

FOCAL POINT: MIXED DICTION In this poem, James combines classical and contemporary language. On the one hand, he uses a classical metaphor to describe the book's new shame: "It has gone with bowed head like defeated legion / Beneath the yoke." We might expect such a line from Homer; indeed, that line might be called an epic simile. On the other hand, sounding much more colloquial and contemporary, he soon after refers to how it is "Knocked into the middle of next week" with the "bummers that no amount of hype could shift, / the unbudgeable turkeys." What is the effect of moving from lofty language to everyday language? Why is it that the poet is associated with grand language and poet's enemy with unpleasant terms (*duds, stiffs, turkeys*)? Ask students to look in the other stanza for examples of mixed diction. Which lines did they find to be the funniest?

> *Students may well react to "The Book of My Enemy Has Been Remaindered" right away, but it is wise to read aloud again after you have discussed it. Their appreciation may be livelier on the second reading. Reactions are impossible to predict, as teachers know, and what is a crowning success with one group may sink unaccountably like a stone with another.*

▶ **POINTS FOR DISCUSSION:** *"Jealousy"*

HALLMARKS *personal essay, colloquial style*

FORM AND CONTENT Lamott's essay explores jealousy in the service of providing advice. It emphasizes its agony and its complexity of sources, and rather than dispensing wisdom from the far-off clouds of the professionally arrived, it speaks writer to writer, but from the vantage point of experience. Use the student questions on page 133 to explore how the essay is shaped, moving from generalities to the specifics of experience. For all its seeming informality, how would they describe its organization? What makes it hang together?

TONE AND AUDIENCE In her essay, Lamott speaks as an adviser to young or inexperienced writers. Ask, who is the audience, the *you* Lamott is addressing? What is Lamott's tone as she discusses her experience with jealousy? How credible do they find her advice? Is she trying to persuade her audience on some particular point? Does she create a sense of fellow feeling with her audience? Ask students to discuss their reaction to it. Did they like it? Was there anything uncomfortable about her more confessional remarks? Did they like her use of personal experience? Were they moved by it? Or put off?

FOCAL POINT: METAPHOR Throughout the piece, Lamott talks about her experience with jealousy in the terms of illness. She has had a "bout" with it, talks about it as a "fever," and references how she got better. You might point out one or two instances of medical language and then ask students to look for more examples. Does this way of talking about it resonate with the students? Do they find it believable? Would they call that metaphoric language? Or do they think Lamott means it quite literally? Is it hyperbolic to call jealousy an illness? Or is it just right, to suggest it is a sickness?

▶ Points for Discussion: *Connecting the Authors*

Ask students to place the two pieces before them. As a starting point, you might ask students to define the purpose of each piece and how well each writer does in shaping his or her discussion. Did they like one piece over another? If so, why? Or are their purposes and forms so different that it is a matter of apples and oranges? What about the gender of the authors: Do they think their pieces seem particularly male or female? Although this sort of gender discussion can quickly unravel in vague and offensive reflections, still it can be interesting to see what sorts of assumptions students have.

FOCAL POINT: COMPARING GENRES One of the writing assignments asks students to consider the differences between poetry and prose. To help students prepare to write, ask someone to read aloud James' poem and the first couple of pages of Lamott's essay. Ask them to listen without reading at the same time. What differences do they notice? Does one seem easier than the other? Ask them next to read over the first stanza and the first paragraph. Where does the writing seem tighter? Which seems more engaging right away?

Reading Questions FOR STUDENTS

CLIVE JAMES   *"The Book of My Enemy Has Been Remaindered"*

"The Book of My Enemy Has Been Remaindered" has been called "a high hymn of schadenfreude." A German word, *schadenfreude*, has been absorbed into English dictionaries. It refers to the idea of exulting over the fall of someone previously elevated. When celebrities land in rehab, when diet doctors suffer heart attacks, when moralists land in jail, the word *schadenfreude* increasingly appears.

1. How would you describe the subject of this poem? How does James discuss it? What is the effect of describing something silly in grand terms?

2. What does the poetic speaker suggest about his enemy and his work?

3. To what end are the titles of other works listed?

4. The refrain is repeated four times, but in the last instance it comes in a new place. Why does he move it to the end of the poem? How does it affect our sense of closure?

5. Does the poet ever seem self-mocking?

ANNE LAMOTT   *"Jealousy"*

1. Who is the *you* of this discussion? To whom does Lamott seem to be addressing her words?

2. What is the effect of hearing the author's personal struggle with jealousy? Does it invest her discussion of it with more, or less, authority? Does what she say sound truer as a result?

3. Did you find Lamott a credible and realistic-sounding narrator?

4. What are some conclusions that the author draws about the effects of jealousy?

5. How would you say the author organizes her discussion? Does she move from specifics to generalities? Or from generalities to specifics?

"Every time a friend succeeds, a little something in me dies." (Gore Vidal)

SPOTLIGHT ON RHETORIC: MOCK EPIC

In the mock epic, a trivial subject is treated in the elevated style of classical literature. The most famous example is Alexander Pope's *The Rape of the Lock*, in which a theft of a lock of hair caused a social uproar in the upper classes. Pope treated this incident with very high style. The comic use of serious forms has a long history in English. In Chaucer's day, for example, there were "sermon joyeux," which used sermon structure for some ridiculous topic.

continued on following page

FIND IT

In Clive James' poem, find examples of three or more of these devices, underlining them and noting in the margin where they appear.

1. alliteration
2. epic simile
3. imperative
4. metaphor
5. refrain

COMPARING POETRY AND PROSE

What is the difference in experience between reading poetry and prose? Before you start writing, reread James' poem and the first couple of pages of Lamott's essay on jealousy.

Questions to Consider: Does one require more concentration? Is one easier? Faster? If you had to choose between reading either of these pieces, which would you select? Why? Why do you think poetry as a form is at present less popular than prose in general and the novel in particular? Why is the novel the fashion of these times?

Your writing should be thoughtful, honest, and clear. Do not worry overly about using poetic terms or being technically correct in some way. Your focus should be on trying to define how you experience the difference between poetry and prose here and elsewhere. Feel free, of course, to use *I*.

IN DEFENSE OF FLAWS

From the Middle Ages on, the Christian tradition observed "seven deadly sins": pride, envy, anger, sloth, gluttony, greed, and lust. In a poem or piece of prose, explore one of these "sins." You might write a confessional exploration and, like Lamott, tell a personal story. Be sure to connect your story to the general problem of whatever it is. What is it that draws people to this particular form of excessive behavior?

Your discussion may be very serious, but not necessarily. You might write something humorous, such as "In Defense of Sloth." If you do this, defend the flaw. Maybe it has some virtues that have gone unconsidered.

CLIVE JAMES ∼ *"The Book of My Enemy Has Been Remaindered"*

1939–
BORN AUSTRALIA

The book of my enemy has been remaindered
And I am pleased.
In vast quantities it has been remaindered
Like a van-load of counterfeit that has been seized
5   And sits in piles in a police warehouse,
My enemy's much-prized effort sits in piles
In the kind of bookshop where remaindering occurs.
Great, square stacks of rejected books and, between them, aisles
One passes down reflecting on life's vanities,
10 Pausing to remember all those thoughtful reviews
Lavished to no avail upon one's enemy's book—
For behold, here is that book
Among these ranks and banks of duds,

cairns—
heaps of stones

These ponderous and seemingly irreducible *cairns*
15 Of complete stiffs.
The book of my enemy has been remaindered
And I rejoice.

legion—
army

It has gone with bowed head like a defeated *legion*
Beneath the yoke.
20 What avail him now his awards and prizes,
The praise expended upon his meticulous technique,
His individual new voice?
Knocked into the middle of next week
His brainchild now consorts with the bad buys
25 The sinker, clinkers, dogs and dregs,

Edsels—
failed Ford motorcars

The *Edsels* of the world of moveable type,
The bummers that no amount of hype could shift,
The unbudgeable turkeys.
Yea, his slim volume with its understated wrapper
30 Bathes in the blare of the brightly jacketed Hitler's War Machine,
His unmistakably individual new voice
Shares the same scrapyart with a forlorn skyscraper
Of The Kung-Fu Cookbook,
His honesty, proclaimed by himself and believed by others,
35 His renowned abhorrence of all posturing and pretense,

Pierrots—
pantomimes

Is there with Pertwee's Promenades and *Pierrots*—
One Hundred Years of Seaside Entertainment,

And (oh, this above all) his sensibility,
His sensibility and its hair-like filaments,
40 His delicate, quivering sensibility is now as one
With Barbara Windsor's Book of Boobs,
A volume graced by the descriptive rubric
"My boobs will give everyone hours of fun."
Soon now a book of mine could be remaindered also,
45 Though not to the monumental extent
In which the chastisement of remaindering has been *meted out*
To the book of my enemy,
Since in the case of my own book it will be due
To a miscalculated print run, a marketing error—
50 Nothing to do with merit.
But just supposing that such an event should hold
Some slight element of sadness, it will be offset
By the memory of this sweet moment.
Chill the champagne and polish the crystal goblets!
55 The book of my enemy has been remaindered
And I am glad.

meted out—
measured out

ANNE LAMOTT ～ **"Jealousy," Excerpt from the Book Bird by Bird: Some Instructions on Writing and Life**

1954–
BORN UNITED STATES

Of all the voices you'll hear on KFKD, the most difficult to subdue may be that of jealousy. Jealousy is such a direct attack on whatever measure of confidence you've been able to muster. But if you continue to write, you are probably going to have to deal with it, because some wonder-
5 ful, dazzling successes are going to happen for some of the most awful, angry, undeserving writers you know—people who are, in other words, not you.

This is going to happen because the public herd mentality is not swayed by the magic that happens when mind and heart and muse and
10 hand and paper work together. Rather, it is guided by talk shows and movie producers and TV commercials. Still, you'd probably like the caribou herd to run in your direction for a while. Most of us secretly want this. But maybe the herd is going to stuff itself on lichen and then waddle after some really undeserving writers instead. Those writers will
15 get the place on the best-seller list, the movie sales, the huge advances, and the nice big glossy pictures in the national magazines where the photo editors have airbrushed out the excessively long eyeteeth, the wrinkles, and the horns. The writer you most admire in the world will give them rave reviews in the *Times* or blurbs for the paperback edition.
20 They will buy houses, big houses, or second houses that are actually as nice, or nicer, than the first ones. And you are going to want to throw yourself down the back stairs, especially if the person is a friend.

You are going to feel awful beyond words. You are going to have a number of days in a row where you hate everyone and don't believe
25 in anything. If you do know the author whose turn it is, he or she will inevitably say that it will be your turn next, which is what the bride always says to you at each successive wedding, while you grow older and more decayed. It can wreak just the tiniest bit of havoc with your self-esteem to find that you are hoping for small bad things to happen
30 to this friend—for, say, her head to blow up. Or for him to wake up one morning with a pain in his prostate, because I don't care how rich and successful someone is, if you wake up having to call your doctor and ask for a finger massage, it's going to be a long day. You get all caught up in such fantasies because you feel, once again, like the kid outside the

35 candy-store window, and you believe that this friend, this friend whom you now hate, has all the candy. You believe that success is bringing this friend inordinate joy and serenity and security and that her days are easier. She's going to live to be one hundred and twenty, he's never going to die—the people who are going to die are the good people, like

40 you. But this is not true. Money won't guarantee these writers much of anything, except that now they have a much more expensive set of problems. The pressure on their lives has actually intensified.

Good, fine, you think. I'm into intensity; those are the problems I want.

But do you really?

45 Yes, you really do.

But some of the loneliest, most miserable, neurotic, despicable people we know have been the most successful in the world.

Right—but it would be different for me. I would not fall for my own press clippings. I would not mention my achievements all the time.

Guggenheim—
prestigious arts fellowship

50 I would not say things like "Boy, you think it's raining hard today? I remember one day—I think it was the year I got my *Guggenheim*—it *really* rained hard." You'd never do that, unlike other people you could mention.

That's very nice. It's all going to happen to somebody else anyway. Bank
55 on it. Jealousy is one of those occupational hazards of being a writer, and the most degrading. And I, who have been the Leona Helmsley of jealousy, have come to believe that the only things that help ease or transform it are (a) getting older, (b) talking about it until the fever breaks, and (c) using it as material. Also, someone somewhere along
60 the line is going to be able to make you start laughing about it, and then you will be on your way home.

I went through a very bad bout of jealousy last year, when someone with whom I am (or rather was) friendly did extremely well. It felt like every few days she'd have more good news about how well her book
65 was doing, until it seemed that she was going to be set for life. It threw me for a loop. I am a better writer than she is. A lot of my writer friends do very well, hugely well, and I'm not jealous of them. I do not know why that is, but it's true. But when it happened for her, I would sit listening to her discuss her latest successes over the phone, praying that
70 I could get off the line before I started barking. I was literally oozing unhappiness, like a sump.

continued on following page

My deepest belief is that to live as if we're dying can set us free. Dying people teach you to pay attention and to forgive and not to sweat the small things. So every time this friend called, I tried to will myself into

75 forgiving both of us. I had been around someone from the South that summer who was always exclaiming, "Isn't that great?"—only she made it almost rhyme with "bright." So when my friend would call with her lastest good news, always presented humbly like some born-again-Christian Miss America contestant, I'd say, "Isn't that gright, huh? Isn't

80 that gright?"

She would say, "You are so supportive. Some of my other friends are having trouble with this."

I'd say, "How could I not be supportive? It's just so darn gright."

But I always wanted to ask, "Could I have the names and numbers of

85 some of your other friends?"

Sometimes I would get off the phone and cry.

After a while I started asking people for help.

One person reminded me of what Jean Rhys once wrote, that all of us writers are little rivers running into one lake, that what is good for one

90 is good for all, that we all collectively share in one another's success and acclaim. I said, "You are a very, very angry person."

My therapist said that jealousy is a secondary emotion, that it is born out of feeling excluded and deprived, and that if I worked on those age-old feelings, I would probably break through the jealousy. I tried to get

95 her to give me a prescription for Prozac, but she said that this other writer was in my life to help me heal my past. She said this writer had helped bring up a lifetime's worth of feeling that other families were happier than ours, that other families had some owner's manual to go by. She said it was once again that business of comparing my insides to

100 other people's outsides. She said to go ahead and feel the feelings. I did. They felt like shit.

My friend, the writer I was so jealous of, would call and say, like some Southern belle, "I just don't know why God is giving me so much money this year." And I would do my Lamaze for a moment, and say, "Isn't that

105 gright?" I have never felt like such a loser in my life.

I called a very wise writer I know who's been in Alcoholics Anonymous for years, who spends half his time helping others get sober. I asked him what he would tell a newcomer who was in the throes of insanity or, say hypothetically, jealousy.

110 "I just listen," he said. "They all tell me these incredibly long, self-important, convoluted stories. And then I say one of three things: I say, 'Uh-huh,' I say, 'Hmmm,' I say, 'Too bad.'" I laughed. Then I started telling him about this awful friend I had who was doing so well. He was silent for a moment. Then he said, "Uh-huh."

115 Next I talked to my slightly overweight alcoholic gay Catholic priest friend. I said, "Do you get jealous?"

He said, "When I see a man my own age in great shape, and I feel all conflicted, wishing I were that thin and yet at the same time wanting to lick him, is that jealousy or is that appreciation?"

120 It was hard to get anyone to say anything that would make the jealousy go away or change into something else. I felt like the wicked stepsister in a fairy tale. I told another friend, and she read me some lines by Lakota Sioux: "Sometimes I go about pitying myself. And all the while I am being carried on great winds across the sky." That is so beautiful,
125 I said; and I am so mentally ill.

Those lines, however, offered the beginning of a solution. They made the first tiny crack in my prison wall. I was waiting for the kind of solution where God reaches down and touches you with his magic wand and all of a sudden I would be fixed, like a broken toaster oven. But this
130 was not the way it happened. Instead, I got one angstrom unit better, day by day.

Another piece of the solution came when a poem by Clive James, called "The Book of My Enemy Has Been Remaindered," appeared one Sunday in *The New York Times Book Review*. "The book of my enemy has
135 been remaindered," it begins, "And I am pleased." It helped more than words can say. Oh, what blessed relief for someone to be as jealous and spiteful as me and to make those feelings funny. I called everyone whose advice I had sought and read it to them. Everybody howled with recognition.

140 Yet another piece of the solution dropped into place when my friend Judy said that the problem was trying to *stop* the jealousy and competitiveness, and that the main thing was not to let it fuel my self-loathing. She said it was nuts for me to try to be happy for this other writer. I cannot tell you how much this helped. I was raised in a culture that pro-
145 motes this competitiveness, this insatiability, this fantasy of needing hundreds of thousands of dollars a year, and then, in the next breath, shames you for any feelings of longing or envy or fear that it will always

continued on following page

be someone else's turn. I was only doing what I had been groomed
to do.

150   So I started getting my sense of humor back. I started telling myself that
if you want to know how God feels about money, look at whom she
gives it to. This cheered me up to no end, even though my closest
friends have lots of money. I told myself that historically when people
do too well too quickly, they are a Greek tragedy waiting to happen. I,
155   who did not do too well too quickly and who was in fact not doing too
well over time, was actually in the catbird seat. I was not going to end
up the cocky heroine in an ugly *hubris* drama. This is not to be under-
estimated. My nerves are shot as it is; the last thing I need would be an
onslaught of thunder and silent screams, with cymbals, fangs, winds
160   pushing forest fires across the land; I mean, who needs it?

Then I started to write about my envy. I got to look in some cold dark
corners, see what was there, shine a little light on what we all have in
common. Sometimes this human stuff is slimy and pathetic—jealousy
especially so—but better to feel it and talk about it and walk through it
165   than to spend a lifetime being silently poisoned.

hubris—
excessive pride

PART **5**

IDENTITY: LITTLE HISTORIES

Joseph Mitchell "The Old House at Home," Excerpt from the Book *Up in the Old Hotel*

Orhan Pamuk "My Grandmother," Excerpt from the Book *Istanbul: Memories and the City*

Richard Rodriguez "Aria," from the Book *Hunger of Memory: The Education of Richard Rodriguez*

Amy Tan "Mother Tongue"

NOTE ON BOOKS AND AUTHORS

Journalist Joseph Mitchell was on the staff of *The New Yorker* for decades, and *Up in the Old Hotel* collects many of his pieces written during his tenure there from the 1930s to the 1960s. Mitchell liked to write profiles of people who were not the luminaries and social high-lifers traditionally chronicled in New York publications, but individuals engaged in farming oysters, tending bar, running Bowery hotels, panhandling, or just drinking too much. Mitchell seemed to eschew celebrity and instead gravitated to small scale, "local" celebrity, the kind true neighborhoods generate.

Writer Orhan Pamuk won the Nobel Prize for Literature in 2006 for *Istanbul: Memories and the City*, which is a remarkable collection of reflections and memories at once about the author, his family, the city, the Ottoman Empire, and the world. He is best known as a novelist for such international, highly literary bestsellers as *My Name Is Red* (2001) and *Snow* (2005).

THE INTERSECTION

With these two chapters from larger works, Joseph Mitchell and Orhan Pamuk call up something elusive and rare about people and places. They are, both of them, great writers of great cities. And one way they get at their big picture, curiously enough, is through small, sharp portraiture. Mitchell especially focuses on individuals and their defining stamp on idiosyncratic places. In "The Old House at Home," he writes about barkeep and bar owner Old John McSorley, a man of strong views and quirky habits, who ran the picturesque McSorley's Ale House in the East Village of Manhattan. No women in *his* pub. And in *Istanbul*, Pamuk writes about his Turkish grandmother, a woman who ruled his family, often from bed. Like her strange bedfellow here in America, she, too, was someone of set views and odd habits. In both these portraits, we seem to touch the present of these characters but somehow, too, we palpably feel their link to a more ancient past. Old Ireland. Old Istanbul. The world and cultures these powerhouses knew in youth are gone. We know that, and the narrators know that.

▶ **POINTS FOR DISCUSSION:** *"The Old House at Home"*

HALLMARKS *portraiture, slice of life (exhaustive detail, metaphor, anthropomorphizing)*

FORM AND CONTENT "The Old House at Home" depicts a highly idiosyncratic place owned by an eccentric individual. Mitchell vividly captures the bar's history and the contributing factors to its organic evolution: its Civil War–era start; the history of Old John, the founder, who came to America during the Irish potato famine; its location at the terminus of the Bowery and its proximity to the old Bowery hotels; and the particular mix of immigrants and industry that made up the clientele during the latter half of the nineteenth century. Ask students to try to define the subject of the piece. What is Mitchell writing about? (Tap into the reading questions for more ways to nudge students to consider the intertwined subjects of person and place.) Further, Mitchell was a journalist: Do they find evidence of that here? Obviously he is not only attentive to facts; he is a masterful shaper of a sense of atmosphere. How does he use descriptors such as *drowsy* to create the

Noted American composer Aaron Copeland's Fanfare for the Common Man *was written in 1942, roughly the same time period during which Mitchell wrote his pieces for* The New Yorker.

feeling of the place? What other modifiers contribute to our sense of the mood of the place and its customs? Help students notice his use of language—for instance, like a small group of disgruntled drunks, "the clocks on the wall have not been in agreement for many years." How in general does he use detail? How does he employ lists to the piece's advantage?

TONE AND AUDIENCE   This character portrait first appeared in *The New Yorker* magazine, which was, and still is, famous for its Reporter at Large and Profile articles. *The New Yorker*'s readership has generally been educated people, lovers of the arts. You might ask your students, "Who is Mitchell's audience? Why does he assume a nationwide audience would be interested in reading about this Lower East Side Irish bar? Further, what is his attitude toward his subject? Is he critical of Old John? Does Mitchell seem to like McSorley's?" Use these questions to kick up discussion about class in America and how we as readers are drawn to read about "others," about people and places that our particular backgrounds might forbid us to actually rub elbows with. There is something completely wonderful about the abundance of detail in this piece—Mitchell seems to revel in specificity. Read aloud favorite parts to help students appreciate it too. Highlight Mitchell's near-sacred evocation of customs and habits of the bar, with its little shrinelike clippings and pictures. Does Mitchell invest his subject with any religious imagery in fact? Would students say that he idealizes or romanticizes this place in any way?

FOCAL POINT: UNCOMMON COMMONERS   Much classical literature tended to emphasize people of high status. Yet one only need read the Mystery Plays or Chaucer's "The Miller's Tale" or the pub scenes of Shakespeare's *Henry V* plays to see how far back in history the broadening of subject matter began: All of these works portrayed regular people—shepherds, millers, clerks, barkeeps. Literature of the Romantic period followed suit. In the highly influential Preface to the Second Edition of *Lyrical Ballads*, William Wordsworth (1800) wrote that he wanted to represent "the language really used by men." And across the pond in nineteenth-century American journalism, there was a tradition of "local color" writing—that is, newspaper journalists depicting people and locales in ways that were quite romanticizing. An interest in people and places showed up in novels too. In Mark Twain's *Huck Finn*, even such minor players as the undertaker are, to brilliant comic effect, treated to close, often, rather affectionate observation. Indeed in many respects, Mitchell's profiles harken back to the work of Twain.

Joseph Mitchell's New York Times *obituary recounts that when "somebody suggested that he wrote about the 'little people,' he replied that there were no little people in his work. 'They are as big as you are, whoever you are,' he said."* Up in the Old Hotel *is an excellent book to keep handy to read aloud for inspiration or when time opens up unexpectedly or events conspire against your classroom preparations.*

▶ POINTS FOR DISCUSSION: *"My Grandmother"*

HALLMARKS   *memoir, narrative sketch writing, general past tense*

FORM AND CONTENT   This rather loosely structured chapter of memories and reflections begins in early childhood and ends in adulthood. Yet it adds up to more than the sum of its parts, I think it's fair to say. It is full of atmosphere, beautifully evoking the mysterious but indelible impressions of youth. Ask students, "What did you think? What struck you? What is Pamuk's subject? Why might Pamuk include a chapter on his grandmother in a book about Istanbul? The author gives us the sense that his grandmother was not really interested actively in political controversies or much driven by questions of East versus West or Atatürk versus the Ottoman past. She stays home. Ask students to consider how the author supports the idea that the home is her little world, one she rules. And yet, do we nonetheless get the sense that the grandmother does have opinions and preferences about the world beyond her home?

TONE AND AUDIENCE Tone is often defined as the attitude of a narrator toward the subject, and thus it is of course shaped by who the narrator is. In the case of memoir, narrator and author are fused, but often complexly. You might ask students to describe in general terms the author's attitude toward his grandmother. Is he worshipful? In awe? Mystified by her? Pamuk recounts a grandchild's experiences of his grandmother. But what, precisely, is the perspective? Is it purely a child's? Indeed, the point of view is more complex, involving the adult retrospective narrator telling us what he remembers of his reactions. The narrative voice is not childlike though he does at times vividly conjure a child's perceptions—the painted toes of his grandmother are vividly described, a source of "fascination and revulsion" recounted in sharp detail in an adult's voice. Does he analyze this sort of image deeply? We hear no Freudian meditations, for example. Rather, this and other images are left to resonate. Some authors meditate at length upon a memory (like Sanders does in "Under the Influence," page 186). In fact, you might ask your students, "Does Pamuk write as if he believes memories and images are fully explicable? Or does he have a sense of the insoluble past? A past that is a mysterious as human beings themselves?"

Further, the question of audience here is an interesting one. Is Pamuk only writing for fellow Turks? Does he stop to explain all his references? Although he does not explain everything, his writing does not seem designed to exclude other readers: It is a recognizable world that an outsider may enter. We may not know what *bezique* is (a pinochle-like card game), but we can tell that it is a game. Do students see any evidence of the author writing for an international audience? Does Pamuk in any sense seem to be explaining Turkish culture to outsiders?

FOCAL POINT: *HÜZÜN* AND PAMUK'S ANATOMY OF TURKISH MELANCHOLY

"My Grandmother" appears in a work that touches on how the Ottoman empire, though gone, is evident everywhere in the city, its vestiges weighing down modern

Mustafa Kemal Atatürk is considered the architect of modern Turkey; he introduced reforms that would move it toward becoming a modern, secular, democratic nation. Atatürk first made a name as a military commander. After the defeat of the Ottoman Empire in World War I, he led the defeat of the troops sent by the Entente Powers. He wanted, and got, an independent republic and in 1922 became its first president.

Atatürk remains highly celebrated in modern Turkey, but not by all. Secularists applaud his dismantling of what they see as backward-looking traditions and customs, including everything from the hereditary Caliphate to the hats men wear—Atatürk mandated that men wear Western-style hats instead of the traditional fez, which he associated with the Ottoman past. But for some Muslims, the shift to secular ways was unwelcome, and some women recounted having been forced to unveil themselves as a result of his reforms.

Turkey with a very particular melancholy called *hüzün*. In the context of this larger meditation on the end of empires, personal vignettes emerge. We learn of Pamuk's grandmother, who approves of Atatürk and secularization, but who observes some aspects of high Ottoman etiquette and has a friend who had been part of a sultan's harem before Atatürk swept out the sultans and ushered in a new era, the Republic of Turkey. The past lives on in the habits of the living. (You might ask students how much they know about Atatürk, which is likely to be nothing. A brief sketch of Atatürk appears earlier in this section.) Does the portrait seem melancholy? What creates a sense of some mysterious sorrow? Point them toward the elements that underscore not progress but some inevitability of decline and fall (such as the fate of the Ottoman Empire, or the downward troping fortunes of his formerly wealthy family). The grandmother urges them to be more careful, but there is no real sense that their fortunes can be reversed. How does that contribute to our sense of melancholy? Is the writing sentimental in any sense? Nostalgic? If so where do they see that?

▶ POINTS FOR DISCUSSION: *Connecting the Authors*

There are many differences in the times and places of these characters, and yet there are also rather striking and amusing similarities. Old John and the grandmother both rule the roost. They are in charge of their domains and seem rather old-fashioned. Ask students to work in pairs to comb the pieces for as many similarities as possible. Ask, "How is it that they could be so similar?"

FOCAL POINT: PARAGRAPHING That writers shape and pace paragraphs in a range of ways, creating a variety of effects, is easily borne out by the juxtaposition of these authors. Have your students place their texts side by side before them. Whose paragraphs are longer and more developed? (Mitchell's are, quite evidently.) Have students examine all of Mitchell's paragraphs. What do they notice? What kinds of decisions did Mitchell seem to make in terms of organizing and pacing his narrative? For example, in the first paragraph, would it be possible to break it into two paragraphs? Could, for example, "It is a drowsy place" (lines 10–11) be the start of a new paragraph? Why do you suppose Mitchell chose to keep it all as one? How is the subject of the first paragraph distinct from the second? And further, what is the effect of such a long, continuous paragraph? In part it allows Mitchell to develop a sustained arc of description that pulls us in quite completely, and by the end of the first paragraph, we have had gained a rich introduction to place that thoroughly sets us up to meet Old John.

After you discuss Mitchell's paragraphing, turn to Pamuk's. How is his approach different from Mitchell's? Pamuk's paragraphs tend to be shorter and are less consistent in length. Guide students to notice that the vignettes Pamuk includes within his paragraphs tend to be briefer. Taken as a whole, we move rather swiftly from reminiscence to reminiscence with few highly amplified scenes. Ask, "Do Pamuk's paragraphing choices reflect the nature of childhood memories? Does the pace set and do the sketchy, yet evocative vignettes underscore the author's message? Which is the longest paragraph? Why?" Pamuk devotes the most room to a scene he considers most worthy of development. Namely, in lines 100–122, which begins "One of the ladies at the game table was from the sultan's harem . . ." This scene creates a sense of his grandmother's connection to the Ottoman past, with her friend from a harem and her little protocol book, which is important to the book's overall theme of the particular melancholy of Istanbul.

JOSEPH MITCHELL   ∽   *"The Old House at Home"*

McSorley's remains a highly popular watering hole, and one step into the place and glance at the old worn wood, sloping floor, and well-used bar sends one flying back to another era. New York University students, merchant marines, construction workers, Wall Streeters, neighborhood folk, and various other regulars as well as tourists all rub elbows there on a cold winter's day next to the old stove. Cats run over the sawdust-strewn floor. And, due to a court order, women have been part of the clientele since 1970 and are generally made welcome today. Much of the memorabilia still exists. Soldiers heading off to World War I would leave a wishbone over the bar and vow to collect it on their return. Wishbones that were never collected again, left by soldiers who perhaps died in battle, still hang there today as a sober, rather eerie reminder of their lives, tragically cut short. You can take a photo tour at www.mcsorleysnewyork.com.

1. Mitchell's writing is highly vivid. How does he create this vivid sense of a certain person living in a certain place?

2. Mitchell attends carefully to the dates and names and places. Is he in some sense a historian?

3. McSorley's Ale House is New York's oldest bar, opening in 1854. What was happening in the United States at that time?

4. Would you say that his subject is the bar itself or Old John? Or both together?

5. In line 31, we are told that Old John had "a lot of unassumed dignity." How does the piece support that idea? Indeed, what does that phrase tell us about Mitchell's attitude toward his subject?

6. This is not celebrity New York. How would you describe the kind of people that Mitchell seems to be interested in?

ORHAN PAMUK   ∽   *"My Grandmother"*

In 2006, Orhan Pamuk was charged with insulting "Turkishness" when he publicly asserted what the Turkish government denies: that the Turks had massacred one million Armenians and thirty thousand Kurds. Eventually the charges were dropped on a technicality after substantial international pressure was applied on his behalf from the European Union and International PEN, a writer's organization. Eight writers signed a letter in his support: José Saramago, Gabriel García Márquez, Günter Grass, Umberto Eco, Carlos Fuentes, Juan Goytisolo, John Updike, and Mario Vargas Llosa.

1. In line 4, the author refers to how people who live comfortably in cities are not interested in its "monuments, history, or 'beauties.'" How does the story of his grandmother support this statement?

2. How do the grandmother and Bekir run the house? What sense does the writer give you about that?

3. What images of the grandmother do you find most striking?

4. What do you learn about the narrative memoirist here? What did you find interesting or notable about him?

5. How would you define the narrative perspective? Is it told from a child's point of view? Or from an adult looking back at his childhood point of view?

6. How figurative does this writing seem to be? Does the author employ a great many similes and metaphors?

SPOTLIGHT ON RHETORIC: WORD CHOICE

The well-chosen word is worthy of consideration on its own. Mitchell's use of language is careful and his choices dead-on. And his choices evoke much. He calls keeping the electric light illuminated over the portrait of Old John a "pious custom" that is still observed. The word *pious* is religious in nature and helps to underscore the worshipfulness the Old John inspired.

FIND IT

Find examples of three or more of these devices, underlining them and noting in the margin where they appear.

1. anecdote

2. anthropomorphism

3. detail

4. metaphor

5. simile

THE WRITER'S DILEMMA

Read the quotation from Orhan Pamuk about the compositional process of writing *Istanbul*. Then, in a page, more or less, answer the questions that follow.

> I thought I would write *Istanbul: Memories and the City* in six months, but it took me one year to complete. And I was working twelve hours a day, just reading and working. My life, because of so many things, was in a crisis; I don't want to go into those details: divorce, father dying, professional problems, problems with this, problems with that, everything was bad. I thought if I were to be weak I would have a depression. But every day I would wake up and have a cold shower and sit down and remember and write, always paying attention to the beauty of the book. Honestly, I may have hurt my mother, my family. My father was dead, but my mother is still alive. But I can't care about that; I must care about the beauty of the book. (Joy E. Stocke, "The Melancholy Life of Orhan Pamuk," *Wild River Review*, November 19, 2007)

Questions: What is your reaction to this statement? Why do you think Pamuk had to keep focusing on the beauty of the book? What do you make of the idea that he couldn't care about his mother being hurt? On the face of it, that is a rather shocking statement. What do you think he means? Why couldn't he care about that? Did you sympathize with that sort of sentiment? Were you upset by it?

PORTRAIT OF A PLACE

Using Joseph Mitchell as a model, write a portrait of a place you know very well in which you create a strong sense of atmosphere and ritual or customs. Like Mitchell, make ample use of details, lists, metaphors, and well-chosen descriptors. If this place has a dominant personality associated with it, be sure to capture it. Consider kitchens, workshops, diners, ice cream parlors, restaurants, local hangouts, doctors' offices, veterinary offices, a room at school. Try to do some research. If you've been eating at a pizzeria for years that has clippings all over the wall, then go there and attend more carefully: What exactly is up on the wall? Why? What do the little idiosyncrasies of a place tell us? Is there a dollar taped on the wall of your favorite diner with a note on it? Try to find out about it. Such details are the stuff of wonderful writing about place.

JOSEPH MITCHELL ~ **"The Old House at Home," Excerpt from the Book** Up in the Old Hotel

1908–1996
BORN UNITED STATES

McSorley's occupies the ground floor of a red-brick tenement at 15 Seventh Street, just off Cooper Square, where the Bowery ends. It was opened in 1854 and is the oldest saloon in New York City. In eighty-eight years it has had four owners—an Irish immigrant, his son, a retired policeman, and his

5 daughter—and all of them have been opposed to change. It is equipped with electricity, but the bar is stubbornly illuminated with a pair of gas lamps, which flicker fitfully and throw shadows on the low, cobwebby ceiling each time someone opens the street door. There is no cash register. Coins are dropped in soup bowls—one for nickels, one for dimes, one for

10 quarters, and one for halves—and bills are kept in a rosewood cashbox. It is a drowsy place; the bartenders never make a needless move, the customers nurse their mugs of ale, and the three clocks on the walls have not been in agreement for many years. The clientele is *motley*. It includes

motley—
diverse

mechanics from the many garages in the neighborhood, salesmen from

15 the restaurant-supply houses on Cooper Square, truck-drivers from Wanamaker's, internes from Bellevue, students from Cooper Union, and clerks from the row of second-hand bookshops just north of Astor Place. The backbone of the clientele, however, is a rapidly thinning group of crusty old men, predominantly Irish, who have been drinking there since they were

20 youths and now have a proprietary feeling about the place. Some of them have tiny pensions, and are alone in the world; they sleep in Bowery hotels and spend practically all their waking hours in McSorley's. A few of these veterans dearly remember John McSorley, the founder, who died in 1910 at the age of eighty-seven. They refer to him as Old John, and they like to sit

25 in rickety armchairs around the big belly stove which heats the place, gnaw on the stems of their pipes, and talk about him.

Old John was quirky. He was normally affable but was subject to spells of unaccountable surliness during which he would refuse to answer when spoken to. He went bald in early manhood and began wearing scraggly,

30 patriarchal sideburns before he was forty. Many photographs of him are in existence, and it is obvious that he had a lot of unassumed dignity. He patterned his saloon after a public house he had known in his hometown in Ireland—Omagh, in County Tyrone—and originally called it the Old House at Home; around 1908 the signboard blew down, and when he ordered a

35 new one he changed the name to McSorley's Old Ale House. That is still the official name; customers never have called it anything but McSorley's.

continued on following page

Old John believed it impossible for men to drink with tranquillity in the presence of women; there is a fine back room in the saloon, but for many years a sign was nailed on the street door, saying, "NOTICE. NO BACK
40   ROOM IN HERE FOR LADIES." In McSorley's entire history, in fact, the only woman customer ever willingly admitted was an addled old peddler called Mother Fresh-Roasted, who claimed her husband died from the bite of a lizard in Cuba during the Spanish-American War and who went from saloon to saloon on the lower East Side for a couple of generations hawking
45   peanuts, which she carried in her apron. On warm days, Old John would sell her an ale, and her esteem for him was such that she embroidered him a little American flag and gave it to him one Fourth of July; he had it framed and placed it on the wall above his brass-bound ale pump, and it is still there. When other women came in, Old John would hurry forward, make a
50   bow, and say, "Madam, I'm sorry, but we don't serve ladies." If a woman insisted, Old John would take her by the elbow, head her toward the door, and say, "Madam, please don't provoke me. Make haste and get yourself off the premises, or I'll be obliged to forget you're a lady." This technique, pretty much word for word, is still in use.

55   In his time, Old John catered to the Irish and German workingmen—carpenters, tanners, bricklayers, slaughter-house butchers, teamsters, and brewers—who populated the Seventh Street neighborhood, selling ale in pewter mugs at five cents a mug and putting out a free lunch inflexibly consisting of soda crackers, raw onions, and cheese; present-day customers
60   are wont to complain that some of the cheese Old John laid out on opening night in 1854 is still there. Adjacent to the free lunch he kept a quart crock of tobacco and a rack of clay and corncob pipes—the purchase of an ale entitled a man to a smoke on the house; the rack still holds a few of the communal pipes. Old John was thrifty and was able to buy the tene-
65   ment—it is five stories high and holds eight families—about ten years after he opened the saloon in it. He distrusted banks and always kept his money in a cast-iron safe; it still stands in the back room, but its doors are loose on their hinges and there is nothing in it but an accumulation of expired saloon licenses and several McSorley heirlooms, including Old John's
70   straight razor. He lived with his family in a flat directly over the saloon and got up every morning at five and took a long walk before breakfast, no matter what the weather. He unlocked the saloon at seven, swept it out himself, and spread sawdust on the floor. Until he became too feeble to manage a racing sulky, he always kept a horse and a nanny goat in a stable
75   around the corner on St. Mark's Place. He kept both animals in the same stall, believing, like many horse-lovers, that horses should have company at night. During the lull in the afternoon a stablehand would lead the horse

around to a hitching block in front of the saloon, and Old John, wearing his bar apron, would stand on the curb and groom the animal. A customer
80 who wanted service would tap on the window and Old John would drop his currycomb, step inside, draw an ale, and return at once to the horse. On Sundays he entered sulky races on uptown highways.

From the time he was twenty until he was fifty-five, Old John drank steadily, but throughout the last thirty-two years of his life he did not take a drop,
85 saying, "I've had my share." Except for a few experimental months in 1905 or 1906, no spirits ever have been sold in McSorley's; Old John maintained that the man never lived who needed a stronger drink than a mug of ale warmed on the hob of a stove. He was a big eater. Customarily, just before locking up for the night, he would grill himself a three-pound T-bone, plac-
90 ing it on a coal shovel and holding it over a bed of oak coals in the back-room fireplace. He liked to fit a whole onion into the hollowed-out heel of a loaf of French bread and eat it as if it were an apple. He had an extraordinary appetite for onions, the stronger the better, and said that "Good ale, raw onions, and no ladies" was the motto of his saloon. About once a
95 month during the winter he presided over an on-the-house beefsteak party in the back room, and late in life he was president of an organization of gluttons called the Honorable John McSorley Pickle, Beefsteak, Baseball Nine, and Chowder Club, which held hot-rock clambakes in a picnic grove on North Brother Island in the East River. On the walls are a number of
100 photographs taken at outings of the club, and in most of them the members are squatting around kegs of ale; except for the president, they all have drunken, slack-mouthed grins and their eyes look dazed. Old John had a bull-frog bass and enjoyed harmonizing with a choir of drunks. His favorite songs were "Muldoon, the Solid Man," "Swim Out, You're Over
105 Your Head," "Maggie Murphy's Home," and "Since the Soup House Moved Away." These songs were by Harrigan and Hart, who were then called "the Gilbert and Sullivan of the U.S.A." He had great respect for them and was pleased exceedingly when, in 1882, they made his saloon the scene of one of their slum comedies; it was called "McSorley's Inflation."

110 Although by no means a handshaker, Old John knew many prominent men. One of his closest friends was Peter Cooper, president of the North American Telegraph Company and founder of Cooper Union, which is a half-block west of the saloon. Mr. Cooper, in his declining years, spent so many afternoons in the back room philosophizing with the workingmen
115 that he was given a chair of his own; it was equipped with an inflated rubber cushion. (The chair is still there; each April 4th for a number of years after Mr. Cooper's death, on April 4, 1883, it was draped with black cloth.)

continued on following page

Also, like other steadfast customers, Mr. Cooper had a pewter mug on which his name had been engraved with an icepick. He gave the saloon a
120 life-sized portrait of himself, which hangs over the mantel in the back room. It is an appropriate decoration, because, since the beginning of prohibition, McSorley's has been the official saloon of Cooper Union students. Sometimes a sentimental student will stand beneath the portrait and drink a toast to Mr. Cooper.

125 Old John had a remarkable passion for memorabilia. For years he saved the wishbones of Thanksgiving and Christmas turkeys and strung them on a rod connecting the pair of gas lamps over the bar; the dusty bones are invariably the first thing a new customer gets inquisitive about. Not long ago, a Johnny-come-lately annoyed one of the bartenders by remarking,
130 "Maybe the old boy believed in voodoo." Old John decorated the partition between barroom and back room with banquet menus, autographs, starfish shells, theatre programs, political posters, and worn-down shoes taken off the hoofs of various race and brewery horses. Above the entrance to the back room he hung a *shillelagh* and a sign: "BE GOOD OR BEGONE."

shillelagh—
club used to control patrons (Irish)

135 On one wall of the barroom he placed portraits of horses, steamboats, Tammany bosses, jockeys, actors, singers, and statesmen. Around 1902 he put up a heavy oak frame containing excellent portraits of Lincoln, Garfield, and McKinley, and to the frame he attached a brass title tag reading, "THEY ASSASSINATED THESE GOOD MEN THE SKULKING DOGS." On the same
140 wall he hung framed front pages of old newspapers; one, from the London Times for June 22, 1815, has in its lower right-hand corner a single paragraph on the beginning of the battle of Waterloo, and another, from the New York Herald of April 15, 1865, has a one-column story on the shooting of Lincoln. He blanketed another wall with lithographs and steel engrav-
145 ings. One depicts Garfield's deathbed. Another is entitled "The Great Fight." It was between Tom Hyer and Yankee Sullivan, both bareknuckled, at Still Pond Heights, Maryland, in 1849. It was won by Hyer in sixteen rounds, and the prize was $10,000. The judges wore top hats. The title tag on another engraving reads, "Rescue of Colonel Thomas J. Kelly and Captain
150 Timothy Deacy by Members of the Irish Revolutionary Brotherhood from the English Government at Manchester, England, September 18, 1867." A copy of the Emancipation Proclamation is on this wall; so, inevitably, is a facsimile of Lincoln's saloon license. An engraving of Washington and his generals hangs next to an engraving of a session of the Great Parliament of
155 Ireland. Eventually Old John covered practically every square inch of wall space between wainscot and ceiling with pictures and souvenirs. They are still in good condition, although spiders have strung webs across many of them. New customers get up on chairs and spend hours studying them.

160 Although Old John did not consider himself retired until just a few years before he died, he gave up day-in-and-day-out duty back of the bar around 1890 and made his son, William, head bartender. Bill McSorley was the kind of person who minds his own business vigorously. He inherited every bit of his father's surliness and not much of his affability. The father was by no means a lush, but the son carried *temperance* to an extreme; he drank 165 nothing but tap water and tea, and bragged about it. He did dip a little snuff. He was so solemn that before he was thirty several customers had settled into the habit of calling him Old Bill. He worshipped his father, but no one was aware of the profundity of his worship until Old John died. After the funeral, Bill locked the saloon, went upstairs to the family flat, 170 pulled the shutters to, and did not come out for almost a week. Finally, on a Sunday morning, gaunt and silent, he came downstairs with a hammer and a screwdriver and spent the day painstakingly securing his father's pictures and souvenirs to the walls; they had been hung hit or miss on wires, and customers had a habit of taking them down. Subsequently he commis-175 sioned a Cooper Union art teacher to make a small painting of Old John from a photograph. Bill placed it on the wall back of the bar and thereafter kept a hooded electric light burning above it, a pious custom that is still observed.

temperance—
abstaining from alcohol

ORHAN PAMUK

1952–
BORN TURKEY

Atatürk—
Mustafa Kemal Atatürk, father
of modern Turkey

"My Grandmother," Excerpt from the Book
Istanbul: Memories and the City

If anyone asked, my grandmother would say she was in favor of *Atatürk's* westernizing project, but in fact—and in this she was like everyone else in the city—neither the East nor the West interested her. She seldom left the house, after all. Like most people who live comfort-

5 ably in a city, she had no interest in its monuments, history, or "beauties"—this despite the fact that she'd studied to be a history teacher. After becoming engaged to my grandfather, and before marrying him, she did something rather brave in Istanbul in 1917—she went out with him to a restaurant. Because they were sitting opposite each other at a

10 table, and because they were served drinks, I like to imagine they were in a restaurant cafe in Pera; and when my grandfather asked her what she'd like to drink (meaning tea or lemonade), she, thinking he was offering her something stronger, answered him harshly.

"I'll have you know, sir, that I never touch alcohol."

15 Forty years later, if she got a bit merry on the glass of beer she allowed herself at our family dinners on New Year's Day, someone would always repeat this story, and she would let out a large embarrassed laugh. If it was an ordinary day and she was sitting in her usual chair in her sitting room, she would laugh for a while and then shed a few tears about the

20 early death of that "exceptional" man, whom I knew only from a collection of photographs. As she cried, I would try to imagine my grandparents sauntering through the city streets, but it was hard to imagine this woman, a round, relaxed matron from a Renoir painting, as a tall thin nervous woman in a Modigliani tableau.

25 After my grandfather had made a large fortune and died of leukemia, my grandmother became the boss of our large family. That was the word her cook and lifelong friend Bekir used with light sarcasm, whenever he tired of her never-ending commands and complaints: "Whatever you say, boss!" But my grandmother's authority did not extend

30 beyond the house she patrolled with a large set of keys. When my father and my uncle lost the factory they had inherited at a very young age from my grandfather, when they entered into large construction projects and made rash investments that ended in failure, forcing her to sell off the family assets one by one, my grandmother would just shed a few

35 more tears and then tell them to be a bit more careful next time.

She would pass her mornings in bed, under thick heavy quilts, propped up against a pile of huge down pillows. Every morning, Bekir would serve her soft-boiled eggs, olives, goat cheese, and toasted bread on a huge tray he would place carefully on a pillow he had arranged on the
40 quilt (it would have spoiled the ambiance to put an old newspaper between the flower-embroidered pillow and the silver tray, as practical-ity would have dictated); my grandmother would linger over her break-fast, reading the paper and receiving her first guests of the day. (It was from her that I learned the joy of drinking sweet tea with a piece of hard
45 goat cheese in my mouth.) My uncle, who could not go to work without first embracing his mother, paid his visit early every morning. After my aunt had sent him off to work, she too would arrive, clutching her handbag. For a short period before beginning school, when it had been decided that it was time I learned to read, I did as my brother had done;
50 every morning I would arrive with a notebook in hand, prop myself up on my grandmother's quilt, and try to learn from her the mystery of the alphabet. As I would discover when I began school, it bored me to learn things from someone else, and when I saw a blank piece of paper, my first impulse was not to write something but to blacken the page with
55 drawings.

Right in the middle of these reading and writing lessons, Bekir would come in and ask, using the same words, "What are we going to serve these people today?"

He treated this question with enormous gravity, as if he were charged
60 with running the kitchen of a large hospital or army barracks. My grandmother and her cook would discuss who was coming from which apartment for lunch and supper and what they should cook for them, and then my grandmother would take out her great almanac, which was full of mysterious information and pictures of clocks; they would
65 look for inspiration at the "menu of the day" as I watched a crow flying between the branches of the cypress tree in the back garden.

Despite his heavy workload, Bekir never lost his sense of humor and had nicknames for everyone in the household, from my grandmother to her youngest grandchild. Mine was "Crow." Years later, he told me it
70 was because I was always watching the crows on the roof next door, and also because I was very thin. My older brother was much attached to his teddy bear and wouldn't go anywhere without it, so to Bekir he was "Nurse." One cousin who had very narrow eyes was "Japan," another who was very stubborn was "Goat." A cousin born prematurely

continued on following page

75 was called "Six-month." For years, he called us by these names, his gentle mockery softened by compassion.

In my grandmother's room—as in my mother's room—there was a dressing table with a winged mirror; I would have liked to open its panels and lose myself in the reflections, but this mirror I was not allowed

80 to touch. My grandmother, who spent half the day in bed and never made herself up, had positioned the table in such a way that she could see all the way down the long corridor, past the service entrance and the vestibule, and right across the sitting room to the windows that looked out to the street, thus allowing her to supervise everything hap-

85 pening in the house—the comings and goings, the conversations in corners, and the quarreling grandchildren beyond—without getting out of bed. Because the house was always so dark, the reflection of a particular maneuver was often too faint to see, so my grandmother would have to shout to ask what was going on—for example, next to

90 the inlaid table in her sitting room—and Bekir would rush in to report who was doing what.

When she wasn't reading the paper or (from time to time) embroidering flowers on pillowcases, my grandmother spent her afternoons smoking cigarettes with other Nişantaşı ladies, mostly of her age, and

95 playing bezique. I remember their playing poker on occasion too. Among the real poker chips, which she kept in a soft blood-red velvet pouch, were old perforated *Ottoman* coins with serrated edges inscribed with imperial monograms, and I liked to take these into the corner and play with them.

Ottoman—
the Ottomans were a Turkish empire (1299–1923)

100 One of the ladies at the game table was from the sultan's harem; after the fall of the empire, when the Ottoman family—I can't bring myself to use the word *dynasty*—was forced to leave Istanbul and they closed the harem, this lady came out of it and married one of my grandfather's colleagues. My brother and I used to make fun of her overly polite way

105 of speaking: despite her being Grandmother's friend, the two would address each other as "madam," while still falling happily upon the oily crescent rolls and cheese toasts that Bekir brought them from the oven. Both were fat, but because they lived at a time and in a culture in which this was not stigmatized, they were at ease about it. If—as happened

110 once every forty years—my fat grandmother had to go outside or was invited out, the preparations would go on for days; until the last step, when my grandmother would shout for Kamer Hanım, the janitor's wife, to come up and pull with all her strength on the strings of her corset. I would watch with my hair on end as the corseting progressed

115 behind the screen—with much pushing and pulling and cries of "Easy, girl, easy!" I was bewitched, too, by the manicurist who would have paid her a visit some days earlier; this woman would sit there for hours with bowls of soapy water and many strange instruments assembled all around her; I would stand transfixed as she painted my revered grand-

120 mother's toenails firehouse red, and the sight of her placing cotton balls between my grandmother's plump toes evoked in me a strange combination of fascination and revulsion.

Twenty years later, when we were living in other houses in other parts of Istanbul, I would often go to visit my grandmother in the Pamuk

125 Apartments, and if I arrived in the morning I would find her in the same bed, surrounded by the same bags, newspapers, pillows, and shadows. The smell in the room—a mixture of soap, cologne, dust, and wood—never varied either. My grandmother always kept with her a slim leather-bound notebook in which she wrote something every day.

130 This notebook, in which she recorded bills, memories, meals, expenses, plans, and meteorological developments, had the strange and special air of a protocol book. Perhaps because she'd studied history, she liked to follow "official etiquette" on occasion, but there was always a note of sarcasm in her voice when she did; her interest in protocol and

135 Ottoman etiquette had another result—every one of her grandsons was named after a victorious sultan. Every time I saw her, I kissed her hand; then she would give me some money, which I would shame-facedly (but also gladly) slip into my pocket, and after I had told her what my mother, father, and brother were up to, my grandmother

140 would sometimes read me what she'd written in her notebook.

"My grandson Orhan came to visit. He's very intelligent, very sweet. He's studying architecture at university. I gave him ten liras. With God's will, one day he'll be very successful and the Pamuk family name will once again be spoken with respect, as it was when his grandfather was

145 alive."

After reading this, she would peer at me through the glasses that made her cataracts look even more disconcerting and give me a strange mocking smile, leading me to wonder, as I tried to smile in the same way, whether she was laughing at herself or because she knew by now

150 that life was nonsense.

RICHARD RODRIGUEZ
"Aria," from the Book *Hunger of Memory: The Education of Richard Rodriguez*
FORM: *Essay*
DATE: 1982

AMY TAN
"Mother Tongue"
FORM: *Lecture*
DATE: 1990

THE INTERSECTION

Immigration is a story of ancient days and modern times, of the biblical past and the Ameri- can present. Families have ever been in search of better safety and more promising means of existence. Here, two children of the immigrant experience explore the role of the English language in their lives. These are personal reflections on language that have (and mean to have) public resonance, and unsurprisingly, between them are some striking similarities. Both Rodriguez and Tan distinguish the intimate language of the family from more public language; both, to different degrees, touch on the matter of English and public education. Their emphases are different, though. Rodriguez's thrust is more polemical; he argues against the suppositions of bilingual education, but he also acknowledges that something can be lost through assimilation. Tan's lecture moves more ruminatively. She evokes the challenges of being an outsider linguistically, focusing on her mother's experience as an immigrant from China. She indicates the complex power of the mainstream language. But she also celebrates her mother's Chinese English, which is her family's own language, and works to rescue her particular Chinese-American English from such terms as "broken." These authors generate vital questions. What is the role of English in American society? How indeed should language be handled in a pluralistic society? What is the right sort of respect to pay to all the differences that exist between people in American society? These highly readable pieces generate a powerful mix of questions . . . a citizen's questions.

▶ **POINTS FOR DISCUSSION:** *"Aria"*

HALLMARKS *memoir form, anecdotal storytelling, argumentation*

FORM AND CONTENT In this opening chapter from *Hunger for Memory: The Educa- tion of Richard Rodriguez*, Rodriguez explores his experience learning English in the Sacramento of the 1950s. Draw from students their general reaction to the piece and get them to try to identify its subject. What is it about? What was Rodriguez's own experience learning English? And why is he a proponent of stu- dents learning in English? Finally, what do they make of the title "Aria" for this chapter? An aria is a solo piece for the voice, usually of some complexity and development. The *aria* is associated, though not exclusively, with opera.

TONE AND AUDIENCE For all his assertion of the efficacy and importance of learning English, Rodriguez acknowledges that something is lost through assimilation. Ask students: What is the tone of this piece of writing? Does it strike them as sad, elegiac, even? Which scenes particularly shape a sense of the poignancy of moving from the intimacy of speaking Spanish to the world of English? How did life change for him once his parents, urged by nuns from the school, begin to speak English at home? What happens to his grasp of Spanish over time? Finally, who do they think is the audience for this work? Is it clearly defined? Is he writing for the general reader?

FOCAL POINT: ARGUMENT In "Aria" Rodriguez characterizes the arguments of bilingual educators and counters them with counter-analysis based on his own experience. How effective is this as a means of argument? How persuasive do the students find him? You might mention that individuals appear before Congress to testify about personal experiences seen as so emblematic that they are weighed in debates of public law and policy. How can personal experience be more powerful than statistics? How can personal experience provide a more complex understanding of the nuances and implications of a debate? And what are the limits of personal experience as a means of making a larger political point? Though Rodriguez has an announced point of view, is making a point his only intention? Is this a memoir that includes an argument? Or an argument that uses the techniques of the memoirist?

▶ POINTS FOR DISCUSSION: *"Mother Tongue"*

HALLMARKS *lecture, anecdotal storytelling*

FORM AND CONTENT In "Mother Tongue," Amy Tan writes about the Englishes she speaks: the standard English of schools and the English that her mother, a Chinese immigrant, speaks. Her essay touches on how she became conscious of her use of these two rather distinct forms and what they suggest about not only her life but the lives of other Asian Americans. Ask your students for their general response to this piece. Did they like it? Did they understand what she meant by levels of English? What does she suggest about the impact of language on her mother's life? On her life? Are they aware of speaking levels of English themselves? What is she saying about the challenges to nonstandard speakers of English in our society?

TONE AND AUDIENCE Tan opens her lecture by saying what she is not, which is a scholar of English or of literature. She then proceeds to make a series of points about English and illustrate them rather amply, too. How would students describe the way she speaks to her audience?

FOCAL POINT: HER MOTHER'S VOICE Amy Tan in *The Joy Luck Club* (1989) and elsewhere writes about the relationship between mothers and daughters. Why is it that she finally imagines her mother to be the audience for her book? She mocks a line from an early story: "That was my mental quandary in its nascent state." Ask students why she finds this line so contemptible. What sort of language did she want to create in her book?

> *Amy Tan has an official website at www.amytan.net and also contributes to redroom.com, an online home for writers.*

Why was Tan so pleased when her mother said of it "So easy to read." Intriguingly, this award-winning author found her voice as an American novelist through the rhythms of Chinese-American English. What do students make of that? (They may need you to explain what we mean by "the voice" of the writer.)

▶ POINTS FOR DISCUSSION: *Connecting the Authors*

Ask students to place both texts on their desks. What are some of the similarities between these pieces? How do they enlarge a reader's understanding of the role of English in the lives of new Americans? Both writers speak about their parents at some length. What is it like to know more of the mainstream language than your parents do? Why, as Rodriguez puts it, was it "unsettling to hear my parents struggle with English"? Which author seems more ambivalent about the status and power of standard English??

FOCAL POINT: STORYTELLING AND DEBATE Which piece has a sharper sense of entering a very specific debate? ("Aria"). Did they like the heightened sense of a particular argument in Rodriguez's piece? How sharply defined is the point of Amy Tan's piece? What would they say is its purpose? Is there anything to be gained from the absence of a central unifying point? Do they prefer one piece over the other? If so, why?

Reading Questions FOR STUDENTS

RICHARD RODRIGUEZ ~ *"Aria"*

1. On the first page Rodriguez describes the first day of school. All children are uneasy, he says, "But I was astonished." Why was he astonished? How is "astonishment" different from "unease"?

2. How does American English sound to the young Richard? What does he mean when he calls Spanish the "language of joyful return"?

3. Rodriguez says that while it would have pleased him to hear Spanish in the classroom, it would have delayed the acquiring of a public identity. What does he mean by this?

4. Rodriguez describes the power of hearing his English name at school: "I also needed my teachers to keep my attention from straying in class by calling out, *Rich-heard*—their English voices slowly prying loose my ties to my other name, its three notes, *Ri-car-do.*" What does the phrase "prying loose" suggest about his relationship to his Spanish name? In what contexts do we typically use the phrase "to pry loose." What sort of figurative language is that? Why did he need to have it pried loose, as he says?

5. On lines 387–389 Rodriguez describes the deep longing summoned by hearing the Spanish word "¿Hijito . . . ?" Why does that word have such an effect?

6. Towards the end of the excerpt Rodriguez discusses those who scorn assimilation: "Those middle-class ethnics who scorn assimilation seem to me filled with decadent self-pity, obsessed by the burden of public life. Dangerously, they romanticize public separateness and they trivialize the dilemma of the socially disadvantaged." (lines 428–431). What is the problem with assimilation in the eyes of some? But what does Rodriguez suggest happens if people do not assimilate?

AMY TAN ~ *"Mother Tongue"*

Amy Tan is a member of a literary garage band called Rock Bottom Remainders together with, among others, Dave Barry, *The Simpsons* creator Matt Groening, Stephen King, and Frank McCourt. She serves as its "lead rhythm dominatrix" (according to her own website).

1. Who does the audience for this lecture seem to be? Why is Tan pointing out that she is not a scholar?

2. What makes a talk she has given before suddenly seem wrong?

3. How does Tan characterize standard English?

continued on following page

4. How has her attitude toward her mother's use of English evolved over time?

5. What are the potential problems for Asian Americans (and other speakers of nonstandard English) whose use of language is highly inflected with another language?

6. Why does Tan start writing her books imagining her mother as her audience?

SPOTLIGHT: STANDARD ENGLISH

Warriner's *English Grammar and Composition* defines Standard English as the English "that is most widely used. It is the language of most educational, legal, governmental, and professional documents." Schools teach Standard English to equip students to participate credibly in the professional world.

Note that some have found the idea of Standard English objectionable, since it implies a hierarchy of the types of English and that Standard English is the model. Recent years have shown a greater interest in all the types of English that are spoken, but respect for dialectical English is not new, as the work of such writers as Mark Twain and Zora Neale Hurston teach us.

FIND IT

Find examples of three or more of these devices, underlining them and noting in the margin where they appear.

1. alliteration

2. anecdotal storytelling

3. metaphor

4. simile

ON SELF-KNOWLEDGE

Choose one of these topics and write a short essay of no more than five paragraphs.

Option One: In his discussion Rodriguez creates a sense that something is gained and lost when students from immigrant families learn English. For him, within his family, what was lost? What was gained? And why, even with something lost, does Rodriguez assert that learning in English at school is ultimately crucial for students from immigrant families?

Option Two: Toward the end of the reading Rodriguez discusses those who scorn assimilation: "Those middle-class ethnics who scorn assimilation seem to me filled with decadent self-pity, obsessed by the burden of public life. Dangerously, they romanticize public separateness and they trivialize the dilemma of the socially disadvantaged." (lines 428–431).

Question: What is Rodriguez's attitude towards assimilation in American society? Be sure to explain what assimilation is, why it has been criticized, and why Rodriguez believes it is important. What is the danger of the failure or inability to assimilate?

Tip: Before you begin read the quotation carefully and be sure you understand it fully. You may use some or all of that quotation in your essay.

TAILORING TALK

Amy Tan talks about the two versions of English that emerged in her life: the English she learned from her mother and standard English. What are all the versions of language you use, to borrow her phrase? Write a few paragraphs about this topic, using the following questions to prompt your thinking.

How would you speak at a job interview? At school? To your grandparents? To your parents? To your friends? Is the English you speak at home influenced by another language? Not at all that your conscious of? Totally? Is the English you speak more rural than urban? Are you influenced by how characters speak on TV? Do you ever find yourself mimicking the English from your favorite sitcom, for example? Have your noticed others doing that?

Think about levels of slang and informality in your use of language. Can you get away with swearing in front of your parents now and then, but never in front of your great aunt? Why is that? And how does language relate to self? Do you ever feel more yourself when speaking a certain way? Do you ever feel like an impostor because of how you're speaking? Or can you slip between worlds easily?

continued on following page

If you are lucky enough to be bilingual and speak a different language at home, write about that, too. What is your language at home? Is it standard, a classic form of language? Is it a Spanish highly influenced by your Colombian grandparents? Upper-middle-class urban Turkish? Or is it informal, slangy, and full of country idioms?

In terms of format, this could be an essay of personal reflection, or you could create a label for each paragraph and reflect on each form of English separately, without creating a transition. Your labels could be quite simple, like "With Friends" and "At the Job Interview" and "To Grandmother's House." You could, though, try to create a catchy phrase for your labels, perhaps referencing songs titles or other works: "To Grandmother's House We Go" or "Rolling with My Homeys."

RICHARD RODRIGUEZ ~ **"Aria," Excerpt from the Book Hunger of Memory**

1944–
BORN UNITED STATES

I

I remember to start with that day in Sacramento—a California now nearly thirty years past—when I first entered a classroom, able to understand some fifty stray English words.

5 The third of four children, I had been preceded to a neighborhood Roman Catholic school by an older brother and sister. But neither of them had revealed very much about their classroom experiences. Each afternoon they returned, as they left in the morning, always together, speaking in Spanish as they climbed the five steps of the porch. And their mysterious books, wrapped in shopping-bag paper, remained on the table next to the door,
10 closed firmly behind them.

An accident of geography sent me to a school where all my classmates were white, many the children of doctors and lawyers and business executives. All my classmates certainly must have been uneasy on that first day of school—as most children are uneasy—to find themselves apart from their
15 families in the first institution of their lives. But I was astonished.

The nun said, in a friendly but oddly impersonal voice, 'Boys and girls, this is Richard Rodriguez.' (I heard her sound out: *Rich-heard Road-ree-guess.*) It was the first time I had heard anyone name me in English. 'Richard,' the nun repeated more slowly, writing my name down in her black leather
20 book. Quickly I turned to see my mother's face dissolve in a watery blur behind the pebbled glass door. Many years later there is something called bilingual education—a scheme proposed in the late 1960s by Hispanic-American social activists, later endorsed by a congressional vote. It is a program that seeks to permit non-English speaking children, many from lower-
25 class homes, to use their family language as the language of school. (Such is the goal its supporters announce.) I hear them and am forced to say no: It is not possible for a child—any child—ever to use his family's language in school. Not to understand this is to misunderstand the public uses of schooling and to trivialize the nature of intimate life—a family's 'language,'

30 Memory teaches me what I know of these matters; the boy reminds the adult. I was a bilingual child, a certain kind—socially disadvantaged—the son of working-class parents, both Mexican immigrants.

continued on following page

In the early years of my boyhood, my parents coped very well in America. My father had steady work. My mother managed at home. They were

35   nobody's victims. Optimism and ambition led them to a house (our home) many blocks from the Mexican south side of town. We lived among *gringos* and only a block from the biggest, whitest houses. It never occurred to my parents that they couldn't live wherever they chose. Nor was the Sacramento of the fifties bent on teaching them a contrary lesson. My mother

40   and father were more annoyed than intimidated by those two or three neighbors who tried initially to make us unwelcome. ('Keep your brats away from my sidewalk!') But despite all they achieved, perhaps because they had so much to achieve, any deep feeling of ease, the confidence of 'belonging' in public was withheld from them both. They regarded the

45   people at work, the faces in crowds, as very distant from us. They were the others, *los gringos.* That term was interchangeable in their speech with another, even more telling, *los americanos.*

I grew up in a house where the only regular guests were my relations. For one day, enormous families of relatives would visit and there would be so

50   many people that the noise and the bodies would spill out to the backyard and front porch. Then, for weeks, no one came by. (It was usually a salesman who rang the doorbell.) Our house stood apart. A gaudy yellow in a row of white bungalows. We were the people with the noisy dog. The people who raised pigeons and chickens. We were the foreigners on the block.

55   A few neighbors smiled and waved. We waved back. But no one in the family knew the names of the old couple who lived next door; until I was seven years old, I did not know the names of the kids who lived across the street.

In public, my father and mother spoke a hesitant, accented, not always

60   grammatical English. And they would have to strain—their bodies tense— to catch the sense of what was rapidly said by *los gringos.* At home they spoke Spanish. The language of their Mexican past sounded in counterpoint to the English of public society. The words would come quickly, with ease. Conveyed through those sounds was the pleasing, soothing, consol-

65   ing reminder of being at home.

During those years when I was first conscious of hearing, my mother and father addressed me only in Spanish; in Spanish I learned to reply. By contrast, English (*inglés*), rarely heard in the house, was the language I came to associate with *gringos.* I learned my first words of English overhearing

70   my parents speak to strangers. At five years of age, I knew just enough English for my mother to trust me on errands to stores one block away. No more.

I was a listening child, careful to hear the very different sounds of Spanish and English. Wide-eyed with hearing, I'd listen to sounds more than words.

75 First, there were English (*gringo*) sounds. So many words were still unknown that when the butcher or the lady at the drugstore said something to me, exotic polysyllabic sounds would bloom in the midst of their sentences. Often, the speech of people in public seemed to me very loud, booming with confidence. The man behind the counter would literally ask,

80 'What can I do for you?' But by being so firm and so clear, the sound of his voice said that he was a *gringo;* he belonged in public society.

I would also hear then the high nasal notes of middleclass American speech. The air stirred with sound. Sometimes, even now, when I have been traveling abroad for several weeks, I will hear what I heard as a boy.

85 In hotel lobbies or airports, in Turkey or Brazil, some Americans will pass, and suddenly I will hear it again—the high sound of American voices. For a few seconds I will hear it with pleasure, for it is now the sound of *my* society—a reminder of home. But inevitably—already on the flight headed for home—the sound fades with repetition. I will be unable to hear it

90 anymore.

When I was a boy, things were different. The accent of *los gringos* was never pleasing nor was it hard to hear. Crowds at Safeway or at bus stops would be noisy with sound. And I would be forced to edge away from the chirping chatter above me.

95 I was unable to hear my own sounds, but I knew very well that I spoke English poorly. My words could not stretch far enough to form complete thoughts. And the words I did speak I didn't know well enough to make into distinct sounds. (Listeners would usually lower their heads, better to hear what I was trying to say.) But it was one thing for *me* to speak English

100 with difficulty. It was more troubling for me to hear my parents speak in public: their high-whining vowels and guttural consonants; their sentences that got stuck with 'eh' and 'ah' sounds; the confused syntax; the hesitant rhythm of sounds so different from the way *gringos* spoke. I'd notice, moreover, that my parents' voices were softer than those of *gringos* we'd

105 meet.

I am tempted now to say that none of this mattered. In adulthood I am embarrassed by childhood fears. And, in a way, it didn't matter very much that my parents could not speak English with ease. Their linguistic difficulties had no serious consequences. My mother and father made themselves

110 understood at the county hospital clinic and at government offices. And yet, in another way, it mattered very much—it was unsettling to hear my

continued on following page

parents struggle with English. Hearing them, I'd grow nervous, my clutching trust in their protection and power weakened.

115 There were many times like the night at a brightly lit gasoline station (a blaring white memory) when I stood uneasily, hearing my father. He was talking to a teenaged attendant. I do not recall what they were saying, but I cannot forget the sounds my father made as he spoke. At one point his words slid together to form one word—sounds as confused as the threads of blue and green oil in the puddle next to my shoes. His voice rushed

120 through what he had left to say. And, toward the end, reached falsetto notes, appealing to his listener's understanding. I looked away to the lights of passing automobiles. I tried not to hear anymore. But I heard only too well the calm, easy tones in the attendant's reply. Shortly afterward, walking toward home with my father, I shivered when he put his hand on my

125 shoulder. The very first chance that I got, I evaded his grasp and ran on ahead into the dark, skipping with feigned boyish exuberance.

But then there was Spanish. *Español:* my family's language. *Español:* the language that seemed to me a private language. I'd hear strangers on the radio and in the Mexican Catholic church across town speaking in Spanish,

130 but I couldn't really believe that Spanish was a public language, like English. Spanish speakers, rather, seemed related to me, for I sensed that we shared-through our language—the experience of feeling apart from *los gringos.* It was thus a ghetto Spanish that I heard and I spoke. Like those whose lives are bound by a barrio, I was reminded by Spanish of my sepa-

135 rateness from *los otros, los gringos* in power. But more intensely than for most barrio children—because I did not live in a barrio—Spanish seemed to me the language of home. (Most days it was only at home that I'd hear it.) It became the language of joyful return.

A family member would say something to me and I would feel myself spe-

140 cially recognized. My parents would say something to me and I would feel embraced by the sounds of their words. Those sounds said: *I am speaking with ease in Spanish. I am addressing you in words I never use with* los gringos. *I recognize you as someone special, close, like no one outside. You belong with us. In the family.*

145 *(Ricardo.)*

At the age of five, six, well past the time when most other children no longer easily notice the difference between sounds uttered at home and words spoken in public, I had a different experience. I lived in a world magically compounded of sounds. I remained a child longer than most; I lin-

150 gered too long, poised at the edge of language—often frightened by the

sounds of *los gringos,* delighted by the sounds of Spanish at home. I shared with my family a language that was startlingly different from that used in the great city around us.

150 For me there were none of the gradations between public and private society so normal to a maturing child. Outside the house was public society; inside the house was private. Just opening or closing the screen door behind me was an important experience. I'd rarely leave home all alone or without reluctance. Walking down the sidewalk, under the canopy of tall trees, I'd warily notice the—suddenly—silent neighborhood kids who stood

155 warily watching me. Nervously, I'd arrive at the grocery store to hear there the sounds of the *gringo*—foreign to me—reminding me that in this world so big, I was a foreigner. But then I'd return. Walking back toward our house, climbing the steps from the sidewalk, when the front door was open in summer, I'd hear voices beyond the screen door talking in Spanish.

160 For a second or two, I'd stay, linger there, listening. Smiling, I'd hear my mother call out, saying in Spanish (words): 'Is that you, Richard?' All the while her sounds would assure me: *You are home now; come closer; inside. With us.*

'*Sí,*' I'd reply.

165 Once more inside the house I would resume (assume) my place in the family. The sounds would dim, grow harder to hear. Once more at home, I would grow less aware of that fact. It required, however, no more than the blurt of the doorbell to alert me to listen to sounds all over again. The house would turn instantly still while my mother went to the door. I'd hear

170 her hard English sounds. I'd wait to hear her voice return to soft-sounding Spanish, which assured me, as surely as did the clicking tongue of the lock on the door, that the stranger was gone.

Plainly, it is not healthy to hear such sounds so often. It is not healthy to distinguish public words from private sounds so easily. I remained clois-

175 tered by sounds, timid and shy in public, too dependent on voices at home. And yet it needs to be emphasized: I was an extremely happy child at home. I remember many nights when my father would come back from work, and I'd hear him call out to my mother in Spanish, sounding relieved. In Spanish, he'd sound light and free notes he never could manage in Eng-

180 lish. Some nights I'd jump up just at hearing his voice. With *mis hermanos* I would come running into the room where he was with my mother. Our laughing (so deep was the pleasure!) became screaming. Like others who know the pain of public alienation, we transformed the knowledge of our public separateness and made it consoling—the reminder of intimacy.

continued on following page

185　Excited, we joined our voices in a celebration of sounds. *We are speaking now the way we never speak out in public.* We *are alone—together,* voices sounded, surrounded to tell me. Some nights, no one seemed willing to loosen the hold sounds had on us. At dinner, we invented new words. (Ours sounded Spanish, but made sense only to us.) We pieced together
190　new words by taking, say, an English verb and giving it Spanish endings. My mother's instructions at bedtime would be lacquered with mock-urgent tones. Or a word like *sí* would become, in several notes, able to convey added measures of feeling. Tongues explored the edges of words, especially the fat vowels. And we happily sounded that military drum roll, the
195　twirling roar of the Spanish *r.* Family language: my family's sounds. The voices of my parents and sisters and brother. Their voices insisting: *You belong here. We are family members. Related. Special to one another. Listen!* Voices singing and sighing, rising, straining, then surging, teeming with pleasure that burst syllables into fragments of laughter. At times it seemed
200　there was steady quiet only when, from another room, the rustling whispers of my parents faded and I moved closer to sleep.

II

Supporters of bilingual education today imply that students like me miss a great deal by not being taught in their family's language. What they seem not to recognize is that, as a socially disadvantaged child, I considered
205　Spanish to be a private language. What I needed to learn in school was that I had the right—and the obligation—to speak the public language of *los gringos.* The odd truth is that my first-grade classmates could have become bilingual, in the conventional sense of that word, more easily than I. Had they been taught (as upper-middle-class children are often taught early) a
210　second language like Spanish or French, they could have regarded it simply as that: another public language. In my case such bilingualism could not have been so quickly achieved. What I did not believe was that I could speak a single public language.

Without question, it would have pleased me to hear my teachers address
215　me in Spanish when I entered the classroom. I would have felt much less afraid. I would have trusted them and responded with ease. But I would have delayed—for how long postponed?—having to learn the language of public society. I would have evaded—and for how long could I have afforded to delay?—learning the great lesson of school, that I had a public
220　identity.

Fortunately, my teachers were unsentimental about their responsibility. What they understood was that I needed to speak a public language. So

May be copied for classroom use. © 2008 Carol Rawlings Miller from *Strange Bedfellows.* (Heinemann: Portsmouth, NH)

their voices would search me out, asking me questions. Each time I'd hear
them, I'd look up in surprise to see a nun's face frowning at me. I'd mum-
225   ble, not really meaning to answer. The nun would persist, 'Richard, stand
up. Don't look at the floor. Speak up. Speak to the entire class, not just to
me!' But I couldn't believe that the English language was mine to use.
(In part, I did not want to believe it.) I continued to mumble. I resisted
the teacher's demands. (Did I somehow suspect that once I learned public
230   language my pleasing family life would be changed?) Silent, waiting for the
bell to sound, I remained dazed, diffident, afraid.

Because I wrongly imagined that English was intrinsically a public language
and Spanish an intrinsically private one, I easily noted the difference
between classroom language and the language of home. At school, words
235   were directed to a general audience of listeners. ('Boys and girls.') Words
were meaningfully ordered. And the point was not self-expression alone
but to make oneself understood by many others. The teacher quizzed:
'Boys and girls, why do we use that word in this sentence? Could we think
of a better word to use there? Would the sentence change its meaning if
240   the words were differently arranged? And wasn't there a better way of saying much the same thing?' (I couldn't say. I wouldn't try to say.)

Three months. Five. Half a year passed. Unsmiling, ever watchful, my teachers noted my silence. They began to connect my behavior with the difficult
progress my older sister and brother were making. Until one Saturday
245   morning three nuns arrived at the house to talk to our parents. Stiffly, they
sat on the blue living room sofa. From the doorway of another room, spy-
ing the visitors, I noted the incongruity—the clash of two worlds, the faces
and voices of school intruding upon the familiar setting of home. I overheard one voice gently wondering, 'Do your children speak only Spanish at
250   home, Mrs. Rodriguez?' While another voice added, 'That Richard especially
seems so timid and shy.'

That Rich-heard!

With great tact the visitors continued, 'Is it possible for you and your husband to encourage your children to practice their English when they are
255   home?' Of course, my parents complied. What would they not do for their
children's well-being? And how could they have questioned the Church's
authority which those women represented? In an instant, they agreed to
give up the language (the sounds) that had revealed and accentuated our
family's closeness. The moment after the visitors left, the change was
260   observed. '*Ahora,* speak to us *en inglés,*' my father and mother united to
tell us.

continued on following page

At first, it seemed a kind of game. After dinner each night, the family gathered to practice 'our' English. (It was still then *inglés,* a language foreign to
us, so we felt drawn as strangers to it.) Laughing, we would try to define
265   words we could not pronounce. We played with strange English sounds,
often over-anglicizing our pronunciations. And we filled the smiling gaps of
our sentences with familiar Spanish sounds. But that was cheating, somebody shouted. Everyone laughed. In school, meanwhile, like my brother
and sister, I was required to attend a daily tutoring session. I needed a full
270   year of special attention. I also needed my teachers to keep my attention
from straying in class by calling out, *Rich-heard*—their English voices slowly
prying loose my ties to my other name, its three notes, *Ri-car-do.* Most of
all I needed to hear my mother and father speak to me in a moment of
seriousness in broken—suddenly heartbreaking—English. The scene was
275   inevitable: One Saturday morning I entered the kitchen where my parents
were talking in Spanish. I did not realize that they were talking in Spanish
however until, at the moment they saw me, I heard their voices change to
speak English. Those *gringo* sounds they uttered startled me. Pushed me
away. In that moment of trivial misunderstanding and profound insight,
280   I felt my throat twisted by unsounded grief. I turned quickly and left
the room. But I had no place to escape to with Spanish. (The spell was
broken.) My brother and sisters were speaking English in another part
of the house.

Again and again in the days following, increasingly angry, I was obliged to
285   hear my mother and father: 'Speak to us *en inglés.' (Speak.)* Only then did I
determine to learn classroom English. Weeks after, it happened: One day in
school I raised my hand to volunteer an answer. I spoke out in a loud voice.
And I did not think it remarkable when the entire class understood. That
day, I moved very far from the disadvantaged child I had been only days
290   earlier. The belief, the calming assurance that I belonged in public, had at
last taken hold.

Shortly after, I stopped hearing the high and loud sounds of *los gringos.* A
more and more confident speaker of English, I didn't trouble to listen to
how strangers sounded, speaking to me. And there simply were too many
295   English-speaking people in my day for me to hear American accents anymore. Conversations quickened. Listening to persons who sounded eccen-
trically pitched voices, I usually noted their sounds for an initial few seconds before I concentrated on *what* they were saying. Conversations
became content-full. Transparent. Hearing someone's *tone* of voice—angry
300   or questioning or sarcastic or happy or sad—I didn't distinguish it from the
words it expressed. Sound and word were thus tightly wedded. At the end

of a day, I was often bemused, always relieved, to realize how 'silent,' though crowded with words, my day in public had been. (This public silence measured and quickened the change in my life.)

305 At last, seven years old, I came to believe what had been technically true since my birth: I was an American citizen.

But the special feeling of closeness at home was diminished by then. Gone was the desperate, urgent, intense feeling of being at home; rare was the experience of feeling myself individualized by family intimates. We 310 remained a loving family, but one greatly changed. No longer so close; no longer bound tight by the pleasing and troubling knowledge of our public separateness. Neither my older brother nor sister rushed home after school anymore. Nor did I. When I arrived home there would often be neighborhood kids in the house. Or the house would be empty of sounds.

315 Following the dramatic Americanization of their children, even my parents grew more publicly confident. Especially my mother. She learned the names of all the people on our block. And she decided we needed to have a telephone installed in the house. My father continued to use the word *gringo.* But it was no longer charged with the old bitterness or distrust. 320 (Stripped of any emotional content, the word simply became a name for those Americans not of Hispanic descent.) Hearing him, sometimes, I wasn't sure if he was pronouncing the Spanish word *gringo* or saying gringo in English.

Matching the silence I started hearing in public was a new quiet at home. 325 The family's quiet was partly due to the fact that, as we children learned more and more English, we shared fewer and fewer words with our parents. Sentences needed to be spoken slowly when a child addressed his mother or father. (Often the parent wouldn't understand.) The child would need to repeat himself. (Still the parent misunderstood.) The young voice, 330 frustrated, would end up saying 'Never mind'—the subject was closed. Dinners would be noisy with the clinking of knives and forks against dishes. My mother would smile softly between her remarks; my father at the other end of the table would chew and chew at his food, while he stared over the heads of his children.

335 My *mother!* My *father!* After English became my primary language, I no longer knew what words to use in addressing my parents. The old Spanish words (those tender accents of sound) I had used earlier—*mamá* and *papá*—I couldn't use anymore. They would have been too painful reminders of how much had changed in my life. On the other hand, 340 the words I heard neighborhood kids call *their* parents seemed equally

continued on following page

unsatisfactory. *Mother* and *Father; Ma, Papa, Pa, Dad, Pop* (how I hated the all-American sound of that last word especially)—all these terms I felt were unsuitable, not really terms of address for *my* parents. As a result, I never

345   used them at home. Whenever I'd speak to my parents, I would try to get their attention with eye contact alone. In public conversations, I'd refer to 'my parents' or 'my mother and father.'

My mother and father, for their part, responded differently, as their children spoke to them less. She grew restless, seemed troubled and anxious at the scarcity of words exchanged in the house. It was she who would question

350   me about my day when I came home from school. She smiled at small talk. She pried at the edges of my sentences to get me to say something more. (What?) She'd join conversations she overheard, but her intrusions often stopped her children's talking. By contrast, my father seemed reconciled to the new quiet. Though his English improved somewhat, he retired into

355   silence. At dinner he spoke very little. One night his children and even his wife helplessly giggled at his garbled English pronunciation of the Catholic Grace before Meals. Thereafter he made his wife recite the prayer at the start of each meal, even on formal occasions, when there were guests in the house. Hers became the public voice of the family. On official business,

360   it was she, not my father, one would usually hear on the phone or in stores, talking to strangers. His children grew so accustomed to his silence that, years later, they would speak routinely of his shyness. (My mother would often try to explain: Both his parents died when he was eight. He was raised by an uncle who treated him like little more than a menial ser-

365   vant. He was never encouraged to speak. He grew up alone. A man of few words.) But my father was not shy, I realized, when I'd watch him speaking Spanish with relatives. Using Spanish, he was quickly effusive. Especially when talking with other men, his voice would spark, flicker, flare alive with sounds. In Spanish, he expressed ideas and feelings he rarely revealed in

370   English. With firm Spanish sounds, he conveyed confidence and authority English would never allow him.

The silence at home, however, was finally more than a literal silence. Fewer words passed between parent and child, but more profound was the silence that resulted from my inattention to sounds. At about the time I no

375   longer bothered to listen with care to the sounds of English in public, I grew careless about listening to the sounds family members made when they spoke. Most of the time I heard someone speaking at home and didn't distinguish his sounds from the words people uttered in public. I didn't even pay much attention to my parents' accented and ungrammatical

380   speech. At least not at home. Only when I was with them in public would

I grow alert to their accents. Though, even then, their sounds caused me less and less concern. For I was increasingly confident of my own public identity.

385 I would have been happier about my public success had I not sometimes recalled what it had been like earlier, when my family had conveyed its intimacy through a set of conveniently private sounds. Sometimes in public, hearing a stranger, I'd hark back to my past. A Mexican farmworker approached me downtown to ask directions to somewhere. '¿Hijito . . . ?' he said. And his voice summoned deep longing. Another time, standing

390 beside my mother in the visiting room of a Carmelite convent, before the dense screen which rendered the nuns shadowy figures, I heard several Spanish-speaking nuns—their busy, singsong overlapping voices—assure us that yes, yes, we were remembered, all our family was remembered in their prayers. (Their voices echoed faraway family sounds.) Another day, a dark-

395 faced old woman—her hand light on my shoulder—steadied herself against me as she boarded a bus. She murmured something I couldn't quite comprehend. Her Spanish voice came near, like the face of a never-before-seen relative in the instant before I was kissed. Her voice, like so many of the Spanish voices I'd hear in public, recalled the golden age of my youth.

400 Hearing Spanish then, I continued to be a careful, if sad, listener to sounds. Hearing a Spanish-speaking family walking behind me, I turned to look. I smiled for an instant, before my glance found the Hispanic-looking faces of strangers in the crowd going by.

Today I hear bilingual educators say that children lose a degree of 'individu-

405 ality' by becoming assimilated into public society. (Bilingual schooling was popularized in the seventies, that decade when middle-class ethnics began to resist the process of assimilation—the American melting pot.) But the bilingualists simplistically scorn the value and necessity of assimilation. They do not seem to realize that there are *two* ways a person is individual-

410 ized. So they do not realize that while one suffers a diminished sense of *private* individuality by becoming assimilated into public society, such assimilation makes possible the achievement of *public* individuality.

The bilingualists insist that a student should be reminded of his difference from others in mass society, his heritage. But they equate mere separate-

415 ness with individuality. The fact is that only in private—with intimates—is separateness from the crowd a prerequisite for individuality. (An intimate draws me apart, tells me that I am unique, unlike all others.) In public, by contrast, full individuality is achieved, paradoxically, by those who are able to consider themselves members of the crowd. Thus it happened for me:

continued on following page

420   Only when I was able to think of myself as an American, no longer an alien in *gringo* society, could I seek the rights and opportunities necessary for full public individuality. The social and political advantages I enjoy as a man result from the day that I came to believe that my name, indeed, is *Rich-heard Road-ree-guess.* It is true that my public society today is often imper-
425   sonal. (My public society is usually mass society.) Yet despite the anonymity of the crowd and despite the fact that the individuality I achieve in public is often tenuous—because it depends on my being one in a crowd—I cele-brate the day I acquired my new name. Those middle-class ethnics who scorn assimilation seem to me filled with decadent self-pity, obsessed by
430   the burden of public life. Dangerously, they romanticize public separateness and they trivialize the dilemma of the socially disadvantaged.

My awkward childhood does not prove the necessity of bilingual education. My story discloses instead an essential myth of childhood—inevitable pain. If I rehearse here the changes in my private life after my Americanization, it
435   is finally to emphasize the public gain. The loss implies the gain: The house I returned to each afternoon was quiet. Intimate sounds no longer rushed to the door to greet me. There were other noises inside. The telephone rang. Neighborhood kids ran past the door of the bedroom where I was reading my schoolbooks—covered with shopping-bag paper. Once I
420   learned public language, it would never again be easy for me to hear inti-mate family voices. More and more of my day was spent hearing words. But that may only be a way of saying that the day I raised my hand in class and spoke loudly to an entire roomful of faces, my childhood started to end.

Amy Tan ~ *"Mother Tongue"*

1952–
BORN UNITED STATES

I am not a scholar of English or literature. I cannot give you much more than personal opinions on the English language and its variations in this country or others.

I am a writer. And by that definition, I am someone who has always
5   loved language. I am fascinated by language in daily life. I spend a great deal of my time thinking about the power of language—the way it can evoke an emotion, a visual image, a complex idea, or a simple truth. Language is the tool of my trade. And I use them all—all the Englishes I grew up with.

10   Recently, I was made keenly aware of the different Englishes I do use. I was giving a talk to a large group of people, the same talk I had already given to half a dozen other groups. The nature of the talk was about my writing, my life, and my book, *The Joy Luck Club*. The talk was going along well enough, until I remembered one major difference that made
15   the whole talk sound wrong. My mother was in the room. And it was perhaps the first time she had heard me give a lengthy speech, using the kind of English I have never used with her. I was saying things like, "The intersection of memory upon imagination" and "There is an aspect of my fiction that relates to thus-and-thus"—a speech filled
20   with carefully wrought grammatical phrases, burdened, it suddenly seemed to me, with nominalized forms, past perfect tenses, conditional phrases, all the forms of standard English that I had learned in school and through books, the forms of English I did not use at home with my mother.

25   Just last week, I was walking down the street with my mother, and I again found myself conscious of the English I was using, the English I do use with her. We were talking about the price of new and used furniture and I heard myself saying this: "Not waste money that way." My husband was with us as well, and he didn't notice any switch in my
30   English. And then I realized why. It's because over the twenty years we've been together I've often used that same kind of English with him, and sometimes he even uses it with me. It has become our language of intimacy, a different sort of English that relates to family talk, the language I grew up with.

35   So you'll have some idea of what this family talk I heard sounds like, I'll quote what my mother said during a recent conversation which I

continued on following page

40   videotaped and then transcribed. During this conversation, my mother was talking about a political gangster in Shanghai who had the same last name as her family's, Du, and how the gangster in his early years wanted to be adopted by her family, which was rich by comparison. Later, the gangster became more powerful, far richer than my mother's family, and one day showed up at my mother's wedding to pay his respects. Here's what she said in part: "Du Yusong having business like fruit stand. Like off the street kind. He is Du like Du Zong—but not

45   Tsung-ming Island people. The local people call putong, the river east side, he belong to that side local people. That man want to ask Du Zong father take him in like become own family. Du Zong father wasn't look down on him, but didn't take seriously, until that man big like become a mafia. Now important person, very hard to inviting him. Chinese way,

50   came only to show respect, don't stay for dinner. Respect for making big celebration, he shows up. Mean gives lots of respect. Chinese custom. Chinese social life that way. If too important won't have to stay too long. He come to my wedding. I didn't see, I heard it. I gone to boy's side, they have YMCA dinner. Chinese age I was nineteen."

55   You should know that my mother's expressive command of English belies how much she actually understands. She reads the Forbes report, listens to Wall Street Week, converses daily with her stockbroker, reads all of Shirley MacLaine's books with ease—all kinds of things I can't begin to understand. Yet some of my friends tell me they understand

60   50 percent of what my mother says. Some say they understand 80 to 90 percent. Some say they understand none of it, as if she were speaking pure Chinese. But to me, my mother's English is perfectly clear, perfectly natural. It's my mother tongue. Her language, as I hear it, is vivid, direct, full of observation and imagery. That was the language that

65   helped shape the way I saw things, expressed things, made sense of the world.

Lately, I've been giving more thought to the kind of English my mother speaks. Like others, I have described it to people as "broken" or "fractured" English. But I wince when I say that. It has always bothered me

70   that I can think of no way to describe it other than "broken," as if it were damaged and needed to be fixed, as if it lacked a certain wholeness and soundness. I've heard other terms used, "limited English," for example. But they seem just as bad, as if everything is limited, including people's perceptions of the limited English speaker.

75   I know this for a fact, because when I was growing up, my mother's "limited" English limited my perception of her. I was ashamed of her

English. I believed that her English reflected the quality of what she had to say. That is, because she expressed them imperfectly her thoughts were imperfect. And I had plenty of empirical evidence to support me:
80   the fact that people in department stores, at banks, and at restaurants did not take her seriously, did not give her good service, pretended not to understand her, or even acted as if they did not hear her.

My mother has long realized the limitations of her English as well. When I was fifteen, she used to have me call people on the phone to
85   pretend I was she. In this guise, I was forced to ask for information or even to complain and yell at people who had been rude to her. One time it was a call to her stockbroker in New York. She had cashed out her small portfolio and it just so happened we were going to go to New York the next week, our very first trip outside California. I had to get on
90   the phone and say in an adolescent voice that was not very convincing, "This is Mrs. Tan."

And my mother was standing in the back whispering loudly, "Why he don't send me check, already two weeks late. So mad he lie to me, losing me money."

95   And then I said in perfect English, "Yes, I'm getting rather concerned. You had agreed to send the check two weeks ago, but it hasn't arrived."

Then she began to talk more loudly. "What he want, I come to New York tell him front of his boss, you cheating me?" And I was trying to calm her down, make her be quiet, while telling the stockbroker, "I can't tol-
100   erate any more excuses. If I don't receive the check immediately, I am going to have to speak to your manager when I'm in New York next week." And sure enough, the following week there we were in front of this astonished stockbroker, and I was sitting there red-faced and quiet, and my mother, the real Mrs. Tan, was shouting at his boss in her
105   impeccable broken English.

We used a similar routine just five days ago, for a situation that was far less humorous. My mother had gone to the hospital for an appointment, to find out about a benign brain tumor a CAT scan had revealed a month ago. She said she had spoken very good English, her best Eng-
110   lish, no mistakes. Still, she said, the hospital did not apologize when they said they had lost the CAT scan and she had come for nothing. She said they did not seem to have any sympathy when she told them she was anxious to know the exact diagnosis, since her husband and son had both died of brain tumors. She said they would not give her any
115   more information until the next time and she would have to make

continued on following page

another appointment for that. So she said she would not leave until the doctor called her daughter. She wouldn't budge. And when the doctor finally called her daughter, me, who spoke in perfect English—lo and behold—we had assurances the CAT scan would be found, promises
120   that a conference call on Monday would be held, and apologies for any suffering my mother had gone through for a most regrettable mistake.

I think my mother's English almost had an effect on limiting my possibilities in life as well. Sociologists and linguists probably will tell you that a person's developing language skills are more influenced by peers.
125   But I do think that the language spoken in the family, especially in immigrant families which are more insular, plays a large role in shaping the language of the child. And I believe that it affected my results on achievement tests, I.Q. tests, and the SAT. While my English skills were never judged as poor, compared to math, English could not be consid-
130   ered my strong suit. In grade school I did moderately well, getting perhaps B's, sometimes B-pluses, in English and scoring perhaps in the sixtieth or seventieth percentile on achievement tests. But those scores were not good enough to override the opinion that my true abilities lay in math and science, because in those areas I achieved A's and scored in
135   the ninetieth percentile or higher.

This was understandable. Math is precise; there is only one correct answer. Whereas, for me at least, the answers on English tests were always a judgment call, a matter of opinion and personal experience. Those tests were constructed around items like fill-in-the-blank sen-
140   tence completion, such as, "Even though Tom was ___, Mary thought he was ___." And the correct answer always seemed to be the most bland combinations of thoughts, for example, "Even though Tom was shy, Mary thought he was charming": with the grammatical structure "even though" limiting the correct answer to some sort of semantic
145   opposites, so you wouldn't get answers like, "Even though Tom was foolish, Mary thought he was ridiculous." Well, according to my mother, there were very few limitations as to what Tom could have been and what Mary might have thought of him. So I never did well on tests like that.

150   The same was true with word analogies, pairs of words in which you were supposed to find some sort of logical, semantic relationship—for example, "Sunset is to nightfall as ___ is to ___." And here you would be presented with a list of four possible pairs, one of which showed the same kind of relationship: red is to stoplight, bus is to arrival, chills is to
155   fever, yawn is to boring. Well, I could never think that way. I knew what

the tests were asking, but I could not block out of my mind the images already created by the first pair, "sunset is to nightfall"—and I would see a burst of colors against a darkening sky, the moon rising, the lowering of a curtain of stars. And all the other pairs of words—red, bus, stoplight, boring—just threw up a mass of confusing images, making it impossible for me to sort out something as logical as saying: "A sunset precedes nightfall" is the same as "a chill precedes a fever." The only way I would have gotten that answer right would have been to imagine an associative situation, for example, my being disobedient and staying out past sunset, catching a chill at night, which turns into feverish pneumonia as punishment, which indeed did happen to me.

I have been thinking about all this lately, about my mother's English, about achievement tests. Because lately I've been asked, as a writer, why there are not more Asian Americans represented in American literature. Why are there few Asian Americans enrolled in creative writing programs? Why do so many Chinese students go into engineering? Well, these are broad sociological questions I can't begin to answer. But I have noticed in surveys—in fact, just last week—that Asian students, as a whole, always do significantly better on math achievement tests than in English. And this makes me think that there are other Asian American students whose English spoken in the home might also be described as "broken" or "limited." And perhaps they also have teachers who are steering them away from writing and into math and science, which is what happened to me.

Fortunately, I happen to be rebellious in nature and enjoy the challenge of disproving assumptions made about me. I became an English major my first year in college, after being enrolled as pre-med. I started writing nonfiction as a freelancer the week after I was told by my former boss that writing was my worst skill and I should hone my talents toward account management.

But it wasn't until 1985 that I finally began to write fiction. And at first I wrote using what I thought to be wittily crafted sentences, sentences that would finally prove I had mastery over the English language. Here's an example from the first draft of a story that later made its way into *The Joy Luck Club*, but without this line: "That was my mental *quandary* in its *nascent* state." A terrible line, which I can barely pronounce.

quandary—
dilemma

nascent—
original

Fortunately, for reasons I won't get into today, I later decided I should envision a reader for the stories I would write. And the reader I decided

continued on following page

195 upon was my mother, because these were stories about mothers. So
with this reader in mind—and in fact she did read my early drafts—
I began to write stories using all the Englishes I grew up with: the English I spoke to my mother, which for lack of a better term might be
described as "simple"; the English she used with me, which for lack of

200 a better term might be described as "broken"; my translation of her
Chinese, which could certainly be described as "watered down"; and
what I imagined to be her translation of her Chinese if she could speak
in perfect English, her internal language, and for that I sought to preserve the essence, but neither an English nor a Chinese structure. I

205 wanted to capture what language ability tests can never reveal: her
intent, her passion, her imagery, the rhythms of her speech and the
nature of her thoughts.

Apart from what any critic had to say about my writing, I knew I had
succeeded where it counted when my mother finished reading my

210 book and gave me her verdict: "So easy to read."

PART **6**

SICK DAYS

THE INTERSECTION

Drinking to excess appears all over literature and has done so from time immemorial. From Plato's *Symposium* (385 B.C.) to A. E. Housman's *Terence, This Is Stupid Stuff* (1896) to Kingsley Amis' *Lucky Jim* (1954) to Caroline Knapp's *Drinking: A Love Story* (1996), alcohol is turned to as the stuff of comedy and tragedy and philosophy. Both of these selections raise the fearsome specter of alcoholism, but they are palpably distinct in form and function. Indeed, their juxtaposition creates an unusually fine opportunity to investigate matters of genre, audience, and diction. One is a sterling example of a personal narrative; the other, an example of expository, namely, medical reference writing for the general reader, but they are, both of them, very cautionary about alcohol abuse (and one of them indeed quite literally a cautionary tale).

▶ POINTS FOR DISCUSSION: *"Under the Influence"*

HALLMARKS *narrative amplification of childhood memories, similes and metaphors, alliteration and assonance, complex and sometimes atypical syntax (such as asyndeton)*

FORM AND CONTENT In one sentence how would students describe the subject of "Under the Influence"? What is it about? What is the writer trying to do in this piece? What does it reveal? Did he love his father? What do we learn? And what sort of piece is it? How would they describe it? Is it a personal essay? A short autobiography?

TONE AND AUDIENCE The first student question (see page 189) asks them to define the tone of the essay. Help them voice their perceptions. Give them about five to ten minutes to talk about their reactions. You might ask them if the word *sad* is a good word for the tone. Is it specific enough? Does the tone change at all? Help them build to a solid characterization, writing and refining their ideas on the board or chart paper. Direct them to look back at the text for evidence that supports their ideas. Ask, "What poetic and narrative devices do you think create the tone of the piece?" What do they consider the most powerful? Who do they think is the audience for this piece?

FOCAL POINT: ALLUSIVENESS Sanders refers to how he interpreted the story of Jesus sending the demons possessing a lunatic into the swine (Mathew 8:28–33). Consider reading this Bible story to your students and investigating Sanders' extended allusion. In his interpretation of this and other stories (like *Metamorphosis* [Kafka 1915]), we see how experience influences vision. Questions for discussion: Why does Sanders discuss this allusion at such length? What does it add to our sense of the setting of his childhood and our understanding of his struggle to understand his father's "demons"? What is the effect later in the piece when Sanders deftly alludes again to the running off the cliff of the swine?

▶ POINTS FOR DISCUSSION: *"Alcoholism"*

HALLMARKS *simple medical diction, paragraphs structured linearly with a focus on definition, use of the imperative (indicating its intention to deter)*

FORM AND CONTENT Ask students to try to identify the genre, audience, and intention of this piece. Is it written for medical personnel? A general audience? How much education does it assume on the part of its reader? Could someone who knew English imperfectly understand it? What is its purpose? Why would someone turn to this article in a medical reference book? Would this article satisfy them?

TONE AND AUDIENCE In informational prose, the writer conveys the meaning of alcoholism and its signs in uncomplicated medical language. Ask students how they would characterize the tone of the piece. Is it sad, like the Sanders' piece? Is it neutral? If it is more neutral than sad, does it ever deviate from its neutrality? What exactly is creating the tone here? Does the structure of paragraphs inform the tone? (See below.) Invite students to read aloud from the text to make their points.

FOCAL POINT: DICTION What kind of language is characteristic of this piece? How would students define it? What is the influence of its medical language in how we hear the piece, so to speak? What does the diction of the piece suggest about its emphasis? How personal is the voice of the writer?

▶ POINTS FOR DISCUSSION: *Connecting the Authors*

In a sense, all writers set out to persuade their audience of something. Although neither of these pieces can be considered persuasive writing in the way an editorial or a book review is, they do each involve persuasion. Which one of these pieces do students believe provides the clearest explanation of alcoholism? Is one more illuminating than the other? Do they each fulfill what they set out to do? What is the special power of a first-person account that a medical explanation lacks? Why do we need a medical explanation? In what situations would the use of "Alcoholism" be fitting? In terms of providing a deterrent to alcohol abuse, is one more powerful? Why?

FOCAL POINT: PARAGRAPHING Ask students to have both texts out on their desks so they can compare the use of paragraphing since narrative and expository paragraphs play by different rules. With your students, look at the paragraphing in both pieces. Begin with the simpler work, "Alcoholism," which generally has paragraphs of definition and exposition, moving in a linear way from a topic sentence. Ask students to describe how the paragraphs are structured in "Alcoholism." Point out as well that, for all its simplicity, there is pleasing sentence and paragraphing variety.

One paragraph begins with an emphatic simple sentence, "Don't fool yourself," and another begins with a question, "What is alcoholism's immediate effect?" Indeed, you might ask students why the author uses a question to start a paragraph.

In "Under the Influence" as well, the paragraphs open in a variety of ways. Sanders uses different lengths of openers. Some are short declarative sentences, such as "My father drank" and "It's all in great fun." At one point, he also speaks in the imperative to the reader, as does "Alcoholism": "Consider a few of our synonyms for *drunk*." Much of Sanders' essay develops memories. How does he lead into those stories of childhood? Are the lead sentences in his paragraphs always topic sentences? Why, in comparison to "Alcoholism," are his paragraphs so much longer?

Reading Questions FOR STUDENTS

SCOTT RUSSELL SANDERS ⁓ *"Under the Influence"*

1. Tone is the literary speaker's attitude toward his subject; characterizing tone in a literary piece involves attending to the emotional undercurrents and manner of expression. Tone has to do with *how* something is being said rather than *what* is being said. What is Scott Russell Sanders' tone as he discusses his father's alcoholism? How does he sound to you?

2. Sanders focuses on a number of scenes from his childhood and scenes that involve his own children. Why does he include them? Why are they powerful?

3. Sanders uses white space between certain paragraphs. There are eight or so of these. How do they affect the pace of the piece? In what sorts of places does he use this device? What would the essay be like without these breaks?

4. When discussing the experience of the children of alcoholics, Sanders refers to how they refuse to believe the Latin maxim *in vino veritas* ("in wine there is truth"). Why do you think Sanders includes this maxim?

6. Early in his piece, Sanders says, "I am only trying to understand the corrosive mixture of helplessness, responsibility, and shame that I learned to feel as the son of an alcoholic." In the essay do you have a sense of his trying to understand rather than understanding in full?

7. Who do you think is the audience for this essay? To whom does he seem to be talking? His children? Children of alcoholics? The general reader? All of these?

Classical Latin and Greek maxims have been important in countless works, such as "Dulce et Decorum Est" (Owen 1920), The Canterbury Tales (Chaucer 1388), and "Essay on Self-Reliance" (Emerson 1841).

ANONYMOUS ⁓ *"Alcoholism"*

1. What type of writing is this? In what sort of setting or reference would you expect to find it?

2. Does this author make any judgments about drinking? Does the pamphleteer just describe what alcoholism is or does he evaluate drinking's value?

3. Would you describe the syntax of this writing as simple or complex?

4. What sort of diction does the writer use?

5. In the margins, note any places where the author uses the imperative. What does this shift into the command form of the verb tell us about the author's intentions?

continued on following page

SPOTLIGHT ON RHETORIC: LINKAGE

The art of connecting ideas has been defined with terms since classical times and in English was sustained in the Elizabethan study of rhetoric and beyond. Though we are perhaps less conscious of these as devices, contemporary authors still turn to them.

asyndeton: a form of verbal compression that consists of the omission of connecting words. In asyndeton, where we expect to find an *and*, we find none (the opposite of polysyndeton).

> "An empty stream, a great silence, a heavy forest. The air was thick, warm, heavy sluggish." (Joseph Conrad, *Heart of Darkness*)

> "Remorseless, treacherous, lecherous, kindless villain." (William Shakespeare, *Hamlet*)

polysyndeton: the repeated use of conjunctions to link together a succession of words, phrases, clauses, or sentences (the opposite of asyndeton), often creating a fluid, or *legato* effect, in conrast to the more staccato, compressed quality of asyndeton. Polysyndeton is strongly associated with the dominant sentence structure in the creation story in Genesis 1:1. Following are other examples.

> "And soon it lightly dipped, and rose, and sank, / And dipped again." (John Keats, 1884, *Endymion*)

> "Neither snow nor rain nor heat nor gloom of night stays these couriers from the swift completion of their appointed rounds" (Herodotus, 430 B.C., Inscription, New York City Post Office)

FIND IT

Find examples in Sanders' piece of three or more of these devices, underlining them and noting in the margin where they appear.

1. alliteration
2. asyndeton
3. biblical allusion
4. listing
5. parallel phrasing
6. simile

SOUND EFFECTS

Early in this piece, immediately following the first insertion of white space, Sanders lists synonyms for *drunk*. This list is readable and lively in part because Sanders makes ample use of poetic devices such as alliteration ("Besotted, blotto, bombed, and buzzed") and assonance and rhyme ("looped, boozy, woozy"). He also pairs phrases of similar structure, like "out of your mind, under the table."

Read over the following list of synonyms and proper names for *jail* (both standard and slang English, including names of prisons). Rearrange them in list form in as poetic a way possible. Create a good sentence that provides segue into the list. It can be quite simple, as Sanders' is: "Consider a few of our synonyms for *drunk*." In addition pay attention to the rhythm of the list. Use a mix of connectives (*and*, *also*, commas, and semicolons). Note that semicolons are often used to delineate a new section or category in a list.

> jail, detention, joint, clink, clinker, slammer, lockup, choky, jug, hoosegow, joint, big house, stone lonesome, mill, death house, Statesville, tank, pen, juvy, poke, downtown, inside, freezer, keep, rack, stockade, coop, big cage, brig, the river, bucket, bull pen, federal pen, up the river, down the river, lockdown, iron city, calaboose, cooler, jug can, pokey, workhouse, Sing Sing, Rikers, Alcatraz, Fulsome, Newgate, Angola, Leavenworth, San Quentin

CAUTIONARY TALE

In the first person, tell a personal story about an experience of yours that might, directly or indirectly, make a reader think twice about their actions. Tell the story with as much detail as possible; take the reader there the way Sanders takes us to that moment when as a small child he pretends to his father that he doesn't notice him drinking. Be as honest and detailed as you can. Remember that it can be hard to write well about why we should behave. Try to avoid sounding Pollyannaish. Really think through what you are writing about and *show* why we should or should not do something.

Possible "should nots": tease, bully, steal, lie, despair, abuse drugs or alcohol, hurt others, remain angry with someone we love, be cruel, cheat, tell hurtful jokes, and so on.

Possible "shoulds": volunteer, study hard, help others, be hopeful, be optimistic, read the paper, do chores, save money, and so on.

My father drank. He drank as a gut-punched boxer gasps for breath, as a
starving dog gobbles food—compulsively, secretly, in pain and trembling.
I use the past tense not because he ever quit drinking but because he quit
living. That is how the story ends for my father, age sixty-four, heart burst-
5   ing, body cooling and forsaken on the linoleum of my brother's trailer.
The story continues for my brother, my sister, my mother, and me, and
will continue so long as memory holds.

In the perennial present of memory, I slip into the garage or barn to see
my father tipping back the flat green bottles of wine, the brown cylinders of
10   whiskey, the cans of beer disguised in paper bags. His Adam's apple bobs,
the liquid gurgles, he wipes the sandy-haired back of a hand over his lips,
and then, his bloodshot gaze bumping into me, he stashes the bottle or
can inside his jacket, under the workbench, between two bales of hay, and
we both pretend the moment has not occurred.

15   "What's up, buddy?" he says, thick-tongued and edgy.

"Sky's up," I answer, playing along.

"And don't forget prices," he grumbles. "Prices are always up. And taxes."

In memory, his white 1951 Pontiac with the stripes down the hood and
the Indian head on the snout jounces to a stop in the driveway; or it is the
20   1956 Ford station wagon, or the 1963 Rambler shaped like a toad, or the
sleek 1969 Bonneville that will do 120 miles per hour on straightaways; or
it is the robin's-egg blue pickup, new in 1980, battered in 1981, the year of
his death. He climbs out, grinning dangerously, unsteady on his legs, and
we children interrupt our game of catch, our building of snow forts, our
25   picking of plums, to watch in silence as he weaves past into the house,
where he slumps into his overstuffed chair and falls asleep. Shaking her
head, our mother stubs out the cigarette he has left smoldering in the ash-
tray. All evening, until our bedtimes, we tiptoe past him, as past a snoring
dragon. Then we curl in our fearful sheets, listening. Eventually he wakes
30   with a grunt, Mother slings accusations at him, he snarls back, she yells,
he growls, their voices dashing. Before long, she retreats to their bedroom,
sobbing—not from the blows of fists, for he never strikes her, but from the
force of words.

Left alone, our father prowls the house, thumping into furniture, rummag-
35   ing in the kitchen, slamming doors, turning the page of the newspaper with
a savage crackle, muttering back at the late-night drivel from television. The

roof might fly off, the walls might buckle from the pressure of his rage. Whatever my brother and sister and mother may be thinking on their own rumpled pillows, I lie there hating him, loving him, fearing him, knowing I

40 have failed him. I tell myself he drinks to ease an ache that gnaws at his belly, an ache I must have caused by disappointing him somehow, a murderous ache I should be able to relieve by doing all my chores, earning A's in school, winning baseball games, fixing the broken washer and the burst pipes, bringing in money to fill his empty wallet. He would not hide the

45 green bottles in his tool box, would not sneak off to the barn with a lump under his coat, would not fall asleep in the daylight, would not roar and fume, would not drink himself to death, if only I were perfect.

I am forty-two as I write these words, and I know full well now that my father was an alcoholic, a man consumed by disease rather than by dis-

50 appointment. What had seemed to me a private grief is in fact a public scourge. In the United States alone some ten or fifteen million people share his ailment, and behind the doors they slam in fury or disgrace, countless other children tremble. I comfort myself with such knowledge, holding it against the throb of memory like an ice pack against a bruise.

55 There are keener sources of grief: poverty, racism, rape, war. I do not wish to compete for a trophy in suffering. I am only trying to understand the corrosive mixture of helplessness, responsibility, and shame that I learned to feel as the son of an alcoholic. I realize now that I did not cause my father's illness, nor could I have cured it. Yet for all this grown-up knowledge, I am

60 still ten years old, my own son's age, and as that boy I struggle in guilt and confusion to save my father from pain.

Consider a few of our synonyms for *drunk:* tipsy, tight, pickled, soused, and plowed; stoned and stewed, lubricated and inebriated, juiced and sluiced; three sheets to the wind, in your cups, out of your mind, under the table, lit

65 up, tanked up, wiped out; besotted, blotto, bombed, and buzzed; plastered, polluted, putrified; loaded or looped, boozy, woozy, fuddled, or smashed; crocked and shit-faced, corked and pissed, snockered and sloshed.

It is a mostly humorous lexicon, as the lore that deals with drunks—in jokes and cartoons, in plays, films, and television skits—is largely comic. Aunt

70 Matilda nips elderberry wine from the sideboard and burps politely during supper. Uncle Fred slouches to the table glassy-eyed, wearing a lamp shade for a hat and murmuring, "Candy is dandy but liquor is quicker." Inspired by cocktails, Mrs. Somebody recounts the events of her day in a fuzzy dialect, while Mr. Somebody nibbles her ear and croons a bawdy song. On the sofa

continued on following page

75   with Boyfriend, Daughter giggles, licking gin from her lips, and loosens the
bows in her hair. Junior knocks back some brews with his chums at the
Leopard Lounge and stumbles home to the wrong house, wonders foggily
why he cannot locate his pajamas, and crawls naked into bed with the ugli-
est girl in school. The family dog slurps from a neglected martini and wob-
80   bles to the nursery, where he vomits in Baby's shoe.

It's all in great fun. But if in the audience you notice a few laughing faces
turn grim when the drunk lurches on stage, don't be surprised, for these
are the children of alcoholics. Over the grinning mask of *Dionysus*, the leer-
ing mask of *Bacchus*, these children cannot help seeing the bloated fea-
85   tures of their own parents. Instead of laughing, they wince, they mourn.
Instead of celebrating the drunk as one freed from constraints, they pity
him as one enslaved. They refuse to believe *in vino veritas,* having seen
their befuddled parents skid away from truth toward folly and oblivion.
And so these children bite their lips until the lush staggers into the wings.

90   My father, when drunk, was neither funny nor honest; he was pathetic,
frightening, deceitful. There seemed to be a leak in him somewhere, and
he poured in booze to keep from draining dry. Like a torture victim who
refuses to squeal, he would never admit that he had touched a drop, not
even in his last year, when he seemed to be dissolving in alcohol before
95   our very eyes. I never knew him to lie about anything, ever, except about
this one ruinous fact. Drowsy, clumsy, unable to fix a bicycle tire, throw a
baseball, balance a grocery sack, or walk across the room, he was stripped
of his true self by drink. In a matter of minutes, the contents of a bottle
could transform a brave man into a coward, a buddy into a bully, a gifted
100   athlete and skilled carpenter and shrewd businessman into a bumbler. No
dictionary of synonyms for *drunk* would soften the anguish of watching our
prince turn into a frog.

Father's drinking became the family secret. While growing up, we children
never breathed a word of it beyond the four walls of our house. To this day,
105   my brother and sister rarely mention it, and then only when I press them.
I did not confess the ugly, bewildering fact to my wife until his wavering
walk and slurred speech forced me to. Recently, on the seventh anniversary
of my father's death, I asked my mother if she ever spoke of his drinking
to friends. "No, no, never," she replied hastily. "I couldn't bear for anyone
110   to know."

The secret bores under the skin, gets in the blood, into the bone, and stays
there. Long after you have supposedly been cured of malaria, the fever can

Dionysus—
Greek God of wind

Bacchus—
Dionysus

in vino veritas—
"there's truth in wine"

flare up, the tremors can shake you. So it is with the fevers of shame. You
swallow the bitter quinine of knowledge, and you learn to feel pity and
115 compassion toward the drinker. Yet the shame lingers in your marrow, and,
because of the shame, anger.

For a long stretch of my childhood we lived on a military reservation in
Ohio, an arsenal where bombs were stored underground in bunkers, vintage airplanes burst into flames, and unstable artillery shells boomed
120 nightly at the dump. We had the feeling, as children, that we played in a
mine field, where a heedless footfall could trigger an explosion. When
Father was drinking, the house, too, became a mine field. The least bump
could set off either parent.

The more he drank, the more obsessed Mother became with stopping him.
125 She hunted for bottles, counted the cash in his wallet, sniffed at his breath.
Without meaning to snoop, we children blundered left and right into damning evidence. On afternoons when he came home from work sober, we
flung ourselves at him for hugs, and felt against our ribs the telltale lump in
his coat. In the barn we tumbled on the hay and heard beneath our sneak-
130 ers the crunch of buried glass. We tugged open a drawer in his workbench,
looking for screwdrivers or crescent wrenches, and spied a gleaming six-
pack among the tools. Playing tag, we darted around the house just in time
to see him sway on the rear stoop and heave a finished bottle into the
woods. In his good night kiss we smelled the cloying sweetness of Clorets,
135 the mints he chewed to camouflage his dragon's breath.

I can summon up that kiss right now by recalling Theodore Roethke's lines
about his own father in "My Papa's Waltz":

> *The whiskey on your breath*
> *Could make a small boy dizzy;*
140 > *But I hung on like death:*
> *Such waltzing was not easy.*

Such waltzing was hard, terribly hard, for with a boy's scrawny arms I was
trying to hold my tipsy father upright.

For years, the chief source of those incriminating bottles and cans was a
145 grimy store a mile from us, a cinder block place called Sly's, with two gas
pumps outside and a moth-eaten dog asleep in the window. A strip of fly-
paper, speckled the year round with black bodies, coiled in the doorway.
Inside, on rusty metal shelves or in wheezing coolers, you could find pop
and Popsicles, cigarettes, potato chips, canned soup, raunchy postcards,

continued on following page

150 fishing gear, Twinkies, wine, and beer. When Father drove anywhere on errands, Mother would send us kids along as guards, warning us not to let him out of our sight. And so with one or more of us on board, Father would cruise up to Sly's, pump a dollar's worth of gas or plump the tires with air, and then, telling us to wait in the car, he would head for that fly-
155 spangled doorway.

Dutiful and panicky, we cried, "Let us go in with you!"

"No," he answered. "I'll be back in two shakes."

"Please!"

"No!" he roared. "Don't you budge" or "I'll jerk a knot in your tails!" So we
160 stayed put, kicking the seats, while he ducked inside. Often, when he had parked the car at a careless angle, we gazed in through the window and saw Mr. Sly fetching down from a shelf behind the cash register two green pints of Gallo wine. Father swigged one of them right there at the counter, stuffed the other in his pocket, and then out he came, a bulge in his coat,
165 a flustered look on his red face.

Because the Mom and Pop who ran the dump were neighbors of ours, living just down the tar-blistered road, I hated them all the more for poisoning my father. I wanted to sneak in their store and smash the bottles and set fire to the place. I also hated the Gallo brothers, Ernest and Julio, whose
170 jovial faces shone from the labels of their wine, labels I would find, torn and curled, when I burned the trash. I noted the Gallo brothers' address, in California, and I studied the road atlas to see how far that was from Ohio, because I meant to go out there and tell Ernest and Julio what they were doing to my father, and then, if they showed no mercy, I would kill them.

175 While growing up on the back roads and in the country schools and cramped Methodist churches of Ohio and Tennessee, I never heard the word *alcoholism,* never happened across it in books or magazines. In the nearby towns, there were no addiction treatment programs, no community mental health centers, no Alcoholics Anonymous chapters, no
180 therapists. Left alone with our grievous secret, we had no way of understanding Father's drinking except as an act of will, a deliberate folly or cruelty, a moral weakness, a sin. He drank because he chose to, pure and simple. Why our father, so playful and competent and kind when sober, would choose to ruin himself and punish his family, we could not fathom.

185 Our neighborhood was high on the Bible, and the Bible was hard on drunkards. "Woe to those who are heroes at drinking wine, and valiant

men in mixing strong drink," wrote Isaiah. "The priest and the prophet reel with strong drink, they are confused with wine, they err in vision, they stumble in giving judgment. For all tables are full of vomit, no place is with-

190 out filthiness." We children had seen those fouled tables at the local truck stop where the notorious boozers hung out, our father occasionally among them. "Wine and new wine take away the understanding," declared the prophet Hosea. We had also seen evidence of that in our father who could multiply seven-digit numbers in his head when sober, but when drunk

195 could not help us with fourth-grade math. Proverbs warned: "Do not look at wine when it is red, when it sparkles in the cup and goes down smoothly. At the last it bites like a serpent, and stings like an adder. Your eyes will see strange things, and your mind utter perverse things." Woe, woe.

200 Dismayingly often, these biblical drunkards stirred up trouble for their own kids. Noah made fresh wine after the flood, drank too much of it, fell asleep without any clothes on, and was glimpsed in the buff by his son Ham, whom Noah promptly cursed. In one passage—it was so shocking we had to read it under our blankets with flashlights—the patriarch Lot fell

205 down drunk and slept with his daughters. The sins of the fathers set their children's teeth on edge.

Our ministers were fond of quoting St. Paul's pronouncement that drunk-ards would not inherit the kingdom of God. These grave preachers assured us that the wine referred to during the Last Supper was in fact grape juice.

210 Bible and sermons and hymns combined to give us the impression that Moses should have brought down from the mountain another stone tablet, bearing the Eleventh Commandment: Thou shalt not drink.

The scariest and most illuminating Bible story apropos of drunkards was the one about the lunatic and the swine. Matthew, Mark, and Luke each

215 told a version of the tale. We knew it by heart: When Jesus climbed out of his boat one day, this lunatic came charging up from the graveyard, stark naked and filthy, frothing at the mouth, so violent that he broke the strongest chains. Nobody would go near him. Night and day for years this madman had been wailing among the tombs and bruising himself with

220 stones. Jesus took one look at him and said, "Come out of the man, you unclean spirits!" for he could see that the lunatic was possessed by demons. Meanwhile, some hogs were conveniently rooting nearby. "If we have to come out," begged the demons, "at least let us go into those swine." Jesus agreed. The unclean spirits entered the hogs, and the hogs

225 rushed straight off a cliff and plunged into a lake. Hearing the story in

continued on following page

Sunday school, my friends thought mainly of the pigs. (How big a splash did they make? Who paid for the lost pork?) But I thought of the redeemed lunatic, who bathed himself and put on clothes and calmly sat at the feet of Jesus, restored—so the Bible said—to "his right mind."

230 When drunk, our father was clearly in his wrong mind. He became a stranger, as fearful to us as any graveyard lunatic, not quite frothing at the mouth but fierce enough, quick-tempered, explosive; or else he grew maudlin and weepy, which frightened us nearly as much. In my boyhood despair, I reasoned that maybe he wasn't to blame for turning into an ogre.
235 Maybe, like the lunatic, he was possessed by demons. I found support for my theory when I heard liquor referred to as "spirits," when the newspapers reported that somebody had been arrested for "driving under the influence," and when church ladies railed against that "demon drink."

If my father was indeed possessed, who would exorcise him? If he was a
240 sinner, who would save him? If he was ill, who would cure him? If he suffered, who would ease his pain? Not ministers or doctors, for we could not bring ourselves to confide in them; not the neighbors, for we pretended they had never seen him drunk; not Mother, who fussed and pleaded but could not budge him; not my brother and sister, who were only kids. That
245 left me. It did not matter that I, too, was only a child, and a bewildered one at that. I could not excuse myself.

On first reading a description of delirium tremens—in a book on alcoholism I smuggled from the library—I thought immediately of the frothing lunatic and the frenzied swine. When I read stories or watched films about grisly
250 metamorphoses—Dr. Jekyll becoming Mr. Hyde, the mild husband changing into a werewolf, the kindly neighbor taken over by a brutal alien—I could not help seeing my own father's mutation from sober to drunk. Even today, knowing better, I am attracted by the demonic theory of drink, for when I recall my father's transformation, the emergence of his ugly second self,
255 I find it easy to believe in possession by unclean spirits. We never knew which version of Father would come home from work, the true or the tainted, nor could we guess how far down the slope toward cruelty he would slide.

How far a man *could* slide we gauged by observing our back-road neigh-
260 bors—the out-of-work miners who had dragged their families to our corner of Ohio from the desolate hollows of Appalachia, the tightfisted farmers, the surly mechanics, the balked and broken men. There was, for example, whiskey-soaked Mr. Jenkins, who beat his wife and kids so hard we could

265 hear their screams from the road. There was Mr. Lavo the wino, who fell asleep smoking time and again, until one night his disgusted wife bundled up the children and went outside and left him in his easy chair to burn; he awoke on his own, staggered out coughing into the yard, and pounded her flat while the children looked on and the shack turned to ash. There was the truck driver, Mr. Sampson, who tripped over his son's tricycle one night

270 while drunk and got so mad that he jumped into his semi and drove away, shifting through the dozen gears, and never came back. We saw the bruised children of these fathers clump onto our school bus, we saw the abandoned children huddle in the pews at church, we saw the stunned and battered mothers begging for help at our doors.

275 Our own father never beat us, and I don't think he ever beat Mother, but he threatened often. The Old Testament Yahweh was not more terrible in his wrath. Eyes blazing, voice booming, Father would pull out his belt and swear to give us a whipping, but he never followed through, never needed to, because we could imagine it so vividly. He shoved us, pawed us with

280 the back of his hand, as an irked bear might smack a cub, not to injure, just to clear a space. I can see him grabbing Mother by the hair as she cowers on a chair during a nightly quarrel. He twists her neck back until she gapes up at him, and then he lifts over her skull a glass quart bottle of milk, the milk running down his forearm, and he yells at her, "Say just one more

285 word, one goddamn word, and I'll shut you up!" I fear she will prick him with her sharp tongue, but she is terrified into silence, and so am I, and the leaking bottle quivers in the air, and milk slithers through the red hair of my father's uplifted arm, and the entire scene is there to this moment, the head jerked back, the club raised.

290 When the drink made him weepy, Father would pack a bag and kiss each of us children on the head, and announce from the front door that he was moving out. "Where to?" we demanded, fearful each time that he would leave for good, as Mr. Sampson had roared away for good in his diesel truck. "Someplace where I won't get hounded every minute," Father would

295 answer, his jaw quivering. He stabbed a look at Mother, who might say, "Don't run into the ditch before you get there," or, "Good riddance," and then he would slink away. Mother watched him go with arms crossed over her chest, her face closed like the lid on a box of snakes. We children bawled. Where could he go? To the truck stop, that den of iniquity? To one

300 of those dark, ratty flophouses in town? Would he wind up sleeping under a railroad bridge or on a park bench or in a cardboard box, mummied in rags, like the bums we had seen on our trips to Cleveland and Chicago? We bawled and bawled, wondering if he would ever come back.

continued on following page

305 He always did come back, a day or a week later, but each time there was a
sliver less of him.

In Kafka's *The Metamorphosis*, which opens famously with Gregor Samsa
waking up from uneasy dreams to find himself transformed into an insect,
Gregor's family keep reassuring themselves that things will be just fine
again, "When he comes back to us." Each time alcohol transformed our
310 father, we held out the same hope, that he would really and truly come
back to us, our authentic father, the tender and playful and competent
man, and then all things would be fine. We had grounds for such hope.
After his weepy departures and chapfallen returns, he would sometimes go
weeks, even months without drinking. Those were glad times. Joy banged
315 inside my ribs. Every day without the furtive glint of bottles, every meal
without a fight, every bedtime without sobs encouraged us to believe that
such bliss might go on forever.

Mother was fooled by just such a hope all during the forty-odd years she
knew this Greeley Ray Sanders. Soon after she met him in a Chicago deli-
320 catessen on the eve of World War II, and fell for his butter-melting Mississippi drawl and his wavy red hair, she learned that he drank heavily. But
then so did a lot of men. She would soon coax or scold him into breaking
the nasty habit. She would point out to him how ugly and foolish it was,
this bleary drinking, and then he would quit. He refused to quit during
325 their engagement, however, still refused during the first years of marriage,
refused until my sister came along. The shock of fatherhood sobered him,
and he remained sober through my birth at the end of the war and right
on through until we moved in 1951 to the Ohio arsenal, that paradise of
bombs. Like all places that make a business of death, the arsenal had more
330 than its share of alcoholics and drug addicts and other varieties of escape
artists. There I turned six and started school and woke into a child's flicker-
ing awareness, just in time to see my father begin sneaking swigs in the
garage.

He sobered up again for most of a year at the height of the Korean War, to
335 celebrate the birth of my brother. But aside from that dry spell, his only
breaks from drinking before I graduated from high school were just long
enough to raise and then dash our hopes. Then during the fall of my senior
year—the time of the Cuban missile crisis, when it seemed that the nightly
explosions at the munitions dump and the nightly rages in our household
340 might spread to engulf the globe—Father collapsed. His liver, kidneys, and
heart all conked out. The doctors saved him, but only by a hair. He stayed

in the hospital for weeks, going through a withdrawal so terrible that Mother would not let us visit him. If he wanted to kill himself, the doctors solemnly warned him, all he had to do was hit the bottle again. One binge would finish him.

345 Father must have believed them, for he stayed dry for the next fifteen years. It was an answer to prayer, Mother said, it was a miracle. I believe it was a reflex of fear, which he sustained over the years through courage and pride. He knew a man could die from drink, for his brother Roscoe had. We children never laid eyes on doomed Uncle Roscoe, but in the stories Mother

350 told us he became a fairy-tale figure, like a boy who took the wrong turning in the woods and was gobbled up by the wolf.

The fifteen-year dry spell came to an end with Father's retirement in the spring of 1978. Like many men, he gave up his identity along with his job. One day he was a boss at the factory, with a brass plate on his door and a

355 reputation to uphold; the next day he was a nobody at home. He and Mother were leaving Ontario, the last of the many places to which his job had carried them, and they were moving to a new house in Mississippi, his childhood stomping grounds. As a boy in Mississippi, Father sold Coca-Cola during dances while the moonshiners peddled their brew in the parking

360 lot; as a young blade, he fought in bars and in the ring, seeking a state Golden Gloves championship; he gambled at poker, hunted pheasants, raced motorcycles and cars, played semiprofessional baseball, and, along with all his buddies—in the Black Cat Saloon, behind the cotton gin, in the woods—he drank. It was a perilous youth to dream of recovering.

365 After his final day of work, Mother drove on ahead with a car full of begonias and violets, while Father stayed behind to oversee the packing. When the van was loaded, the sweaty movers broke open a six-pack and offered him a beer.

"Let's drink to retirement!" they crowed. "Let's drink to freedom! to fishing!

370 hunting! loafing! Let's drink to a guy who's going home!"

At least I imagine some such words, for that is all I can do, imagine, and I see Father's hand trembling in midair as he thinks about the fifteen sober years and about the doctors' warning, and he tells himself *Goddamnit, I am a free man*, and *Why can't a free man drink one beer after a lifetime of*

375 *hard work?* and I see his arm reaching, his fingers closing, the can tilting to his lips. I even supply a label for the beer, a swaggering brand that promises on television to deliver the essence of life. I watch the amber liquid pour down his throat, the alcohol steal into his blood, the key turn in his brain.

continued on following page

380 Soon after my parents moved back to Father's treacherous stomping ground, my wife and I visited them in Mississippi with our five-year-old daughter. Mother had been too distraught to warn me about the return of the demons. So when I climbed out of the car that bright July morning and saw my father napping in the hammock, I felt uneasy, for in all his sober

385 years I had never known him to sleep in daylight. Then he lurched upright, blinked his bloodshot eyes, and greeted us in a syrupy voice. I was hurled back helpless into childhood.

"What's the matter with Papaw?" our daughter asked.

"Nothing," I said. "Nothing!"

390 Like a child again, I pretended not to see him in his stupor, and behind my phony smile I grieved. On that visit and on the few that remained before his death, once again I found bottles in the workbench, bottles in the woods. Again his hands shook too much for him to run a saw, to make his precious miniature furniture, to drive straight down back roads. Again he

395 wound up in the ditch, in the hospital, in jail, in treatment centers. Again he shouted and wept. Again he lied. "I never touched a drop," he swore. "Your mother's making it up."

I no longer fancied I could reason with the men whose names I found on the bottles—Jim Beam, Jack Daniels—nor did I hope to save my father by

400 burning down a store. I was able now to press the cold statistics about alcoholism against the ache of memory: ten million victims, fifteen million, twenty. And yet, in spite of my age, I reacted in the same blind way as I had in childhood, ignoring biology, forgetting numbers, vainly seeking to erase through my efforts whatever drove him to drink. I worked on their place

405 twelve and sixteen hours a day, in the swelter of Mississippi summers, digging ditches, running electrical wires, planting trees, mowing grass, building sheds, as though what nagged at him was some list of chores, as though by taking his worries on my shoulders I could redeem him. I was flung back into boyhood, acting as though my father would not drink himself to death

410 if only I were perfect.

I failed of perfection; he succeeded in dying. To the end, he considered himself not sick but sinful. "Do you want to kill yourself?" I asked him. "Why not?" he answered. "Why the hell not? What's there to save?" To the end, he would not speak about his feelings, would not or could not give a name

415 to the beast that was devouring him.

In silence, he went rushing off the cliff. Unlike the biblical swine, however, he left behind a few of the demons to haunt his children. Life with him and

the loss of him twisted us into shapes that will be familiar to other sons
and daughters of alcoholics. My brother became a rebel, my sister retreated
420   into shyness, I played the stalwart and dutiful son who would hold the
family together. If my father was unstable, I would be a rock. If he squan-
dered money on drink, I would pinch every penny. If he wept when drunk—
and only when drunk—I would not let myself weep at all. If he roared at
the Little League umpire for calling my pitches balls, I would throw nothing
425   but strikes. Watching him flounder and rage, I came to dread the loss of
control. I would go through life without making anyone mad. I vowed never
to put in my mouth or veins any chemical that would banish my everyday
self. I would never make a scene, never lash out at the ones I loved, never
hurt a soul. Through hard work, relentless work, I would achieve something
430   dazzling—in the classroom, on the basketball floor, in the science lab, in
the pages of books—and my achievement would distract the world's eyes
from his humiliation. I would become a worthy sacrifice, and the smoke of
my burning would please God.

It is far easier to recognize these twists in my character than to undo them.
435   Work has become an addiction for me, as drink was an addiction for my
father. Knowing this, my daughter gave me a placard for the wall: WORKA-
HOLIC. The labor is endless and futile, for I can no more redeem myself
through work than I could redeem my father. I still panic in the face of other
people's anger, because his drunken temper was so terrible. I shrink from
440   causing sadness or disappointment even to strangers, as though I were still
concealing the family shame. I still notice every twitch of emotion in the
faces around me, having learned as a child to read the weather in faces,
and I blame myself for their least pang of unhappiness or anger. In certain
moods I blame myself for everything. Guilt burns like acid in my veins.

445   I am moved to write these pages now because my own son, at the age of
ten, is taking on himself the griefs of the world, and in particular the griefs
of his father. He tells me that when I am gripped by sadness he feels
responsible; he feels there must be something he can do to spring me
from depression, to fix my life. And that crushing sense of responsibility is
450   exactly what I felt at the age of ten in the face of my father's drinking. My
son wonders if I, too, am possessed. I write, therefore, to drag into the light
what eats at me—the fear, the guilt, the shame—so that my own children
may be spared.

I still shy away from nightclubs, from bars, from parties where the solvent
455   is alcohol. My friends puzzle over this, but it is no more peculiar than for a

continued on following page

man to shy away from the lions' den after seeing his father torn apart. I took my own first drink at the age of twenty-one, half a glass of burgundy. I knew the odds of my becoming an alcoholic were four times higher than for the sons of nonalcoholic fathers. So I sipped warily.

460   I still do—once a week, perhaps, a glass of wine, a can of beer, nothing stronger, nothing more. I listen for the turning of a key in my brain.

ANONYMOUS ∾ *"Alcoholism"*

Alcoholism is often thought of as a disorder, but it's actually a chronic, progressive disease. Alcoholism, alcohol abuse, and alcohol dependence are all characterized by a person's misuse of alcohol. If a person has difficulty controlling the amount of alcohol he or she drinks; if

5   alcohol is a repeated activity; if the drinking has caused problems with work, school, family, or society, then a diagnosis of alcoholism is likely.

Alcoholism is a drug dependency. To depend on alcohol means your body has become so accustomed to the intake of alcohol that when it doesn't get it, physical symptoms occur. The disease creates a psycho-

10 logical dependency as well—a marked need for its effects. Current research has shown that alcoholism significantly alters brain function, and so the intertwined physical and psychological dependency is no surprise.

Family history may make you more likely to become alcoholic. Studies

15 show that sons of alcoholic men who began drinking at an early age are especially prone. Research has also shown that children who are born to alcoholic parents are four times more likely to become alcoholics than children who do not have alcoholic family histories. This finding holds true even when the children are raised away from their biological

20 parents.

What is alcohol's immediate effect? A mere two sips of alcohol goes straight to the brain, where it produces a numbing effect. Sometimes, called a "feel good" effect, the alcohol loosens inhibitions. A person may experience mild mood swings, including states of elation, sadness,

25 irritability, and rage. An individual may slur words and lose coordination. The physical impairment and impairment in judgment lead to accidents in the home or on the roads. High alcohol levels can cause a person to fall into a coma and even die, a situation that too frequently happens in college settings.

30 Teenagers and adults alike often wonder what the distinction is between habitual use of alcohol and alcoholism. It's a fine distinction, and a slippery slope between the two. Many alcoholic rehab organizations use the rule of thumb that if you're worried about it, you probably have a problem with alcohol. Other questions asked of individuals who

35 may be alcohol dependent include: Do you have trouble stopping drinking without experiencing unpleasant physical and psychological effects? Do you have a tendency to overdrink? Do you ever drink

continued on following page

instead of attending school or work? Has drinking ever led to problems in personal relationships? Problems in your self concept and sense of
40 well-being?

Classic warning signs of a physical dependence on alcohol are tolerance to the effects of alcohol or withdrawal symptoms you experience when you abstain from its use. These symptoms are relieved when the alcoholic imbibes a drink. Signs of withdrawal may range from a pro-
45 tracted headache, anxiety, trouble sleeping, and nausea to tremors, delirium, and seizures.

Many individuals heading toward alcoholism fool themselves into thinking they can't be alcoholic because they can "hold their liquor" well. This can even be seen as a positive trait by themselves and peers.
50 However, this tolerance may be a first sign of alcohol dependence. Tolerance occurs when, after a period of alcohol use, the drug effects that are usually seen are not as readily apparent. Thus, the alcoholic may appear sober even if he or she has a blood alcohol concentration that would normally indicate intoxication. A long-time user of alcohol
55 may also metabolize (break down) the alcohol slightly more rapidly than someone whose body is not accustomed to chronic alcohol consumption.

Don't fool yourself! This mistaken understanding of tolerance is what leads to dead drunk individuals getting behind the wheel of a car and
60 endangering themselves and others. No matter how sober you feel, your liver is still unable to metabolize pure alcohol at a rate faster than approximately 1 ounce of 80-proof liquor every hour. After heavy drinkers develop a high tolerance, they may discover that their tolerance gradually declines and that they become drunk on progressively
65 smaller amounts of alcohol. This decrease in tolerance probably occurs because their damaged livers metabolize or break down more slowly. In addition, the effects of aging and the involvement of your nervous system may play a role. High tolerance is a sign of probable alcohol dependence.

SENECA THE YOUNGER
"Asthma"

FORM: *Letter*
DATE: A.D. 60

JOAN DIDION
"In Bed," Excerpt from the Book *The White Album*

FORM: *Personal Essay*
DATE: 1968

FORMAL NOTE

One can easily see in Seneca how the letter anticipated the later personal essay. Letters, like personal essays, are an occasion for relaying observations in the first person. Seneca's letters, written to a civil servant named Lucilius, were meant to be circulated. In fact, Seneca's writing seems quite similar to a modern personal essay such as Didion's. Seneca is seen as a classical forerunner not only of the personal essay but of modern prose style. His emphasis on simplicity and clarity are virtues famously praised in *The Elements of Style* (William Strunk Jr. and E. B. White 1959). As a form, the personal essay began to flower in the Elizabethan period when writers were branching out from satire and character sketch writing. And other forms, such as the sermon, also influenced the rise of the essay.

THE INTERSECTION

Two thousand years and an ocean—not to mention sex—separate Seneca the Younger and Joan Didion. Yet between these writers there is something kindred as they describe their experience with the onset of a recurrent illness. In a letter Seneca writes about asthma; Didion, in a personal essay from *The White Album* (1979) writes about her history of migraine headaches. In both we gain a sharp sense of coming to terms with an incurable, recurrent illness. Though they emphasize different aspects of it—Seneca is more explicitly philosophical—both speak of learning to live with illness, and both, in a sense, seem to be enlarged by illness, too.

▶ POINTS FOR DISCUSSION: *"Asthma"*

HALLMARKS *letter form, simple lucid prose style, declarative sentences, epigrammatic statements, moving from personal experience to general truth, didacticism*

FORM AND CONTENT Seneca's letter to Lucilius builds a discussion that moves with deft seamlessness from a single asthma attack to assertions about life and death. Ask students what the subject of the piece is. If they say it is about asthma, as the title suggests, ask them what that means. Is it only about asthma? Why is he discussing it? To complain to Lucilius? What is he saying about death? If they were going to subtitle this letter, what would they call it? Is there any indication that this is in response to something Lucilius has said about death? Do we feel that we are coming into the middle of a conversation?

TONE AND AUDIENCE How is Seneca speaking to Lucilius? What does Seneca's attitude toward Lucilius seem to be? With what tone does Seneca address Lucilius? Do students find Seneca respectfully instructive? Condescending? Who seems to be of higher status? Letter writer? Or addressee?

FOCAL POINT: DIDACTICISM Lead them to a discussion of the didactic aspect of the letter. Where is Seneca at his most instructive? The student questions ask if Seneca is an epigrammatic writer, someone who makes quite quotable statements. In such a statement, one tends to speak declaratively and in general terms. In Seneca's case, he speaks of what the wise man does and whom he should emulate: "The man, though, whom you should admire and imitate is the one who finds it a joy to live and in spite of that is not reluctant to die." Is this didacticism here overt or covert, would they say? How common is overt didacticism today? Are we as concerned about what the wise man does?

▶ POINTS FOR DISCUSSION: *"In Bed"*

HALLMARKS *personal essay, narrative, listing technique, lively sentence variety, sentence fragments*

FORM AND CONTENT "In Bed" provides occasion for interesting questions about the memoir genre. Here a writer recounts her personal history with a recurrent illness: What makes it interesting? Does she only want the reader to learn about her experience? In part, she is also explaining the illness, its history, its public perception (misperception), and the challenges it presented. The personal history touches continually on larger matters (like the American view of illness) but stays firmly rooted in her own experience. Why can it be important to hear an individual's perspective? What can it teach us? What did they think? Did they learn something about migraines? How does her attitude toward it change?

TONE AND AUDIENCE What is Didion's tone as she describes her illness? How much grief does she convey about its effect on her life? How does her tone shift at the end of the essay when she discusses her changing attiude? Memoir writing is sometimes faulted for its self-indulgence; this might be an interesting question—ask students if they found "In Bed" self-pitying in any places. Or was it appropriately vivid and dramatic in its evocation of her experience with the illness? Does she ever use humor? Is she fairly sustained in the seriousness of her discussion?

FOCAL POINT: SENTENCE VARIETY Sentence variety is one of the hallmarks of fine prose, and students are often encouraged toward it (indeed, sentence variety is highlighted on many grading rubrics and standards, including those of the twenty-five-minute essay on the SAT in English). Didion's essay provides an exceptional model. Ask students to look for different types of sentences. Her sentences expand and contract in size. Their types vary. She includes lists. She allows fragmentary sentences. Sometimes her sentences run wonderfully long, and sometimes, only sometimes, she lands neatly at the end of a paragraph with a simple lucid sentence. Look with students at the second paragraph of the essay and at its last paragraph. In the second paragraph, where she describes the onslaught of her illness, she creates a long sentence, linking together verb phrases. How does the very length of the sentence help convey what the experience is like? Then again, in the last paragraph, where she describes life after an attack, what kinds of sentences are characteristic? What is the effect of those shorter sentences? How do they help create mood?

▶ POINTS FOR DISCUSSION: *Connecting the Authors*

Ask the students to place both essays on their desks. Consider with them the degree to which these authors use illness to discuss something larger. Seneca, obviously, is the more philosophical of these two writers. He speaks explicitly about how his illness is a catalyst for reflection on life and death, building off the idea that doctors refer to asthma as "rehearsing for death." Other themes emerge: How do we handle death? Whom should we emulate? Are these thematic points ultimately more emphasized than what it is like to have asthma? How are Didion's intentions different? Why does she describe her illness to such an extent? How might her descriptions help dispel the misperceptions common in the general public? What does her essay suggest about illness and Americans?

FOCAL POINT For all their differences, these pieces share something essential: they investigate what illness reveals about the human condition, that certain things are nonnegotiable. How do we live in the face of that? Indeed, dealing with our physical realities and necessities is surely a most universal theme. Why do they think Seneca's writings have lasted as they have? What makes his writing classic, in every sense? It was said that Shakespeare's writing was "not of an age, but for all time." Is Didion's essay for all time, do they think? Or is it "of an age," so rooted in its moment that it would probably not translate into the future? What do they think?

SENECA THE YOUNGER ～ *"Asthma"*

1. This is a letter. How formal does it seem to you to be? Does it seem wholly personal? Would you suspect that it was written with the expectation that it would be shared?

2. In the first sentence, what figure of speech does Seneca employ when he says "Ill health"?

3. Why do doctors call asthma "rehearsing death"?

4. Why does he say he is not overjoyed by having escaped death by asthma after his recent attack?

5. What is Seneca's way of handling an attack?

6. What is his attitude toward death?

7. To what degree does Seneca generalize about reality and truth?

8. Philosophy is the study of wisdom. In what lines do you see Seneca speaking about wisdom?

9. Would you call Seneca an epigrammatic writer, the sort one would be inclined to quote? If so, pick a line or two that seem to you most generally quotable.

JOAN DIDION ～ *"In Bed"*

1. In a sentence, describe the subject of this essay. Go further than "It is about migraines." Think of the full scope of the essay. You might begin your sentence "'In Bed' is about how migraines . . ."

2. Do you see any signs of confessional writing here? Where does Didion give the sense of talking about something previously secret?

3. How does she characterize the public attitude toward migraine? How well understood was it when she was a child?

4. What was her attitude toward her illness as a child?

5. Why do you think she was ashamed of her illness? Why did she lie on questionnaires about how often she had headaches?

6. Didion makes use of listing in her essay. She lists triggers for her illness, lists things she does when in the migraine aura, lists its symptoms. What do these lists add to the piece? How do they enlarge our understanding? Try to imagine the essay without them.

7. In line 21 the author tells us that she "fought migraine then." How does her attitude change, as she recounts it in the last two paragraphs of the piece?

8. Is there anything positive about her essay?

Author Joan Didion has been a prolific American writer for decades now. Her recent memoir, *The Year of Magical Thinking* (2005), went onto the *New York Times* best-seller list and became a one-woman show on Broadway starring Vanessa Redgrave. It recounts a year of personal tragedy during which her daughter and husband both died in separate illnesses.

Spotlight on Rhetoric: The Intentional Sentence Fragment

The intentional sentence fragment, while considered ungrammatical, is often used in contemporary writing. It can be used to create the breathless pace of some experience. It can create drama. Note how Didion's two fragments here are preceded by a list. The fragments create emphasis; they alter the pace; they create variety:

> Almost anything can trigger a specific attack of migraine: stress, allergy, fatigue, an abrupt change of barometric pressure, a contretemps over a parking ticket. A flashing light. A fire drill.

Indeed, in practice writers, particularly fiction writers, are rule-benders. In fact, the rules of grammar emerged from how people wrote rather than the other way around. However, keep in mind intentional fragments are indeed intentional and not the result of poor proofreading or sloppy prose style or ignorance.

Find It

Find examples of three or more of these devices, underlining them and noting in the margin where they appear.

1. listing technique
2. metaphor
3. sentence fragments
4. simile

WHY CAN'T YOU GET WHAT YOU WANT?

You can't always get what you want, not only according to The Rolling Stones, but also according to mothers everywhere. But why not? What is it about life?

Write unabashedly about what you want and try to be as honest and specific as possible. Consider developing your piece with some or all of these questions. What do you really want? In the long run? In the short term? What did you want when you were little? What about now? How badly do you want it? In fact, do you really want it? Do you feel good about wanting it? And then again, what do you really need? How are want and need different?

THE LETTER

Write a letter to someone (that you would care to share with your teacher), and in your letter describe a personal experience from which you learned. What happened? How were you enlarged by your experience?

Like Seneca, open with the story of what happened, and then move to the broader issue of what you learned. In other words, use formal structure for your personal essay, proceeding from your specific experience to your learnings (which, in a sense, is the opposite of an expository essay, where you move from the general to the specific). Your language may well be informal if that is what is appropriate but give your discussion a clear shape.

SENECA THE YOUNGER ~ *"Asthma"*

**C. 4 B.C.–A.D. 65
BORN ROME**

*i.e. its medical name, asthma.

5

10

15

Ill health which had granted me quite a long spell of leave—has attacked me without warning again. "What kind of ill health?" you'll be asking. And well you may, for there isn't a single kind I haven't experienced. There's one particular ailment, though, for which I've always been singled out, so to speak. I see no reason why I should call it by its Greek name,* difficulty in breathing being a perfectly good way of describing it. Its onslaught is of very brief duration—like a squall, it is generally over within the hour. One could hardly, after all, expect anyone to keep on drawing his last breath for long, could one? I've been visited by all the troublesome or dangerous complaints there are, and none of them, in my opinion, is more unpleasant than this one—which is hardly surprising, is it, when you consider that with anything else you're merely ill, while with this you're constantly at your last gasp? This is why doctors have nicknamed it "rehearsing death," since sooner or later the breath does just what it has been trying to do all those times. Do you imagine that as I write this I must be feeling in high spirits at having escaped this time? No, it would be just as absurd for me to feel overjoyed at its being over—as if this meant I was a healthy man again— as it would be for a person to think he has won his case on obtaining an extension of time before trial.

20

25

30

Even as I fought for breath, though, I never ceased to find comfort in cheerful and courageous reflections. "What's this?" I said. "So death is having all these tries at me, is he? Let him, then! I had a try at him a long while ago myself." "When was this?" you'll say. Before I was born. Death is just not being. What that is like I know already. It will be the same after me as it was before me. If there is any torment in the later state, there must also have been torment in the period before we saw the light of day; yet we never felt conscious of any distress then. I ask you, wouldn't you say that anyone who took the view that a lamp was worse off when it was put out than it was before it was lit was an utter idiot? We, too, are lit and put out. We suffer somewhat in the intervening period, but at either end of it there is a deep tranquillity. For, unless I'm mistaken, we are wrong, my dear *Lucilius*, in holding that death follows after, when in fact it precedes as well as succeeds. Death is all that was before us. What does it matter, after all, whether you cease to be or never begin, when the result of either is that you do not exist?

Lucilius—
civil servant (and addressee)

35

I kept on talking to myself in these and similar terms—silently, needless to say, words being out of the question. Then little by little the affliction in my

continued on following page

40

45

50

breathing, which was coming to be little more than a panting now, came on at longer intervals and slackened away. It has lasted on, all the same, and in spite of the passing of this attack, my breathing is not yet coming naturally. I feel a sort of catch and hesitation in it. Let it do as it pleases, though, so long as the sighs aren't heartfelt. You can feel assured on my score of this: I shall not be afraid when the last hour comes—I'm already prepared, not planning as much as a day ahead. The man, though, whom you should admire and imitate is the one who finds it a joy to live and in spite of that is not reluctant to die. For where's the virtue in going out when you're really being thrown out? And yet there is this virtue about my case: I'm in the process of being thrown out, certainly, but the manner of it is as if I were going out. And the reason why it never happens to a wise man is that being thrown out signifies expulsion from a place one is reluctant to depart from, and there is nothing the wise man does reluctantly. He escapes necessity because he wills what necessity is going to force on him.

(Translated by Robin Campbell)

JOAN DIDION ～ ## "In Bed," Excerpt from the Book The White Album

1934–
BORN UNITED STATES

Three, four, sometimes five times a month, I spend the day in bed with a migraine headache, insensible to the world around me. Almost every day of every month, between these attacks, I feel the sudden irrational irritation and flush of blood into the cerebral arteries which tell me that

5   migraine is on its way, and I take certain drugs to avert its arrival. If I did not take the drugs, I would be able to function perhaps one day in four. The physiological error called migraine is, in brief, central to the given of my life. When I was 15, 16, even 25, I used to think that I could rid myself of this error by simply denying it, character over chemistry.

10 "Do you have headaches *sometimes? frequently? never?*" the application forms would demand. "Check one." Wary of the trap, wanting whatever it was that the successful circumnavigation of that particular form could bring (a job, a scholarship, the respect of mankind and the grace of God), I would check one. "*Sometimes*," I would lie. That in fact

15 I spent one or two days a week almost unconscious with pain seemed a shameful secret, evidence not merely of some chemical inferiority but of all my bad attitudes, unpleasant tempers, wrongthink.

For I had no brain tumor, no eyestrain, no high blood pressure, nothing wrong with me at all: I simply had migraine headaches, and migraine

20 headaches were, as everyone who did not have them knew, imaginary. I fought migraine then, ignored the warnings it sent, went to school and later to work in spite of it, sat through lectures in Middle English and presentations to advertisers with involuntary tears running down the right side of my face, threw up in washrooms, stumbled home by

25 instinct, emptied ice trays onto my bed and tried to freeze the pain in my right temple, wished only for a neurosurgeon who would do a lobotomy on house call, and cursed my imagination.

It was a long time before I began thinking mechanistically enough to accept migraine for what it was: something with which I would be liv-

30 ing, the way some people live with diabetes. Migraine is something more than the fancy of a neurotic imagination. It is an essentially hereditary complex of symptoms, the most frequently noted but by no means the most unpleasant of which is a vascular headache of blinding severity, suffered by a surprising number of women, a fair number of

35 men (Thomas Jefferson had migraine, and so did Ulysses S. Grant, the

continued on following page

40

day he accepted Lee's surrender), and by some unfortunate children as young as two years old. (I had my first when I was eight. It came on during a fire drill at the Columbia School in Colorado Springs, Colorado. I was taken first home and then to the infirmary at Peterson Field, where my father was stationed. The Air Corps doctor prescribed an enema.) Almost anything can trigger a specific attack of migraine: stress, allergy, fatigue, an abrupt change in barometric pressure, a contretemps over a parking ticket. A flashing light. A fire drill. One inherits, of course, only the predisposition. In other words I spent yesterday in bed with a headache not merely because of my bad attitudes, unpleasant tempers and wrongthink, but because both my grandmothers had migraine, my father has migraine and my mother has migraine.

45

No one knows precisely what it is that is inherited. The chemistry of migraine, however, seems to have some connection with the nerve hormone named serotonin, which is naturally present in the brain. The amount of serotonin in the blood falls sharply at the onset of migraine, and one migraine drug, Methysergide, or Sansert, seems to have some effect on serotonin. Methysergide is a derivative of lysergic acid (in fact Sandoz Pharmaceuticals first synthesized LSD-25 while looking for a migraine cure), and its use is hemmed about with so many contraindications and side effects that most doctors prescribe it only in the most incapacitating cases. Methysergide, when it is prescribed, is taken daily, as a preventive; another preventive which works for some people is old-fashioned ergotamine tartrate, which helps to constrict the swelling blood vessels during the "aura," the period which in most cases precedes the actual headache.

50

55

60

Once an attack is under way, however, no drug touches it. Migraine gives some people mild hallucinations, temporarily blinds others, shows up not only as a headache but as a gastrointestinal disturbance, a painful sensitivity to all sensory stimuli, an abrupt overpowering fatigue, a stroke-like aphasia, and a crippling inability to make even the most routine connections. When I am in a migraine aura (for some people the aura lasts fifteen minutes, for others several hours), I will drive through red lights, lose the house keys, spill whatever I am holding, lose the ability to focus my eyes or frame coherent sentences, and generally give the appearance of being on drugs, or drunk. The actual headache, when it comes, brings with it chills, sweating, nausea, a *debility* that seems to stretch the very limits of endurance. That no one dies of migraine seems, to someone deep into an attack, an ambiguous blessing.

65

70

75

debility—
weakness

My husband also has migraine, which is unfortunate for him but fortunate for me: perhaps nothing so tends to prolong an attack as the accusing eye of someone who has never had a headache. "Why not take a couple of aspirin," the unafflicted will say from the doorway, or "I'd have a headache, too, spending a beautiful day like this inside with all the shades drawn." All of us who have migraine suffer not only from the attacks themselves but from this common conviction that we are perversely refusing to cure ourselves by taking a couple of aspirin, that we are making ourselves sick, that we "bring it on ourselves." And in the most immediate sense, the sense of why we have a headache this Tuesday and not last Thursday, of course we often do. There certainly is what doctors call a "migraine personality," and that personality tends to be ambitious, inward, intolerant of error, rather rigidly organized, perfectionist. "You don't look like a migraine personality," a doctor once said to me. "Your hair's messy. But I suppose you're a compulsive housekeeper." Actually my house is kept even more negligently than my hair, but the doctor was right nonetheless: perfectionism can also take the form of spending most of a week writing and rewriting and not writing a single paragraph.

But not all perfectionists have migraine, and not all migrainous people have migraine personalities. We do not escape heredity. I have tried in most of the available ways to escape my own migrainous heredity (at one point I learned to give myself two daily injections of histamine with a hypodermic needle, even though the needle so frightened me that I had to close my eyes when I did it), but I still have migraine. And I have learned now to live with it, learned when to expect it, how to outwit it, even how to regard it, when it does come, as more friend than lodger. We have reached a certain understanding, my migraine and I. It never comes when I am in real trouble. Tell me that my house is burned down, my husband has left me, that there is gunfighting in the streets and panic in the banks, and I will not respond by getting a headache. It comes instead when I am fighting not an open guerrilla war with my own life, during weeks of small household confusions, lost laundry, unhappy help, canceled appointments, on days when the telephone rings too much and I get no work done and the wind is coming up. On days like that my friend comes uninvited.

And once it comes, now that I am wise in its ways, I no longer fight it. I lie down and let it happen. At first every small apprehension is magnified, every anxiety a pounding terror. Then the pain comes, and I concentrate only on that. Right there is the usefulness of migraine, there in

continued on following page

that imposed yoga, the concentration on the pain. For when the pain recedes, ten or twelve hours later, everything goes with it, all the hidden resentments, all the vain anxieties. The migraine has acted as a circuit breaker, and the fuses have emerged intact. There is a pleasant convalescent euphoria. I open the windows and feel the air, eat gratefully, sleep well. I notice the particular nature of a flower in a glass on the stair landing. I count my blessings.

120

Glossary of Literary Terms

AD-LIB to make a spontaneous remark while delivering a speech or prepared lines; to improvise speech

ALLITERATION repetition of initial consonant sounds ("While I nodded nearly napping," Edgar Allen Poe, "The Raven")

ALLUSION a reference, explicit or implicit, to something in previous literature and history ("Since the siege and the assault were ended at Troy," The Gawain-poet, *Sir Gawain and the Green Knight*)

ANAPHORA the repetition of words, phrases, or clauses in successive lines, stanzas, or paragraphs. ("Fog everywhere. Fog up the river, where it flows among green aits and meadows; fog down the river, where it rolls deified among the tiers of shipping and the waterside pollutions of a great (and dirty) city. Fog on the Essex marshes, fog on the Kentish heights." Charles Dickens, *Bleak House*)

ANECDOTE an interesting story, humorous or otherwise, that is briefly recounted

ANTHROPOMORPHISM assigning human traits to an animal, God, or an object

APHORISM a memorable, brief expression of some principle or truth; a saying or adage. ("A foolish consistency is the hobgoblin of little minds." Ralph Waldo Emerson, *Self-Reliance*)

APOSTROPHE figure of speech in which someone absent or dead or something nonhuman is addressed as if it were alive and able to reply ("O Rose, thou art sick!" William Blake, "The Sick Rose")

ASSONANCE repetition of vowel sounds in a sequence of words with different endings. ("I heard a fly buzz when I died." Emily Dickinson)

ASYNDETON the omission of connecting words such as *and* (the opposite of polysyndeton) ("An empty stream, a great silence, a heavy forest. The air was thick, warm, heavy, sluggish." Joseph Conrad, *Heart of Darkness*)

BLANK VERSE unrhymed lines in iambic pentameter, widely used in English drama

CHORUS a group of lines repeated at various intervals during a song

COLLOQUIAL informal language, often seeming spoken; conversational language

CONCEIT an elaborate metaphor sustained over a number of lines or paragraphs

CONNOTATION what is suggested by a word, apart from what it explicitly describes (see *denotation*)

DECLARATIVE SENTENCE a sentence that makes a declaration

DENOTATION the direct, specific meaning(s) of a word (see *connotation*)

DIALECT language of a distinct region or social stratum differing in grammar and vocabulary from the standard language of mainstream culture

DICTION characteristic word choice in a work or in a passage; a writer's language may be characterized by archaisms or scientific language or words of Germanic origin; one also speaks of formal versus colloquial diction and other oppositions

DIDACTIC having an intention to teach or preach; fables, parables, and allegories are didactic in a strict sense (The Wedding Guest in Samuel Taylor Coleridge's *The Rime of the Ancient Mariner* has heard a harrowing tale that makes him wake the next day "a sadder and a wiser man.")

ELEGIAC mournful, sorrowful tone, for something (or someone) dead or lost

ELEGY a poem or song of lamentation for someone who has died (Walt Whitman, *When Lilacs Last in the Dooryard Bloom'd* for Abraham Lincoln)

END-STOPPED in poetry, the stopping of grammatical structures at the ends of lines; not enjambed

ENJAMBMENT in poetry, the carrying on of sense and grammatical structure from one poetic line to the next poetic line; not end-stopped

ENUMERATION to list; to determine the number of

EPIC a poem that celebrates, in a continuous narrative, the achievements of mighty heroes and heroines and uses elevated language and a grand style

EXHORTATION language meant to persuade someone to take action ("Once more into the breach, dear friends, once more." William Shakespeare, *Henry V*)

FIGURATIVE LANGUAGE employs figures of speech and exists on more than a literal level; figurative language heightens meaning by implicitly or explicitly representing something in terms of some other thing

FOOT a group of syllables taken as a unit of poetic meter; fixed combination of syllables, each of which is counted as being either stressed or unstressed

HYPERBOLE overstatement or exaggeration in poetry or prose (though in casual speech we also speak hyperbolically: "I was so embarrassed I almost died.")

IMAGERY words and phrases that appeal to our senses, including "word images" but also images that appeal to our senses of taste, touch, and hearing

IMPERATIVE the command form of the verb ("Make my bed straight." Emily Dickinson, or "Go back to Mississippi." Dr. Martin Luther King Jr.)

INTERROGATIVE in question form

INVOCATION the act or process of invoking an appeal to a higher power for assistance; when someone calls on a God; a prayer

JARGON a specialized language pertaining to a certain work context; nonsensical talk

LAMPOON a sharp satiric attack, usually directed at an individual

METAPHOR a comparison or identification of one thing with another unlike it

METONYMY when a name is substituted with the name of something or some place associated with it ("The White House" for "the president")

PARODY the imitation of a person, an author, a work, or type of work for comic effect

PERIODIC SENTENCE an often relatively long sentence in which the grammatical sense and meaning are suspended until the end of the sentence

PERSONIFICATION a figure of speech in which human attributes are given to an animal, object, or when a character becomes the embodiment of a concept ("Good things of day . . . drowse" or "Devouring Time, blunt thou the lion's paws"; allegory often employs sustained personification, with characters that have names like "Sin" and "Good Times")

POLEMIC a controversial argument usually attacking another point of view or policy

POLYSYNDETON the repeated use of conjunctions to link together a succession of words, phrases, clauses, or sentences (the opposite of asyndeton) ("And soon it lightly dipped, and rose, and sank, And dipped again, . . ." John Keats, *Endymion*)

PROPAGANDA material distributed and created by the proponents of a cause

PROSE the common form of written language; stories, textbooks, speeches are all written in prose; in comparison to poetry, prose is language that is irregular in its rhythms and is often more similar to natural, spoken speech than verse

REFRAIN a frequently repeated part of a song

RHETORIC the art of language—of using its resources effectively and usually with a certain goal or effect in mind. These resources include word choice, any and all figures of speech, and structure of composition. They are all the forms and strategies available to writers. As an area of study rhetoric has both a classical and Elizabethan background and was a conscious part of curricula in the past.

A Note on Rhetoric in Daily Usage: The word *rhetoric* comes up in terms of a "rhetorical question," a question that is posed to make an assertion, not elicit a reply ("Are we not all honorable men?" William Shakespeare, *Julius Caesar*). A rhetorical question is usually part of a self-contained speech act. Another contemporary use of the word *rhetoric* occurs when someone says "that's just rhetoric," which implies that speech has been used manipulatively and is devoid of genuine logic or meaning. These uses are related to the classical sense of rhetoric, but distinct from it, too.

RHETORICAL QUESTION a statement constructed as a question that is not intended to be answered

SATIRE a literary work in which human folly or vice is attacked through the use of irony, or wit

SCANSION the process of analyzing the rhythm of a line of poetry—that is, of marking stressed and unstressed syllables, dividing the lines into feet, identifying the metrical patterns, and noting significant variations from that pattern

SIMILE a comparison or identification of one thing with another unlike it, connected by *like* or *as* ("Though I sang in my chains like the sea." Dylan Thomas)

SLICE OF LIFE an anecdote or experience presented realistically, often conveying the nature of some social or regional niche

SONNET a fourteen-line poem in iambic pentameter with a variable rhyme scheme. (Two traditional types are the *Petrarchan sonnet* with an octave and sestet and the *Shakespearian sonnet* with three quatrains and a rhyming couplet.)

SPOOF a form of comic parody that tends to be light in nature

STRATEGY any technique employed by a writer to achieve the goal of persuading others

SYMBOL a figure of speech in which something means more than what it is, for example, the cross, which is literally pieces of crossed wood used for execution, is a symbol of Christ (and his story and his crucifixion)

THEME central or dominant idea or concern of a work

TONE the writer's or speaker's attitude toward his subject, his audience, or himself; the emotional coloring, or emotional meaning of a work

UNDERSTATEMENT a figure of speech that consists of saying less than one means and thus creating emphasis, or of saying it with less force or apparent emphasis than the occasion warrants

VERBAL IRONY a figure of speech in which what is meant is the opposite of what is said (In Shakespeare's *Macbeth*, Ross tells Macduff his wife is "Well" when we know she has been slaughtered. Verbal irony often plays with double meanings or double-entendres: here "well" means that she is in heaven, free from worldly harm.)

WORKS CONSULTED FOR THIS LIST

Abrams, M. H., Editor. 1979. "Glossary." In *The Norton Anthology of English Literature,* Volume I. New York: W. W. Norton.

Baldick, Chris. 1990. *The Concise Oxford Dictionary of Literary Terms.* Oxford: New York University Press.

Gove, Phillip B., Editor in Chief. 1970. *Webster's Seventh New Collegiate Dictionary.* Springfield, MA: G. & C. Merriam Company.

Hamilton, Shannon. 2007. *Essential Literary Terms with Exercises.* Saddlebrook, NJ: Peoples Education Inc.

Perrine, Laurence, and Thomas R. Arp. 1992. *Sound and Sense.* 8th ed. Orlando, FL: Harcourt Brace.

Saint Ann's School English Department. 2008. Literary Terms Master List. Brooklyn, NY: unpublished.

Bibliography
(Works and Persons Consulted)

PART 1 PERSUASION POLITICS

Dr. Martin Luther King Jr. / William Shakespeare

Branch, Taylor. 1989. *Parting the Waters: America in the King Years.* New York: Simon & Schuster.

Churchill, Winston. 1897. *The Scaffolding of Rhetoric* (unpublished essay). www-adm.pdx.edu/user/frinq/pluralst/churspek.htm (accessed June 30, 2008)

Conversation with Adele Oltman. Brooklyn, New York. April 5, 2008.

Conversation with the Reverend Charles W. Rawlings. South Orange, New Jersey. January, 30, 2008.

Barack Obama / Arnold Schwarzenegger

Obama, Barack. 2007. *Dreams from My Father: A Story of Race and Inheritance.* New York: Crown Books.

Olympe de Gouges / Sojourner Truth

Gage, Frances. 1889. *A History of Woman Suffrage.* 2nd ed. Vol.1. Rochester, NY: Charles Mann.

History Matters: The U.S. Survey Course on the Web. " 'Ain't I a Woman?': Reminiscences of Sojouner Truth Speaking." http://historymatters.gmu.edu/d/5740/ (accessed June 5, 2008)

Hugo, Victor. 1875. *The New York Times*, Editorial Page.

Lewis, Jone Johnson. Last revised, 2001. "Olympe de Gouges and the Rights of Woman: Women's Rights During the French Revolution." About.com: Women's History. http://womenshistory.about.com/library/weekly/aa01099.htm (accessed June 1, 2008)

Scholastic Online in conjunction with Groliers Online. "History of Women's Suffrage." http://teacher.scholastic.com/activities/suffrage/history.htm (accessed June 5, 2008)

PART 2 WARTIME

President George W. Bush / Susan Sontag / Melissa Byles

Acocello, Joan. 2005. "Postscript: Susan Sontag." *The New Yorker,* January 10.

Byles, Melissa (a pen name for Ricardo Lida Nirenberg). 2001. "Open Letter to Susan Sontag." *Offcourse: A Literary Journal.* www.albany.edu/offcourse/fall01/sontag.html (accessed March 29, 2008)

Faulkner, William. 1954. Novel Prize Acceptance Speech. *The Faulkner Reader.* New York: Random House.

Fox, Margalit. 2004. "Susan Sontag, Social Critic, Dies at 71." *The New York Times,* December 28. Obituary Page.

National Commission on Terrorist Attacks Upon the United States. 2003. *9/11 Commission Report,* Authorized Edition. New York: W. W. Norton.

Sontag, Susan. 2001. Comment. *The New Yorker,* September 24.

White, E. B. 1948. *Here Is New York.* New York: Little Bookroom.

Wilfred Owen / Erich Maria Remarque

Abrams, M. H., General Editor. 1979. "Wilfred Owen." In *The Norton Anthology of English Literature,* Volume II. New York: W. W. Norton.

Fussell, Paul. 1975. *The Great War and Modern Memory.* New York: Oxford University Press U.S.A.

Remarque, Erich Maria. 1987. *All Quiet on the Western Front.* New York: Ballantine Books.

Yeats, W. B. 1936. *Introduction to The Oxford Book of Modern Verse, 1892–1935,* W. B. Yeats, Editor. Oxford: Oxford University Press.

———. 1940. Letter to Dorothy Wellesley, December 26, 1936. *Letters on Poetry from W. B. Yeats to Dorothy Wellesley.* Oxford: Oxford University Press.

PART 3 SATIRIC PENS

Jonathan Swift / Leonard Lewin

Abrams, M. H., General Editor. 1979. "Jonathan Swift." In *The Norton Anthology of English Literature,* Volume I. New York: W. W. Norton.

The Hoaxipedia. *Report from Iron Mountain.* www.museumofhoaxes.com/hoax/Hoaxipedia/Report_From_Iron_Mountain/

Lewin, Leonard C. 1996. *Report from Iron Mountain on the Possibility and Desirability of Peace.* Free Press.

Unsigned article. 1967. "Hoax or Horror? A Book That Shook White House." *U.S. News & World Report,* November 20.

Unsigned Articles from *The Onion*

Eliot, T. S. 1968. *Four Quartets.* New York: Harvest Books.

Weil, Dr. Andrew. 1996. *Spontaneous Healing: How to Discover and Enhance Your Body's Natural Ability to Heal Itself.* New York: Ballantine Books.

Wikipedia. "The Onion." http://en.wikipedia.org/wiki/The_onion (accessed April 23, 2008)

Ira C. Herbert of Coca-Cola / Richard Seaver of Grove Press

Seaver, Richard. 2008. Email message to author, April 22.

PART **4** TEXT TALK

Rudyard Kipling / H. T. Johnson

Abrams, M. H., General Editor. 1979. "Rudyard Kipling." *The Norton Anthology of English Literature*, Volume 2. New York: W. W. Norton.

Brown, Justin. 2002. "Should Tiger Woods Carry the Black Man's Burden?" *The Christian Science Monitor.* August 16.

Conversation with Ruth Chapman. Brooklyn, New York. June 1, 2008.

Culp, Dr. D. W. 1902. *One Hundred of America's Greatest Negroes.* Toronto: J. L. Nichols. (Online at *The Project Gutenburg eBook of Twentieth Century Negro Literature*, accessed June 23, 2008.)

History Matters: The U.S. Survey Course on the Web. "The Black Man's Burden: A Response to Kipling." http://historymatters.gmu.edu/d/5476/ (accessed February 5, 2008)

Neil Young / Lynyrd Skynyrd / Warren Zevon

Conversation with Nicole Rosenthal Hartnett. New York. April 2, 2008.

Conversation with William Hogeland. New York. March 19, 2008.

Lynyrd Skynyrd official website. www.lynyrdskynyrd.com

McDonough, Jim. 2002. *Shakey: Neil Young's Biography.* New York: Random House.

Neil Young official website. www.neilyoung.com

Wallace, George. 1963. Reprint of Public Statement. *The New York Times,* May 8.

Warren Zevon official website. www.warrenzevon.com

Clive James / Anne Lamott

Clive James official website. www.clivejames.com

Lamott, Anne. 1995. *Bird by Bird: Some Instructions on Writing and Life.* New York: Anchor Books.

PART **5** IDENTITY: LITTLE HISTORIES

Joseph Mitchell / Orhan Pamuk

Brenner, Angie. 2008. "Turkish Authors Face Controversy". *The Wild River Review.* www.wildriverreview.com/spotlight_turkishauthors.php (accessed May 1, 2008)

Lord Kinross. 1965. *Ataturk, Rebirth of a Nation.* London: Weidenfeld and Nicholson.

McSorley's official website. www.mcsorleysnewyork.com

Mitchell, Joseph. 1991. *Up in the Old Hotel.* New York: Vintage.

Orhan Pamuk official website. www.orhanpamuk.net

Pamuk, Orhan. 2004. *Istanbul: Memories and the City.* New York: Alfred A. Knopf.

Severo, Richard. 1996. "Joseph Mitchell, Chronicler of the Unsung and Unconventional, Dies at 87." *The New York Times,* May 25. Obituary.

Sumner-Boyd, Hillary, and Jonathan Freely. 2001. *Strolling Through Istanbul.* London: Kegan Paul International.

Swacker, Robert, and Leslie Jenkins. 2006. *Irish New York.* New York: Universe Publishing.

Richard Rodriguez / Amy Tan

Amy Tan official website. www.amytan.net

California Department of Education. Data and Statistics. www.cde.ca.gov/ds/

———. Specialized Programs—English Learners. www.cde.ca.gov/sp/el/

Education Data Partnership Home Page. www.ed-data.k12.ca.us/welcome.asp

PBS: Richard Rodriguez Essays. www.pbs.org/newshour/essays/richard_rodriguez.html

Red Room website. Amy Tan. www.redroom.com/author/amy-tan (accessed May 6, 2008)

Sadie, Stanley, Editor. 2000. *The New Grove Dictionary of Music and Musicians.* New York: Oxford University Press USA.

Tan, Amy. 1990. *The Joy Luck Club.* New York: Ballantine Books.

———. 1991. "Mother Tongue." *Best American Essays.* New York: Houghton Mifflin.

PART **6** **SICK DAYS**

Scott Russell Sanders / Anonymous

Scott Russell Sanders. 1989. "Under the Influence." New York: HarperCollins.

Seneca the Younger / Joan Didion

Didion, Joan. 1979. "In Bed." In *The White Album.* New York: Farrar, Straus, and Giroux.

Conversation with Thomas Kingsley. Brooklyn, New York. February 20, 2008.

GENERAL REFERENCE

AmericanRhetoric.com

Baldick, Chris. 1990. *Oxford Concise Dictionary of Literary Terms.* Oxford: New York University Press.

Wikipedia.com